T0247896

Glorious Lessons

Glorious Lessons

John Trumbull, Painter of the American Revolution

RICHARD BROOKHISER

Yale UNIVERSITY PRESS/NEW HAVEN & LONDON

Published with assistance from the Annie Burr Lewis Fund and
with assistance from the foundation established in memory of
Philip Hamilton McMillan of the Class of 1894, Yale College.

Yale University Press books may be purchased in quantity for
educational, business, or promotional use. For information,
please e-mail sales.press@yale.edu (U.S. office) or sales@yaleup.
co.uk (U.K. office).

Set in Minion type by IDS Infotech, Ltd.
Printed in the United States of America.

Library of Congress Control Number: 2023947493
ISBN 978-0-300-25970-4 (hardcover : alk. paper)

A catalogue record for this book is available from the
British Library.

This paper meets the requirements of ANSI/NISO Z39.48-1992
(Permanence of Paper).

10 9 8 7 6 5 4 3 2 1

For
Leo Eaton (RIP)
Michael Pack
artists, friends

Contents

A Note on Spelling

Rules of spelling and punctuation have changed between John Trumbull's time and ours, and letter writers then as now often made their own rules. I have regularized and modernized liberally for ease of reading.

I have followed Trumbull's usage in writing "Bunker's Hill," and his age's usage in writing "Indian" and "Indians."

Glorious Lessons

INTRODUCTION

W hen Colonel John Trumbull, artist and Revolutionary War veteran, was an old man, he said, "Let those who think it is an easy
thing to paint a picture, go to that wall and make it tell a story."[1]

From youth—he was born in 1756—to old age—he died in 1843—he
painted stories and subjects drawn from many sources: history; sacred and
secular literature; people he knew, people who paid him, people he observed on the sly. He produced or designed many other works besides, both
graphic and three-dimensional: battle maps, a college campus, a church.
But for half a century, he worked on a series of paintings that told one
story, the most important story of his life, the most important (he believed)
of all political history.

I first saw the wall that tells this story when I was a student. Trumbull left his most important paintings to Yale College. The gallery he
designed to hold them was torn down long ago, but the collection remains, as per the terms of his bequest, in a room devoted to it, where I
happened upon it one day.

I am a writer. Books, columns, reporting are my life. I have never
held a painter's brush in my hand. But this wall got my attention, as its
creator intended.

The paintings on it were then arranged approximately as Trumbull
had first grouped them (they have been rearranged since). The colors
and the furnishings of the room mimicked a gallery of the early nineteenth century—green banquettes, red walls. In the center of the most
important wall hung a life-size portrait of a Revolutionary War officer in

full uniform. Ranged around it were eight paintings, four on a side, three feet long by two feet tall, depicting multiple characters, military and civilian, also of the late eighteenth century. At the extremities of the wall were two arrays of small portraits, each about four inches tall. Some of the faces rendered in these reappeared in the larger works, most did not. They were like a casting call.

The man in the standing portrait was George Washington. He also dominated four of the medium-sized paintings, whether on horseback or standing. Two of the Washington-less images I recognized from textbooks, or middlebrow coffee-table books, or who knows where, so familiar were they. The rest were new to me.

There was a lot of color, a lot of information, many moods. There was darkness and death, smoke and panic; a rearing horse, blasted trees. There was also the formality of surrender, when warfare assumes the mask of civility. Away from the battlefield were scenes of political deliberation. White women were there, as well as a number of Native American men, and one black man. I grasped some themes—Washington, I concluded, was a star of the show, which is true, though he is not the only one. Other themes I missed entirely. The labels affixed to the frames were confusing as often as they were helpful: I noticed that the dates of completion were years apart and often out of sync with the order of the events being depicted; the artist had evidently painted out of sequence, and in bursts of activity long removed from each other.

But the wall, as a whole, succeeded in its primary purpose: it got the viewer's attention. *This is important; pay attention. These men and women are dead, but they live here. You do not know them (you do not know them yet) but they had you in mind.* Although words can be compelling, the eyes have it. This wall has our eyes.

It anticipated visual forms Trumbull never knew. It was a graphic novel, its images less numerous than those in a book, but each one larger and more packed. Glimpsed quickly, it was a movie trailer; studied slowly, it was the film itself.

The story Trumbull aimed to tell was the story of the American Revolution. But it was more than a recap of engagements and parleys, or of sessions of Congress, the revolutionary tribunal. In a letter to Thomas Jefferson, one of his subjects, he defined his purpose: "to give the present and future sons of oppression and misfortune, such glorious lessons of their rights, and of the spirit with which they should assert and support them."[2] Trumbull wanted to tell the creation story of America—what it should mean to Americans, and what it could mean to the world, and to the future.

Trumbull put his story on more than a single wall in a collegiate art gallery. He commissioned engravings that would replicate his images as prints, spreading his lessons nation- and world-wide (and making, he hoped, a profit for himself). He toured his paintings, before hanging them in their destined home; one of the venues in which he showed his depiction of the Declaration of Independence being presented to Congress was Independence Hall in Philadelphia, where the Declaration had been presented to Congress. He labored and schemed to hang vast copies of four of his paintings in the Rotunda of the Capitol in Washington, D.C., and worked with the architects to make sure that the Rotunda would be a space, both grand and simple, best calculated to display them. He asked, in vain, to hang copies of four more of his paintings there. At the end of his artistic life, his talent all but gone, he busied himself with somewhat less vast copies that now hang in Hartford, Connecticut. He wrote an autobiography, whose first edition included plates of his works. Other books, over the years, commemorative or instructive, have done the same. Now and again a Trumbull will appear on letters or in wallets, on stamps or bills. They are in America's mind's eye.

Trumbull's authority for telling this story was personal. He was born into a political family. His father, Jonathan Trumbull, Sr., was the last colonial and first revolutionary governor of Connecticut—"the rebel governor," the British called him. His three older brothers all served the cause. John himself was briefly on the staffs of two generals, George Washington and Horatio Gates. He served on the fringes of several battles, in the thick of one. He was shot at; he saw men wounded, killed. Out of uniform he was jailed by the enemy as a spy. He stayed interested in American politics all his life, and met everybody—French and British generals, Creek and Seneca chiefs, six presidents. He worshipped Washington; he was successively Jefferson's protégé and wingman, his enemy, and finally his respected long-ago colleague.

More important, Trumbull's authority as a storyteller was a product of thought and desire, conviction and will. He made the story of the American Revolution visible because he wanted to. For a little country with no tradition, an ignorant public, and powerful anti-aesthetic impulses, late eighteenth-century America produced a surprising number of capable painters: Benjamin West, John Singleton Copley, Charles Willson Peale, Gilbert Stuart. The world of art was so small that Trumbull knew them all. His peers left revolutionary-era portraits and battle scenes, many interesting, some brilliant; two of them contemplated telling the story of the Revolution in a connected way themselves. But Trumbull alone did it.

It took him many years, half of a long life. Many of those years were wasted, as far as his great project was concerned: spent painting other things; spent painting nothing at all. He tried his hand at dealing art, buying and selling Old Masters; he served as a diplomat in Britain and France.

His personal life presented various obstacles. Governor Trumbull never understood why his youngest son wanted to paint. When John explained that he wished to glorify his country as ancient artists had glorified Athens, the governor responded with a line that would have supplied Henry James with a novel, or Cole Porter with a lyric: "*Connecticut is not Athens.*"[3] The artist married a woman he adored, whom he painted as both the Madonna and the woman taken in adultery. His family did not adore her; she took to drink. He had sired, by another woman, an illegitimate son who chose a career he disapproved of: serving in the British army. When Trumbull tried to talk his son out of it, the young man replied, reasonably enough, "You ... follow[ed] your own inclination in the choice of your profession."[4]

Milton wrote of that one talent which is death to hide. Trumbull could be very good at hiding his. But despite distractions, temptations, vexations, and sloth, Trumbull's story kept drawing him back.

Because he had lived through it, his story has the immediacy of news; it also achieves the comprehensiveness of history. The enemy is not demonized. Trumbull painted British officers into his canvases from life; one of his most sympathetic figures is a mortally wounded Hessian. He depicted a Native American ally, and did studies of several more. He produced a canvas showing an armed black man, at a time when black men in much of America were not allowed to bear arms. He knew the war could not have been won without French help; he knew it would scarcely have been worth winning without the principles that animated it.

Still there are gaps. One, which he meant to fill, though he never got around to it, was geographic. You would not know, from his telling, that anything important in the Revolution happened south of Virginia. One gap never seems to have occurred to him: many Americans fought for or sympathized with the other side.

Because Trumbull's story was so important to him—and, he believed, to America and to the world—his eight-part narrative of the Revolution and his standing portrait of Washington, which he wanted hung with it, will be described in this book when they are finished, displayed in the gallery he built for them and arranged as he chose. The rest of his life—other paintings he painted; paintings he studied; family, teachers, lovers, battles, quarrels—will be told as it unfolds.

How many Americans today sympathize with the story Trumbull tells? Trumbull never sculpted; if he had, his statues might have been graffitied and smashed as those of other artists, depicting his same subjects, have recently been. Trumbull's paintings, hung too high to be easily damaged, witnessed a mob bent on overturning a presidential election pass through the Capitol.

Most Americans are not vandals or rioters. But we have been revolutionaries; we still wage wars. Trumbull knew that. Even successful wars can bring as many defeats as victories; Trumbull knew that too. War and politics—history itself—are tales of slaughter and oppression, unless they lead to freedom and peace. But brave and thoughtful men and women can achieve those ends. Trumbull believed that, and wants to show it.

When I first saw Trumbull's wall I was not an art historian in training, nor have I become one. Now as then I am a visitor with a pair of open eyes. I do come to him as a historian, and a citizen. Trumbull understood the American Revolution to be more than an episode of power politics, or even of colonials resisting imperial overlords. It was a true revolution, a profound change in how people thought about their political condition: the first chapter in a worldwide revolution of self-rule. How to win self-rule and how to keep it has been an issue for every people, east and west, north and south, for two hundred and fifty years.

Trumbull's story may inspire those struggling with despots or invaders. It can challenge those who do not understand what, or how fragile, self-rule is. It is still worth seeing and pondering.

ONE

John Trumbull drew his first pictures on the floor of his family's house in Lebanon, Connecticut, copying pictures made by his older sister Faith that hung over the mantel in the parlor.

Embroidering and painting were skills taught to genteel young ladies in eighteenth-century England, and even in transatlantic colonies. As an old man, Trumbull recalled copying his sister's productions. "I endeavored to imitate them, and for several years the nicely sanded floors . . . were constantly scrawled with my rude attempts at drawing."[1]

Faith's paintings have not survived. But some of her embroideries have—pieces painted on cloth, then worked over in stitched thread. Although the figures in them are crude, the scenes are elaborate. Groups of men, women, and animals, in poses copied from seventeenth- and eighteenth-century European prints, are arranged in landscapes with local houses and trees (oaks, by the look of the leaves). Some of the activities depicted are drawn from ordinary life—a woman milks a cow (plate 1). Others are fanciful, or at least fanciful for eighteenth-century Connecticut— another woman in a striped formal dress plays a guitar for a small dog. In the larger pieces there is rudimentary perspective—people shrunken by distance standing in remote fields, or on the far shore of a pond.

The paintings and embroideries that young John saw in the parlor resemble the world—yet each one creates a new world. Like every artist's world, these worlds are simpler than the one we inhabit: the bombardment of visual data that we learn as infants to construe as bodies in space is further pared down and focused. These worlds are also timeless: the people and creatures in them may have come from elsewhere or be about to do something else, but now they are arrested. Spare and still as they are, however, the artists' worlds allow a viewer to imagine: to wonder why the figures before him are there, or what might happen next; to put himself in the scene. They unlock imagination. If a viewer is so inclined and so gifted, he could re-create them, or in re-creating alter them. Painters always begin by painting other paintings.

The Psalmist says, "The days of our years are threescore years and ten." John Trumbull's life as a painter would last at least that long; it began with a boy scrawling on the floor.

The Trumbull house still stands in Lebanon, at one end of the long town green (figure 1). It is simultaneously plain and imposing for a rural village: two stories, four rooms down, four rooms up. On the back wall of a closet off the second-floor girls' room—John had two sisters, Faith and Mary—there is a wispy chalk sketch of two figures, a man and a woman. Scratched into the wall of one of the ground-floor rooms are floral doodles, traced with a compass. The sketch and the compass-work might be John's. His own second-floor room was once undeniably, if discreetly, ornamented by him: he painted the inner side of a cupboard door with a noble Roman, defending his daughter's honor with a sword. The Roman is now in a museum in Hartford; the cupboard in John's old room yawns, doorless. No other traces of John's youthful efforts remain in the house where he grew up.

We do not know what his mother, also named Faith, or Flora, the family's slave, thought of his floor work. It must have complicated their work in keeping the floor "nicely sanded." John was the baby of the family, the youngest of six children, and the pet of his sisters; they may have humored his imitations of Faith's handiwork. We can with more confidence imagine what Jonathan Trumbull, Sr., John's father, thought of his son's artistic efforts: very little. Genteel boys were not taught painting and embroidery, but were groomed to take up serious work—business, the ministry, the law—as Jonathan himself had been; as his older sons, Joseph, Jonathan, Jr., and David, were.

Indifference to visual arts had deep roots in the world of John's youth. Connecticut and its neighboring colonies in British North America were children of Calvin. The Congregational Church was established by law and supported by taxes; the Word, as revealed in the Bible, and

Figure 1. The house of Governor Jonathan Trumbull, Sr., fronts the village green in Lebanon, Connecticut. John, youngest of his six children, frequently disagreed with his father about his future career.

expounded by the clergy, was its lone art form. Religious painting and sculpture were tools of Rome (not noble ancient Rome, but degenerate Catholic Rome). The Congregationalist meetinghouses of New England were undecorated except, in some older ones, for the Almighty's all-seeing and unwinking Eye, depicted on the pulpit.[2] Thus Calvinism as established by the first wave of settlers.

As the decades passed, prosperity and commerce—in a word, luxury—softened these foundational prejudices. The wealthy and the aspiring in port cities and towns, and even inland crossroads, acquired a taste for rich fabrics and elegant furniture, imported from London or made to order by local artisans. Yet radicals and rabble-rousers would periodically appear to denounce finery, even as the pious were liable to worry that it betokened vanity. John's talents bucked a slackening but still powerful current.

One other feature of the Trumbull house, John believed, marked his later artistic life. The main staircase, with a sleek banister and a curved landing at the top, rose in the center of the house; but there was a back stairs, leading from his sisters' room, as steep as a ladder, plunging thirteen steps straight down, from the second to the ground floor. Playing with Faith and Mary one day—"frolicking," as he put it—John fell down these stairs and was knocked out, with a great bruise over his left eye.[3] After he recovered, he squinted for a few days, then thought no more of his injury—until "several years after," when he found in closing his right eye that he could no longer see out of his left. His partial loss of sight was a fact that lay in the back of his mind for the rest of his life. When John was a young man, Gilbert Stuart, a fellow painter, joked that one of his canvases looked as if it had been painted by a one-eyed man. John blazed up, thinking that Stuart knowingly mocked him. Stuart had no idea of his friend's condition; it was a josh gone wrong. John was not amused.

Trumbull blamed his disability on his accident, but his fall could not have produced such a long-delayed reaction. His partial blindness must have had some other cause, unless, as sometimes happens, the damage was immediate and it took a long time for it to be noticed (people seldom blink alternately and deliberately unless they are performing some special task—threading a needle, sighting a gun). Seeking causes and explanations, Trumbull linked two shocks: his fall, his loss of the use of an eye. Eyes are how painters see the world, and the new worlds they make. Trumbull only had one left. The desire to paint, and the possibility that he might be unable to, both came from home; they were twin inheritances.

Lebanon lies in the gently rising highlands of eastern Connecticut. The town brook drains ultimately into the Thames River at Norwich, twelve miles to the southeast; twenty miles south of Norwich lay New London and Long Island Sound. Hartford, the colony's capital, was thirty miles west of Lebanon; Boston, one of the largest ports in Britain's new world, was a hundred miles to the northeast.[4] A post road connecting these two towns passed Lebanon a few miles to the north. Lebanon, the year John was born, was one of Connecticut's larger towns, and was within easy distance of yet more prominent places.

Jonathan Trumbull, John's father, was born in Lebanon in 1710, the second son of Joseph Trumbull, a farmer and drover. Joseph prospered to the point of marketing his cattle in Boston, and dreamed of trading with Barbados. He tapped Joseph, Jr., his eldest son, to be his merchant partner, and sent Jonathan to Harvard, intending him for the clergy. But after Joseph, Jr., went down with the family's first ship on its maiden voyage, Jonathan was called to replace him in the family business. Jonathan never lost the marks of his religious training. Every year he read the Old Testament in Hebrew; his considered opinion as an adult was that the two great enemies of Christianity in the modern world were the Sultan and the Pope.

In 1735 he married Faith Robinson, the daughter of a Massachusetts minister. There was a shipwreck in her own past, which had taken the life of her mother; Mrs. Robinson's body was found, washed ashore, minus the ring finger, which had been cut off by a scavenger. Over the first twenty-one years of marriage, Faith bore six children: yet another Joseph (b. 1737), Jonathan, Jr. (b. 1740), Faith (b. 1743), Mary (b. 1745), David (b. 1751), and finally John (b. 1756).

Jonathan Trumbull's merchant career flourished along with his family. By the 1760s he was buying and selling as far afield as London; Halifax, Nova Scotia; Newport, Rhode Island; and the West Indies. He owned a thousand acres of land in and around Lebanon, most of which he rented to farmers. His eldest son, Joseph, managed a family office in Norwich; his second son, Jonathan, Jr., oversaw a warehouse on the Sound.

The flush times ended in 1767, when John was eleven. As with most financial crashes, there were more than enough causes. Hard times, felt throughout the British empire, found creditors demanding payment; Jonathan's land holdings, though valuable, were illiquid; still other ships had been lost at sea. Jonathan managed to give his creditors just enough to avoid technical bankruptcy. But a third son, David, who should have been enrolled at Harvard at this time, as his father and older brothers had been before him, could not be sent there.

One other factor contributed to Jonathan Trumbull's business travails, and it had to do with his other business, which had become his primary one: politics. When customers are also constituents, there is a disincentive to collecting their debts rigorously.[5] Hence another pinch on his resources. And Jonathan Trumbull had been serving, and appealing to, constituents for decades.

Connecticut, according to its seventeenth-century charter, had both an elected legislature and executive (only Rhode Island, among Britain's North American colonies, enjoyed an equivalent degree of self-rule). Jonathan was first elected to the General Assembly, the lower, larger house, as early as 1733. He missed serving for the next two years, but was reelected in 1736; and for almost half a century thereafter voters would send him, without interruption, to that office, or to more exalted ones. He served in the judiciary as well, starting at the county level (there was no separation of powers in colonial Connecticut). In 1766 he became simultaneously deputy governor and chief justice of the colony's Superior Court. In 1769, his near-bankruptcy notwithstanding, he was elected governor.

With his jobs came responsibilities in Britain's imperial wars. The mother country had been fighting France on and off since the end of the seventeenth century. In North America these conflicts pitted Britain's colonies, strung along the Atlantic from Newfoundland to Georgia, against an arc of French possessions that swung from Quebec, along the shores of the Great Lakes and the Mississippi River, down to New Orleans.

Connecticut, buffered from the frontier by its neighboring colonies, was not a battlefield. Its role was to support the empire with supplies and men. Jonathan helped the wheels of war turn. In 1756, the year of John's birth, the Seven Years' War (called the French and Indian War in North America) was declared. Jonathan was commissioned to represent Connecticut at intra-colonial strategy sessions in New York, Hartford, and Boston. As a merchant/lawmaker he oversaw the production and distribution of flintlocks and cutlasses, cartridge boxes and belts. The conflict in North America turned decisively in 1759, when British regulars, after a daring night march, captured the French citadel of Quebec; the thirty-two-year-old commander of the attack, Major General James Wolfe, died at the moment of victory.

Politics and war surrounded John's childhood. Art was his personal passion, but he would come to share his father's absorption in public life.

John's formal education began close to home. Nathan Tisdale, a Lebanon native and a Harvard graduate, ran a grammar school facing the town green. (John's father had helped establish it.) Tisdale's was a well-regarded establishment, attracting students from colonies as distant as the West Indies. The pupils were almost all boys (Faith and Mary Trumbull had been sent for their education to an instructress of girls in Boston). The curriculum was the standard classical curriculum of the day—poets (Homer, Vergil, Horace), orators (Cicero), divinity (the New Testament in Greek).

John was particularly impressed by the history of ancient Rome, as told by Charles Rollin, a French pedagogue, in a popular English translation. The ancient Romans were not Christians, yet despite lacking the blessings of revelation, they had managed, according to Rollin's and their own accounts, to be brave, virtuous—and all-conquering. In times of intense civic engagement, such as Connecticut had experienced, Rome's example came to the fore.

John showed a precocious gift for languages, learning Latin and Greek faster and better than his peers. He also showed the temperament of a loner. He attributed this in later life to a frail constitution, which made him reluctant to compete in boys' games. Drawing and reading offered two solitary pursuits to occupy him.

Besides the Trumbull family's slaves—a 1745 list of assets shows another, Hector, in addition to Flora—Lebanon had a number of blacks, both enslaved and free. They do not figure in John's memories of his early life. Indians do.

The Mohegans, an Algonquian-speaking nation, had allied with white settlers in a seventeenth-century war against the Pequots. (Whites profited from the internecine rivalries of Native Americans even as Indians played competing European empires against each other.) As a reward for their friendship, the Mohegans retained a swath of eastern Connecticut, on which they took up agriculture and Christianity. Every year a Mohegan sachem or some other dignitary would pay a courtesy visit to the General Assembly meeting in Hartford. On the way, these men called at the Trumbull house.

All his life John would remember, to his shame, a prank he tried to play on one Mohegan guest. This man, Zachary, had been a drunkard in his youth. Alcohol was the white man's second-most deadly weapon, after smallpox. But Zachary, realizing that drunkenness did not become someone of his station, had been sober for years. "One day," John later recalled, "the mischievous thought struck me to try the sincerity of the old man's temperance." John offered him some home-brewed beer. Zachary put down his knife and fork and looked the boy in the face. "John," he said, "you don't know what you are doing. . . . If I should but taste your beer, I could never stop until I got to rum." He concluded with a maxim: "While you live, never again tempt any man to break a good resolution."[6] Zachary's words, recorded decades after the fact, were no doubt polished by frequent retelling, but there is no reason to doubt that they had been impressive when uttered; white men often commented admiringly on native eloquence. John had been given a lesson in morality, and respect. An older man told a youth how to behave; a red man showed a white boy what was owed him, and the boy listened.

In January 1772, age fifteen, John was sent to complete his education at Harvard. His entry fee was paid by his brother, Jonathan, Jr., not by his straitened father. John had proposed an alternative course of study. In Boston there lived an American painter—a real one, not a teenage decorator like his sister Faith, but a prodigy. John Singleton Copley, son of Anglo-Irish immigrants, had begun painting portraits professionally in his teens, about the time John was born. His fame had reached London, to say nothing of Lebanon. If John could study with him, the expense would be the same as attending Harvard, and he would be prepared when his apprenticeship ended for a career. "This argument seemed to me not bad," wrote John.[7] His father sent him to Harvard.

Harvard was over a century old when John entered it. It lay in Cambridge, a still-rural village north of Boston. Travelers between the two places had to take a ferry across the Charles River; the tolls went to the support of the college. The student body was not much larger than that of Nathan Tisdale's grammar school; it consisted of the sons of the ambitious and of the elite of eastern New England, bound to join the elite themselves. John's father, class of 1727, was now governor of Connecticut; one of his classmates, Thomas Hutchinson, had just been appointed governor of Massachusetts by the crown. John boarded with William Kneeland, a former tutor.

John was so well prepared that he began as a junior, or third-year student. This lateral entry, combined with his youth, and a shortage of surplus funds, kept him as isolated in Cambridge as he had been in Lebanon. "I was not a speaker," he wrote in later years, explaining his failure to graduate with honors despite his linguistic skills.[8] He did not speak in public; he spoke little more to his fellow students.

He got two benefits from his college years. In Cambridge there lived a family of refugees, the Robichauds, expelled by the British from the conquered French colony of Acadia. Trumbull scrimped on his pocket money to pay them to teach him their language. His fluency in French would ease many an artistic and political endeavor.

The greatest benefit of his time away from home was proximity to Copley and his work. John called on him as he passed through Boston on his way to Cambridge, introduced by a Trumbull family friend who was also a friend of the artist. Copley lived in a house on Boston Common; when John arrived he was about to host a dinner party. The impression Copley made was still vivid to John sixty years later: "an elegant looking man, dressed in a fine maroon cloth, with gilt buttons—this was dazzling to my unpracticed eye!"[9] So painters could be colorful themselves—and rich (or at least richly dressed). What impressed John even more were Copley's paintings, "the first I had ever seen deserving the name"—they "riveted, absorbed my attention."[10]

Copley had made his transatlantic reputation with a 1765 painting, *A Boy with a Flying Squirrel,* which he sent to London to be exhibited the following year (figure 2).[11] The boy was Copley's younger half brother, shown sitting at a table with a chained flying squirrel; the pet was imaginary, created by Copley to add a touch of Americana to his canvas. The dominant hues are sober—shades of maroon (the artist must have liked the color)—but the details are bravura. The boy's fingers twiddle the squirrel's golden chain; fingers are the downfall of mediocre portraitists, but these are precisely rendered. The boy's cuffs, the squirrel's bright underbelly, a glass of water are all reflected in the shiny tabletop. The textures of the boy's jacket, collar, and hair, and of the wall-hanging behind him, are richly evoked and nicely distinguished;

Figure 2. John Singleton Copley, *A Boy with a Flying Squirrel*
(Henry Pelham), 1765. This is the painting that made the young
American known in London. The pet is imaginary, the details
precise. (Photograph © 2024 Museum of Fine Arts, Boston.)

you can almost feel them, and feel the differences between them. The
painting shows Copley's characteristic flaw too: the boy's pallor is extreme; almost everybody Copley ever painted would come out looking
a little dead. But Copley's subjects, even in portraits that are more con-
ventional, inhabit realistic spaces, lit and shadowed, filled with objects—
especially fabrics—that have an almost tactile presence. John was right
to be riveted.

Harvard owned several Copley portraits of local eminences, which were hung in its Philosophy Chamber, a combination museum and classroom. In the college library were a handful of art books: gloomy engravings of Roman ruins by Giambattista Piranesi, a contemporary Italian: a mixture of the classical and the fantastic, which provided examples of applied perspective. There was an edition of *The Art of Painting,* a didactic Latin poem by Charles du Fresnoy, a seventeenth-century French artist. John could read it in the original, but the English edition carried a translation on facing pages by John Dryden. Du Fresnoy gave practical tips—how to arrange subjects in a composition, where to focus the highlights—but he opened with a paean to the value of the art itself. Painters "dive … into all the past ages; and search their histories for subjects which are proper for their use; with care avoiding to treat of any but those which by their nobleness … have deserv'd to be consecrated to eternity. … And by this, their care and study, it comes to pass, that the glory of Heroes is not extinguish'd with their lives: and those admirable works, those prodigies of skill, which even yet are objects of our admiration, are still preserv'd." Artists immortalizing the deeds of heroes become immortal in turn.[12]

John copied two of the works that he saw at Harvard (not Copleys—that might have been aiming too high): an oil painting of Vesuvius in eruption, and an engraving of Rebecca at the well, at the moment when Abraham's servant recognizes her as the future wife of Isaac (Genesis 24). John had to come up with his own colors for his copy of the black and white engraving; as he put it, "I managed as well as I could."[13] He took the result across the Charles to Copley, who encouraged the teenager.

Back in Lebanon, Jonathan Trumbull, Sr., was mindful of the persistence of his youngest son's artistic inclinations, and anxious to squelch, or at least redirect them.

His representative on the spot was John's landlord, William Kneeland. In April 1772, three months after John's arrival in Cambridge, Kneeland wrote to the governor to tell him that his son was off to a good start and that he, Kneeland, was on the case: "It gives me very great pleasure to acquaint you, that your son's character and reception here are such as a tender parent would wish a child to have. His tutors speak well of him as a scholar; and I believe all with whom he is conversant approve of his modest and affable deportment. I mention these things, because I know the anxious care of a prudent parent to learn the knowledge of his child's behavior from such as are likely to communicate it without partiality or prejudice."

In July, Kneeland wrote again.

"I find [John] has a natural genius and disposition for limning." *Limning* literally means "painting" or "describing"; in colonial America, it carried a class taint. A limner was a painter of likenesses, probably self-taught, possibly even itinerant; an artisan, on the level of a carpenter, or a shoemaker. Not a line of work fit for a Harvard graduate, much less a governor's son. Kneeland went on: "As a knowledge of that art will probably be of no use to him, I submit to your consideration whether it would not be best to endeavor to give him a turn to the study of perspective, a branch of mathematics, the knowledge of which . . . may be greatly useful in future life."[14] A lad who knew perspective could become a surveyor or a mapmaker. In young countries there was always a demand for them, and doing the community's work was praiseworthy.

The governor wrote back in August. "I am sensible of [John's] natural genius and inclination for limning; an art I have frequently told him will be of no use to him." Trumbull, Sr., approved Kneeland's suggested remedy. "I have mentioned to him the study of the mathematics, and among other branches that of perspective, hoping to bring on a new habit and turn of his mind."[15]

John's father could manage Connecticut politics and military logistics; John was harder to control, for his mind was already turned to art. But ironically, the governor's thoughts about the usefulness of perspective were prescient; John's knowledge of it would have a decisive impact on his military, political, and artistic career.

In July 1773 John graduated from Harvard and returned to Lebanon.

T W O

J ohn found employment as soon as he returned home. Nathan Tisdale
suffered a stroke in the summer of 1773 and asked his former scholar
to take over the running of his school. Until the schoolmaster recovered
the following spring, the seventeen-year-old managed everything from
teaching the youngest students how to read to preparing the oldest for
college.

In his free time John played an instrument he had learned, the
flute, and flirted with his female neighbors, whom he called the "Demoiselles."[1] The young man who would not speak in public had no trouble
speaking to young women, evidently; perhaps being his sisters' pet
smoothed the way.

He also made his first history painting. He picked, as du Fresnoy
recommended, a noble subject. At the climax of the Battle of Cannae,
Rome's most crushing loss in its wars with Carthage, a Roman officer
offered his horse to his wounded commander, Aemilius Paulus, to spare
his being killed by the enemy. Aemilius refused the mount so that his
subordinate might bring tidings of the defeat to Rome. John arranged
fighting and dying figures imitated from engravings of classical subjects
in a tableau of battlefield disaster. The coloring is garish—the cloaks and
tunics are unpleasant shades of blue and orange—and the figures,
though they are gesturing, stabbing, and expiring, have the rigidity of
copies. But they all hang together in a coherent scene.

Governor Trumbull did not forbid his youngest son from painting,
but he followed up on his correspondence with William Kneeland by
giving John another, practical project. Connecticut had claimed and

settled a portion of the Susquehanna River valley, relying on an expansive colonial charter. But Pennsylvania's boundaries, according to its charter, overlapped Connecticut's. Rival settlers had come to blows. John prepared maps of the area supporting Connecticut's claims.

All the business of daily life was soon consumed by politics. General Wolfe's great victory at Quebec generated a crisis for the British empire. By expelling France from the continent, Wolfe removed the enemy that kept colonists and homeland united, while the debts incurred by supporting his campaign and those of other commanders on far-flung fronts could only be paid down by taxes levied on Americans. Burdens grew after the threat had vanished.

The new burdens were more than monetary requisitions; they were requisitions of a new kind. Colonial taxes were now being set in Parliament, in which colonists had no voice, not in America, where, even in colonies without elected governors—that is, most of them—there was at least one elected house of the legislature. The problem of imperial taxation was political and ultimately moral, as much as it was economic.

Governor Trumbull had been alive to the problem for years. He was a servant of the empire, but he was a servant of Connecticut first and foremost. "When [the mother country] tries to enslave us," he had written as early as 1770, "the strictest union must be dissolved."[2] For a year and a half, John himself had been living across the Charles River from Boston, a hotspot of colonial protest. In the decade before he arrived, rioters had looted and all but demolished Thomas Hutchinson's house, and British soldiers had fired on another mob pelting them with snowballs and ice chunks, killing five (a toll immortalized as the Boston Massacre). Firebrands churned out angry polemics even during periods of relative peace. Youth, school, and art had kept the imperial crisis from the forefront of John's mind; when he painted great men in desperate situations, he painted Romans. But in his postgraduate year, politics became unignorable. As he would later write, "A moral storm was at hand."[3]

Five months after John returned home, yet another Boston mob, this one well-organized and well-directed, dumped 324 chests of tax-bearing tea into the harbor. Parliament responded by voting to close the port to all marine traffic. The empire was blockading its own people. When the Port Bill went into effect on June 1, 1774, Congregational churches across New England, Lebanon's included, tolled their bells all day, a double message: mourning, and warning of more danger to come. A congress of delegates from a dozen colonies met in Philadelphia in the fall to plan a continental response to Britain's oppressive acts.

Connecticut's response was to put itself on a war footing. The General Assembly ordered the colonial militia to train and mobilized new regiments. Each town was directed to supply a quota of gunpowder, balls, and flint. More ammunition was bought in New York City and the West Indies.

As Connecticut readied itself for the worst, the situation in Massachusetts continued to deteriorate. On April 19, 1775, British troops sweeping the countryside around Boston for weapons and malcontents clashed with local militias at Lexington and Concord. The news reached Connecticut the next day. Governor Trumbull called the General Assembly into special session at Hartford; he wrote to Thomas Gage, the British general in charge of Boston, at the end of the month, hoping even then for reconciliation, but adding that Connecticut would defend its rights "to the last extremity."[4]

Governor Trumbull became, and remained for eight years, Connecticut's war leader. As in the French and Indian War, the state was not a theater of action (at least at first). But it acted as the strategic reserve for Boston, New York City, and northern New York, which all became battlegrounds. Connecticut supplied men, ammunition, cannons, and food. When an American commander in northern New York needed to fell trees to slow a British invasion from Canada, Connecticut sent him four thousand axes. An outbuilding of Trumbull's Lebanon home that he had used for his business affairs became his war office; he and a state-appointed Committee of Safety would meet there over a thousand times.

When France, the old enemy, allied with Britain's rebellious colonies, aristocratic officers posted to Lebanon found it an unlikely command center and its most prominent citizen an unlikely commander. The duc de Lauzun compared the town to Siberia: "cabins scattered through immense forests."[5] The marquis de Chastellux wrote that the governor loved public affairs "with a passion, whether they be great or small; or, rather there are none for him of this latter class."[6] John's father was a merchant revolutionary, devoted to his cause, tending to details— a type new to French noblemen.

The Trumbull family threw itself into the cause along with their patriarch. Joseph became commissary general for the entire American army; Jonathan, Jr., paymaster for the army's Northern Department (responsible for operations in Canada and northern New York), then comptroller of the American Treasury. David collected arms and supervised the transit of provisions as needed. The Trumbull brothers' jobs were a product of nepotism and merit. They got them because they were their father's sons, but they held them because they executed them competently. When Massachusetts patriot John Hancock—rich, ambitious, and gifted with a knack for putting his foot wrong—observed that all the Trumbulls seemed "well provided for," John, the youngest, agreed: they were "secure of four halters" if the cause failed.[7]

John himself went into active military service. After the battles of Lexington and Concord, militia poured into eastern Massachusetts to besiege the British in Boston. Connecticut sent six thousand men. Its First Regiment was commanded by Joseph Spencer, a sixty-year-old judge and friend of the governor; John was his adjutant, or assistant.

Before landfill transformed its geography, Boston occupied a tadpole-shaped peninsula, projecting into an inner harbor encircled by outlying villages. Spencer's regiment, which arrived in early May, was posted on the heights of Roxbury southwest of the city.

The Americans ringing Boston were initially an uprising of New Englanders. But the Continental Congress, convening for a second year in Philadelphia, wanted a national effort. In mid-June it tapped George Washington of Virginia as commander in chief; the four major generals under him represented New York and Virginia as well as Massachusetts and Connecticut. John's commander, Spencer, was one of eight brigadier generals.

Before Washington could arrive to take command, there was another engagement.

On the morning of June 17, John was inspecting the regiment's men on guard duty when he heard British ships firing in the channel north of Boston, four miles away. Charlestown, a village of a thousand people, fronted the channel on the north shore, backed by two hills, Breed's Hill and Bunker's Hill. "Some movement was making in that quarter," John wrote sixty years later, "but we knew not what. . . . As the day advanced, the firing continued to increase, and our anxiety to know the cause was extreme." Americans, they learned, had dug trenches and breastworks on the hills, and the enemy was firing to dislodge them. "About three o'clock ... the firing suddenly increased, and became very heavy and continuous; and soon after, with the help of glasses, the smoke of fire-arms became visible along the ridge of the hill, and fire was seen to break out among the buildings of the town, which soon extended rapidly, and enveloped the whole in flames."[8] The British fired a few shots over Roxbury for good measure; a soldier at John's side dropped dead of a heart attack. John and his comrades did not learn the details of the main battle on the heights above Charlestown until late that night.

The entrenchments on Breed's Hill and the slope before them had become a charnel house. The British had chosen to take the American position by frontal assault. Although the guns of the British ships incinerated the town, they could not be elevated enough to support the troops marching uphill. The Americans met the attackers with a stream of musket fire. The advance faltered, then fell back, decimated. A second assault suffered the same fate; a third took the American trenches only because the defenders had finally run out of ammunition. "The dead," wrote an American officer, "lay as thick as sheep in a fold."[9] A thousand British had been killed or wounded, half as many Americans.

The British kept firing toward Cambridge, the American reserve position, through the night. The roar of cannons, the shells trailing sparks like comet tails, and the glare of still-burning Charlestown made "a fearful breaking in for young soldiers," John wrote.[10] And for young adjutants: he had turned nineteen eleven days earlier.

The Battle of Bunker's Hill made a fearful breaking in for another Trumbull. John's sister Faith, whose artwork had first inspired his own, had been married to Jedediah Huntington, a Norwich merchant, for eight years. Huntington was also an officer in the militia and had led his company to Cambridge after the battles of Lexington and Concord. The Trumbull and Huntington families planned a reunion in Roxbury on June 17, expecting to view a static siege, but as the fighting to the north waxed in intensity, Faith was hurried away to safety. She had glimpsed, John wrote, war's "horrible realities."[11] A first battle shocks anyone; this shocked her profoundly.

George Washington arrived in Cambridge on July 2. John's brother Joseph tipped him that the new commander in chief was anxious to get an accurate map of the enemy's position. John made his way from Roxbury, creeping through high grass as close as he could come to the neck of the peninsula that connected Boston to the mainland. He found that the British had erected a wall across it with bastions at either end. He counted their cannons and made a sketch, the details of which were afterward confirmed by the information of a British deserter. Washington, who had worked as a surveyor himself when he was John's age, appreciated both his boldness and his precision, and put him on his staff as the second of two aides-de-camp. So Governor Trumbull's career advice bore fruit.

George Washington had already earned a military reputation. He had gathered intelligence, fought battles, and organized frontier defense in the French and Indian War. Indeed, he had started the war, by firing on a party of French in the upper Ohio valley.

He seemed well cast for greater glory. He attended the 1775 session of the Continental Congress as a delegate from Virginia, dressed in his old uniform, wearing his willingness to fight. He wore it, as he wore everything, well; he was six foot four, 190 pounds, masterly and graceful. On horseback, which is where most strangers encountered him, he became still more imposing, a modern centaur. Thomas Jefferson, a younger Virginia politician, would call him "the best horseman of his age."[12]

Women felt the spell. Abigail Adams, wife of one of Massachusetts's delegates to Congress, sent a swoony description of him to her husband, John, in Philadelphia. "You had prepared me to entertain a favorable impression of him, but I thought the one half was not told me. . . . Those lines of Dryden instantly occurred to me.

> Mark his Majestick fabric! He's a temple
> Sacred by birth, and built by hands divine.
> His soul's the Deity that lodges there,
> Nor is the pile unworthy of the God."[13]

Men felt his force. When a fight broke out in camp between a Virginia and a Massachusetts regiment—the Massachusetts men, sailors from Marblehead, included Indians and blacks, so there may have been a racial tinge to the ruckus—Washington, seeing it from a distance, leapt off his horse and strode to the center of the brawl, grabbing two sluggers by their necks and shaking them like dogs. The fight stopped.

Washington would prove, over time, to be as good at listening as he was at manly display. When New Englanders took offense at some stray remarks of his, critical of their raggedy appearance and rough manners, he never breathed such thoughts again. Deep into the siege of Boston, when his generals criticized a plan he had devised to attack the town over the frozen bay with men on ice skates, he dropped it, resuming the waiting game. He learned to keep his temper to himself, and to save his energy and aggression for the right moments.

Washington was a man such as John had never seen. His father, sixty-three years old, was a planner and a politician. Washington, forty-three, was both, but could lead in the camp and the field.

John's first reaction to being so close to the commander in chief was to be overwhelmed. Washington's aides were responsible for more than the occasional map. Their chief conferred regularly with the army's senior officers and hosted locally prominent persons and their wives, like Mrs. Adams, as well. John explained his unhappiness in his new job by saying that he was "unequal" to its "*elegant* duties."[14] Since his experience of social life had been confined to the Trumbull, Kneeland, and Robichaud families, this was probably true. After only a month, a Virginian replaced him as aide-de-camp, and he was sent back to his Connecticut regiment in Roxbury as brigade major, or regimental chief of staff—a position with more administrative responsibility than he had held as adjutant. In spare moments he played his flute, which he had asked his brother David back in Lebanon to send him.

He also asked about his sister Faith. Bunker's Hill was not the first shock in her life. Two years earlier she and her husband had given their only child, a five-year-old boy, to Governor and Mrs. Trumbull to raise; evidently motherhood was too much for her to handle. But she needed her husband's companionship: his departure for the war left her feeling lonely and fearful. In October, John invited her to return to Roxbury for a change of scene—an odd plan considering her previous experience of life at the front. But he assured her, "We live . . . as if our enemies were a thousand miles from us, they do nothing to molest us at all." To David he wrote, "What can ail her?. . . . I hope however that a little riding will restore her health."[15] Faith's health was beyond the reach of a little riding. She suffered from what her age called melancholy, ours clinical depression. She wept uncontrollably, she had delusions. She saw a doctor who prescribed "a course of physicks," probably herbals.[16] There were passing improvements, false dawns, but on Thanksgiving she hanged herself. One Trumbull did perish by a halter. "She was a woman," John wrote, "of deep and affectionate sensibility," but of "too sensitive mind."[17]

The long siege finally succeeded after the winter of 1775–76, not because of soldiers on ice skates, but because the Americans had hauled sixty tons of ordnance, captured the previous spring in northern New York, over three hundred miles of snowy trails and frozen rivers to Cambridge. Washington received his new weaponry at the beginning of March. The regiments occupying Roxbury were ordered to fortify the Dorchester heights a few miles to the east, and closer to the Boston peninsula. This was done in one night, as John wrote, "with perfect order, secrecy and success."[18] The British now lay at the mercy of American batteries. On St. Patrick's Day, 1776, they evacuated the city and sailed to Nova Scotia.

They would certainly be back. New York, with its splendid harbor, was the likeliest target. John's regiment redeployed there at the end of March.

Meanwhile the war had been raging hundreds of miles away from the coast. In the French and Indian War, the long, slender lakes of northern New York—Lake Champlain and Lake George—formed a natural invasion corridor between British America and French Canada. Now they served the same purpose for rebellious America and British Canada. In the spring of 1775 the Americans had captured forts Ticonderoga and Crown Point on the shore of Lake Champlain—a brilliant stroke. Thereafter the northern war waxed in scope, and in violence. In September, Richard Montgomery, a British army veteran who had settled in America and taken up the cause of his new home, led an American army via Lake Champlain to the St. Lawrence River. He took Montreal in November and moved downstream to invest the fortified aerie of Quebec. There he was joined by a second American army, led by Benedict

Arnold, a Connecticut merchant, which had bushwhacked across the wilderness of Maine. On New Year's Eve, 1775, they attacked the citadel in a raging snowstorm. Montgomery was killed by a blast of grape— small metal shot fired from a cannon, as if it were a gigantic shotgun. The failed assault was the turning point of the invasion. After the British reinforced Quebec in the spring, they counterattacked, pushing the Americans back from all the territory they had gained.

In June 1776, Horatio Gates, another Americanized British veteran, was sent by Congress to retrieve the situation. Gates's previous role in the American army had been adjutant general, overseeing administrative operations (he was a by-the-book officer, suited to the task; his nickname in the service was "Granny Gates"). He had been impressed with John's work as brigade major, and asked him to be his adjutant, with the rank of colonel. John agreed, and three weeks after his twentieth birthday set off with Gates to the north.

They reached Lake Champlain in July. Ticonderoga lies on the west shore, twenty miles above the lake's southern tip; Crown Point is also on the west shore, ten miles further north. At Crown Point, John found the wreck of the army that had retreated from Canada. The men were ravaged by smallpox. The disease, which had broken out in Boston shortly before the siege, had spread as fast as men could travel. George Washington combatted it in the army he commanded with quarantines, and eventually inoculations, but no coherent plan to contain it had been adopted in the northern army. The American general who had succeeded Montgomery had died of it on the retreat. The troops, healthy and ill alike, had been ferried down Lake Champlain in open, leaking boats, subsisting on salt pork and lake water cut with rum. "I found not an army but a mob," John wrote to his father in July, "ruined by sickness, fatigue, and desertion, and void of every idea of discipline."[19] Decades later the memory of that mob still dismayed him. "I did not look into [a] tent or hut in which I did not find either a dead or dying man. I can scarcely imagine any more disastrous scene."[20] John tallied the sick and the effectives for Gates, and the shadow army was ordered to fall back to Ticonderoga.

John was assigned to strengthen the fortifications there; while doing so he made a prescient observation. On the eastern shore of the lake, opposite Fort Ticonderoga, lay Rattlesnake Hill, renamed Mount Independence by the Americans. Western fort and eastern hill projected into the lake like claws, pinching it, and the Americans had manned both. To the southwest rose an even taller hill, Sugar Loaf, renamed Mount Defiance—unoccupied, because its summit seemed too distant for any artillery atop it to threaten Mount Independence or the fort, and too steep to be accessible to artillery, in any case. John thought Mount Defiance was close enough to be dangerous, and accessible enough to be armed. Perhaps his artist/mapmaker's eye gave him special clarity. With the help of Ebenezer Stevens, a Massachusetts artilleryman, he arranged demonstration shots to show that cannon on Mount Defiance could cover both American positions; on one of his test fires the gun exploded, almost wiping out him and his gun crew. He also took a party of officers clambering up the slope, to prove that it could be scaled. John's higher-ups observed, and, in a spell of paralysis that often overcomes war planners, did nothing.

Washington, meanwhile, was having a bad war. A British expeditionary force appeared off New York City at the end of June and drove him, in a series of autumn battles, from the state and across New Jersey toward Philadelphia. Gates was ordered to reinforce Washington on the Pennsylvania side of the Delaware River. John, sent south, was briefly back under Washington's command at the end of December, as Washington meditated a counterstroke. But battle seldom threatens at only one point. A detachment of British and Hessians, their hired German auxiliaries, took Newport, Rhode Island. John was sent to the American covering force at Providence, where he went into winter quarters.

John had spent a year and a half on the fringes of battles— observing them, observing their aftermaths, preparing for future ones. For the past six months he had, in addition, been preoccupied with his rank. Gates had promised him a colonelcy back in June, but Congress had not yet confirmed it. "I have made it a rule never to ask promotion," John proudly wrote to his brother Joseph in August, but he certainly hungered for it.[21] When it finally came in February 1777, it was dated from September 1776—three months later than he had expected. That meant that men who had been made colonels in the interval were now senior to him. His promotion, instead of being a gratification, seemed like an affront. John sent a brusque note to the president of Congress—John Hancock, the very man who had sneered at his family's various assignments—asking that his commission be redated: "A soldier's honor forbids the idea of giving up the least pretension to rank."[22] He sent a longer note to James Lovell, a Massachusetts congressman who had been a Harvard classmate of Joseph's, explaining that he must resign if this were not done. "From this day . . . I lay aside my cockade and sword, with a determination *fixed as fate,* never to resume them until I can do it with honor."[23] Lovell tried to soothe him: there had been confusion concerning the scope of Gates's own appointment, he explained, which necessarily affected John's. Congress, Lovell added, had been "piqued at the style and manner of your demand."[24] If John asked again in a softer tone, he would surely get what he wanted.

John was unmoved. "I have never asked any office in the public service, *nor will I ever.* . . . I forbear saying anything further on a subject of perfect indifference to me."[25] At the time he wrote this second letter to Lovell, he was already back home in Lebanon.

What a touchy twenty-year-old. Yet John was not the only officer in the American Revolution to be obsessed with points of rank. That spring, John Adams wrote to his wife Abigail from Congress, "I am worried to death with the wrangles between military officers . . . scrambling for rank and pay like apes for nuts."[26] Pay was important, especially when Congress failed to pay the men it had summoned. But questions of rank reflected an officer's honor as a warrior, and as a man.

Congress too was touchy. Politicians in a republic were rightly wary of the lengths to which military men may pursue their sense of honor. A classical education provided numerous accounts of overbearing officers; Shakespeare had dramatized several—*Julius Caesar, Coriolanus.*

Trumbull's brothers Joseph and Jonathan, Jr., also had spats with Congress over their job performance. This was not the pathological sensitivity of their sister Faith, but the concern of sons anxious to measure up to their father, the governor and war leader of their state. Public service was an ongoing Trumbull family test. Jonathan, Jr., would ultimately pass with honors, becoming governor of Connecticut himself one day. John, the runt of the litter, had chosen to distinguish himself as the only

Trumbull in arms. Now Congress was downgrading his distinction in his own (and therefore, said vanity, everyone's) eyes. So he quit.

Back in Lebanon, John took up painting again. He depicted more scenes from classical history. One subject, the late Roman general Belisarius begging, may have resonated specially with him. Legend had it that Belisarius was reduced to beggary because he had been blinded on the orders of the emperor Justinian. The wronged one-eyed colonel painted the wronged no-eyed hero. But John's treatment does not cohere. He put down three parallel groups of figures, Belisarius flanked by observers, like badly hung strips of wallpaper.

He also did a number of family portraits. The governor, despite his reservations about John becoming a painter, sat for a double portrait of himself and Mrs. Trumbull. John had much still to learn about representing anatomy. His mother's face is warm and affectionate, his father's dour but dignified. But the proportions of their heads are faulty, and the fingers of the governor's right hand hang limp at his side, as if invertebrate. A family group of Jonathan, Jr., his wife, and daughter shows the same problem with head size. A standing portrait of Jabez Huntington, Faith's father-in-law, gives him a peculiar pointing left arm, more suited to a scarecrow.

Better than these was a self-portrait (plate 2). John wears his dark hair short in front, long in back, in the current military fashion. He sits at a table, leaning his trim torso slightly forward. His left arm, and his painter's palette, rest on a book by the English artist William Hogarth; the binding is nicely reflected in the tabletop, a Copleyesque touch. Hogarth was best known for moralizing prints that showed sin punished and virtue rewarded in bustling scenes of London life. His book, which John had read at Harvard, was a practitioner's guide to beauty, explaining to artists what it was, and how to achieve it. (Hogarth believed that S-curves winding their way through a composition engaged the eye.) John's pose says, *I know this,* or *I will soon know this. Let me show you. (Forget my family's ill-shaped heads.)* His lips curve in an attractive half-smile.

Before he could make good his artistic boast, the war claimed him once more.

While John was painting, the British mounted a major invasion of New York. Their main army, under General John Burgoyne, captured

Fort Ticonderoga in the summer of 1777, by scaling and arming Mount Defiance, just the means that John had warned against. But after losing two battles near Saratoga in the fall, they surrendered to John's old commander Horatio Gates. This victory encouraged France, which had been helping the Americans on the sly, to do so openly. The first joint operation of the new allies was to be a land-sea attack on Newport, with French ships and American troops, in the summer of 1778.

Newport is only sixty miles east of Lebanon; John volunteered to act as an aid to John Sullivan, the general in command of the American troops, and set off to join him in August.

Newport lies at the mouth of Narragansett Bay, on the southwest corner of the island that gives the state its name. Sullivan occupied Butts Hill at the island's northern end. After a gale dispersed the French fleet, however, he thought it wiser to give the operation up.

The British attacked him at the end of the month, before he could evacuate the island. John was ordered to warn Sullivan's rearguard that they were about to be outflanked. They were posted on Quaker Hill, a mile south of Butts Hill. John's ride to them was his first experience of enemy fire aimed directly at him. A comrade watching from a distance expected "every instant to see you fall. . . . Your preservation . . . I have ever considered as little short of a miracle."[27] Others were less lucky. John passed a colonel missing an arm, a captain shot through the body, an officer being carried to have a leg amputated. The last made a joke of it. His foot had been crushed in the morning by a spent cannonball. "If this had happened to me in the field," he told John, "the loss of a leg might be borne, but to be condemned through all future life to say I lost my leg under the breakfast table, is too bad."[28] Marching, reconnoitering, skirmishing continued throughout the afternoon.

The next day the Americans withdrew to the mainland; the battle was over.

So was John's military career. It had been neither long nor conspicuous. Yet he had held responsibilities and risked his life. Angry enough to resign, he was eager enough to serve again when the fighting came near him, and as the years passed he would grow ever more proud of his service. In 1777 he blustered that he had laid aside his sword. In a self-portrait in middle age he shows himself holding it, next to his palette.

THREE

H is military service over, John returned to painting. He marked his career choice by moving from Lebanon to Boston. There he had first seen paintings worthy of the name, and there the twenty-two-year-old would be physically separated from his family.

John boarded in a house that had once belonged to John Smibert, a Scottish artist, dead for almost thirty years, who had kept a shop that sold paints and displayed copies of European paintings—Raphael, Rubens, Van Dyck. The shop and the collection still existed in the 1770s, and John bought a number of the replicas from the estate of Smibert's nephew.[1]

His family still supplied him with a subject, a seated portrait of Joseph. John had to paint this from memory, for his oldest brother had died in July 1778, age forty-one. The family story was that Joseph succumbed from the burden of his revolutionary duties. John shows him beside a table, slightly hunched. The face is fatigued and brooding. It is an image of an unhappy man. There is some awkwardness in the arrangement of the limbs and the furniture, but the mental state of the subject—Joseph's interior—rings true. It was the best portrait John had produced so far.

For the rest, he socialized with a coterie of recent Harvard graduates. Christopher Gore, class of 1776, and Rufus King, class of 1777, would become lifelong, devoted friends. They met in John's room, drank tea, and talked, like the young sophisticates they were, about literature and the state of the world.

Boston politics was dominated by John's old nemesis, John Hancock, and by Samuel Adams. Hancock pretended to be a radical populist; Adams was the real thing. He had failed at several quotidian jobs—brewer, tax collector—but as a polemicist, a wire-puller, and a talent spotter he was a genius (he had introduced his younger second cousin John Adams to politics). He and Hancock now labored to keep patriot spirits high even in the wake of disappointments like the Newport campaign. John disliked their ceaseless agitation; he was not the first military man, retired or on active duty, to think ill of civilian shouters.

The fact was, Boston, so far from being a step up, was a dead end. Copley, Boston's best painter, had fled to London as a Loyalist at the beginning of the war. Smibert's copies of the European masters—models of what painting should be—were copies. A copy can repeat a general effect, not necessarily the details that make an original throb. Boston offered no one from whom, and little from which, John could learn. He needed to live somewhere with a sophisticated art world if he was to progress.

His next step, as logical as it was unusual for the son of a rebel governor in wartime, was to go to London.

The man who first suggested it was John Temple, a former British official who was still trying, four years into the Revolution, to reconcile the two sides. Temple had been born in Boston to a British army officer and his American wife. After growing up in England, he had returned to New England as a colonial administrator—employment he lost on the eve of the Revolution when he passed sensitive information to American patriots. On one side of the Atlantic, he knew opposition members of Parliament; on the other, Sam Adams and John's father. Temple, the governor wrote, "hath done and suffered much for the cause of this his native and much injured country."[2] He was an American patriot, who longed to keep America within the empire on the best possible terms.

There was a moment, after the Battles of Saratoga, when the British government, panicked at the prospect of a world war against both America and France, temporarily adopted Temple's program. London sent peace commissioners to America in the summer of 1778, offering everything short of independence, and paid Temple to go himself to see what he could accomplish behind the scenes. Stopping in his native Boston, Temple met John and suggested that he go to London to study with Benjamin West.

West's trajectory had been even more unusual than Temple's. Born and raised in Pennsylvania's Quaker heartland, he would claim in later life that Indians had taught him how to make colors from plants.[3] Rich Philadelphians, impressed with his budding artistic skills, sent him to Italy to learn his art. He moved on to London in 1763, where the elite first noticed him because of his skill as a skater. When they found that he also painted in a pleasing style, he became a sensation, taken up by noblemen, clergymen, and ultimately George III himself.

For all his transatlantic success, West was always hospitable to Americans who came to study with him.

John's first reaction to Temple's suggestion was reasonable enough: "I did not think this could be done with safety, during the war."[4] But Temple assured him he could make it happen. Back in London after the failure of his peace mission, Temple wrote to say that no less a person than Lord George Germain, the secretary of state, had told him that if John "chose to visit London for the purpose of studying the fine arts," he "might rely upon being unmolested."[5]

Like other young men early in the race of life, John had more than one possible goal in mind. In Boston he had joined his brothers in buying (with borrowed money) shares in merchant vessels. He might be able to do even better for their investments by monitoring voyages from their European end. "My father's opinion," he wrote to his brother David, "I believe will favor the design."[6] So he could buck his father by pursuing painting, and please him at the same time by making money.

After returning to Lebanon in the fall of 1779, John sailed in May 1780 from New London on a French merchant ship. His voyage was a greater leave-taking than he had planned: his mother died, age sixty-one, while he was at sea. He had painted what turned out to be a farewell portrait during his stay at home.

Trumbull traveled with a fellow American officer, Major John Tyler, from a wealthy Boston family. They landed at Nantes and stopped in Paris, where John hobnobbed with America's diplomats—Benjamin Franklin and John Adams, and Adams's teenage son, John Quincy (it is good to be well-connected). Bad military news from America blighted

John's commercial hopes: the British had captured Charleston, South Carolina, a major victory, which shook the value of American securities. It was time then for John to paint in earnest.

Franklin, who had lived many years in England, knew West and gave John a letter of introduction. John and Tyler arrived in England via a packet ship from the neutral Austrian Netherlands.

Lebanon, John's home, had a population of not quite four thousand; Boston, his recent address, under twenty thousand. London, his new abode, was pushing one million—the largest city in Europe. John arrived on the heels of the Gordon Riots, five days of mayhem inspired by Lord George Gordon, a mentally unbalanced nobleman who feared that Britain was sliding into popery. Mobs set fires, threatened Parliament, and were quelled only by the army. The vast urban organism took the blow and moved on. John, intent on his career, notified Temple of his arrival and called as soon as possible on West.

So much did the king admire West that the transplanted American had rooms assigned to him at Windsor Castle. But his main residence and studio was "a very large elegant house" in the artsy West End.[7] William Hogarth, author of the book on beauty that John had studied at Harvard, had lived in the neighborhood years earlier. Living there now was Sir Joshua Reynolds, a painter superior, certainly in his own mind, to West. Reynolds kept a carriage with gilded wheels and was attended by liveried servants. John Singleton Copley, John's first mentor, had settled nearby after he arrived from Boston. John, still aspiring to these circles, roomed with Tyler off the Strand, the city's main artery.

The art that these Englishmen and Anglo-Americans emulated was classic, realistic, and international. The Italian Renaissance, epitomized by Raphael, supplied the foundation. Painters from other countries who had absorbed its lessons—Velázquez (Spain), Van Dyck and Rubens (the Netherlands), Poussin (France)—completed the canon. The baroque, the fashion that succeeded the Renaissance, added shade and swirls, but was still recognizably related. Roman painting, discovered at Pompeii early in the eighteenth century, was a bit stiff, but Greek and Roman statues and busts offered useful models of the human form.

This visual world, though rich, was limited. Italian art before the Renaissance was ignored; gothic figured only as a setting for horror stories and a source of eccentric decoration. There was a vogue for Chinese porcelain, and American Indian clothing might provide exotic details in painted descriptions of overseas empires, but that was as far as cultural appropriation went.

England itself was a relative newcomer to the world of art. Charles I, though he had lost his throne and his head in the century before, had been a sophisticated patron. Sir Robert Walpole, an early eighteenth-century prime minister, accumulated a magnificent collection of paintings, the jewels of which had been sold to Catherine the Great of Russia just the year before John's arrival. But other aristocrats were eager to acquire what pictures they could—recognized masterpieces, bought on the continent, or, would-be ones, newly painted.

Local artists who aimed to satisfy this demand yearned in turn for status: to be recognized as, if not the peers of their noble customers, capable at least of appearing in their drawing rooms. The stigma of artisan needed to be effaced in England no less than in New England. Hence Reynolds's carriage wheels and servants. Hence, more important, the Royal Academy of the Arts—an institution, modeled on similar bodies in Europe, that exhibited the works of established artists, taught aspiring ones, and sought to educate the public. When Trumbull arrived in London, the Royal Academy was quartered in Somerset House, a palatial complex between the Strand and the Thames. The king himself acted as patron. Reynolds was the first president, installed in 1768 and knighted the following year. West was a founding member.

West's first question to John when he presented himself at his studio was, had the young man brought any samples of his work? (Oil paintings can be rolled and carried as conveniently as fishing rods.) John had not. West then invited him to look around his studio and pick something to copy, so that the master could judge his skill. John picked a copy of a seated Madonna by Raphael, which West called "a good omen," since the original was one of Raphael's most admired works. Describing the scene decades later, John wrote that he had not known the masterpiece he had chosen, though he had in fact seen another copy of it in Smibert's Boston shop.[8] West then took him into an adjoining room, where he introduced him to one of his students, like him an American, who would show him where the paints, brushes, and easels were.

John's new partner was Gilbert Stuart, a year older than he was. Stuart had come to London from his native Rhode Island at the start of the Revolution. He was talented, improvident, and brash. Samuel Johnson, the great essayist and lexicographer, meeting the young man, was impressed with his talk and asked him where he had learned English, as if Americans did not know the language. "Not from your dictionary," Stuart replied.[9] He could turn his humor on his teacher too. West drew curly hair, Stuart once explained, "with a flourish of his brush ... like a figure three. Here, Trumbull," he went on, showing John an unfinished portrait on West's easel, "do you want to know how to paint hair? ... Our master figures out a head of hair like a sum of arithmetic ... three and three make six, and three are nine, and three are twelve." West, eavesdropping in the next room, came in and gave Stuart a scolding. But when the portrait was done, the two pupils noticed there were no longer any threes in the hair.[10] Opposites attracted. The merchant/governor's son and the scapegrace became friends. Stuart too had a flute, and the pair played duets together.

West had already painted his most famous picture, one that would help set the course of John's life.

Charles du Fresnoy had urged painters to preserve the glory of heroes. West's sensational painting immortalized General James Wolfe and his greatest victory, the capture of Quebec (figure 3). In 1759, as the tide of the Seven Years' War began to run in England's favor, Wolfe's assignment was to take France's citadel on the St. Lawrence River. After a three-month siege, the British made a night climb up a cliffside path to the Plains of Abraham, a field stretching behind the town's walls. The next morning the defenders marched out to meet them and were defeated. Wolfe, shot in the stomach and chest early in the engagement, heard shouts of "They run!" as he lay dying. "Who?" he asked, and when told it was the French, he said, "Now, God be praised, I will die in peace." Unlike General Richard Montgomery sixteen years later, he had taken Quebec. But, as would his American successor, he perished in the attempt.

West immortalized the moment of death. To do so he mimicked the iconography of Christ's deposition from the cross. Quebec is Golgotha. Wolfe dies in the center, supported by anxious officers. Two groups

Figure 3. Benjamin West, *The Death of General Wolfe,* 1770. West's blockbuster
painting violated Sir Joshua Reynolds's strictures against contemporary detail.
But painters, including Reynolds, and the public admired it.

of men stand on either side; those to the viewer's left point to the retreating French. An Indian in the left foreground is a geographical marker,
and a representative of Britain's Iroquois allies. A tableau of the battle
space fills the background, including a spire of the town, the field itself,
and the St. Lawrence dotted with British ships, all under a stormy sky.

Strict accuracy is not the point. One of West's supporting characters, Sir William Johnson, depicted in a green coat on the left, was hundreds of miles away when the Battle of Quebec was fought. West
included him because he marshalled Indian allies for other British victories. Of the other figures who can be identified, five or six were engaged in the battle, though only one—the lieutenant in the central group
carrying the flag—was with Wolfe when he died.[11]

Why paint a historical painting that is not historical? West wanted to capture more than a moment; he aimed to show its significance. The scenery and the turbulent sky suggest the stakes—nothing less than control of North America. The expressions of some of the witnesses capture the emotion of death-in-victory. Even gestures that are naively rendered—the pointing of the men on the left—fill a narrative need.

The picture is not without flaws on its own terms. Poor Wolfe himself is beyond dying—he looks almost boneless. Where did West study anatomy? The Indian in the foreground sits, with his chin on his hand, as if observing some indoor activity—a game of billiards, or a performance on the clavier—not one empire triumphing over another. Yet to a great extent West preserved the glory of a hero—a hero, moreover, who was virtually a contemporary: born only eleven years before George III, seventeen years after Jonathan Trumbull, Sr.

West put his characters in contemporary military dress (he was much more accurate about what they were wearing than who wore it). He encountered some resistance for doing this, according to an account he gave his own biographer years later. Sir Joshua Reynolds came to West when the picture was in contemplation and urged him to put his figures in classical garb, as if he were young John Trumbull painting noble Romans in Lebanon. Historical paintings in modern dress, Reynolds argued, would be a new thing, and all innovations risk "repulse or ridicule." West persisted with his original intention and invited Reynolds to view the finished product. After studying it for half an hour, Reynolds said, "Mr. West has conquered. . . . I retract my objections."[12]

Why had Reynolds objected in the first place? There had already been two paintings before West's of Wolfe dying, neither very good, but both showing their subjects in their actual uniforms. Continental painters had long depicted contemporary battles in which everyone appears as they were. But Reynolds argued, in a lecture delivered as president of the Royal Academy no less, that painters who aspired to the "grand style" must depict human nature unadorned, "disregard[ing] all local and temporary ornaments."[13] Yet West had packed a canvas unquestionably grand with sword hilts and sashes, buttons and beaded gunpowder pouches. Here was a battle all right, but bigger and bolder. If that broke or bent a genre, so be it.

As soon as *The Death of General Wolfe* was exhibited in 1771, it was a sensation. West was asked to copy it, by George III among others, and a print of the painting sold handsomely. A year later the king made West his official history painter, with an annual salary of £1,000.[14]

John's first essay in history painting was a standing portrait of George Washington. He showed Washington in uniform, on some rocky outcrop, perhaps near West Point, the great fort of the lower Hudson River valley. John worked from memory, and this Washington looks leaner in the face than he actually was. But the pose is both imposing and natural, a great advance on John's awkward standing portrait of Jabez Huntington.

Behind Washington a black groom in a turban holds his horse. The exotic black attendant was a feature of English military portraits, a status marker, almost a fashion accessory. Joshua Reynolds had included one each in two portraits of officers who served during the Seven Years' War.[15] Washington's black body servant, his slave William Lee, rode with him on his fox hunts in peacetime and attended him throughout the war. During his days in the army John would have seen Lee almost as often as he had seen Washington. He nevertheless gives him an orientalizing turban, rather than the simple livery and hat he actually wore.

John's portrait was a contemporary history painting, even more current than West's *Death of General Wolfe*. It filled a visual need, a news hole: who is this man we have been fighting? After being driven from New York in 1776, Washington had commanded in five battles in two years: a mix of victories (Trenton and Princeton, in the winter of 1776–77, a mere month after John had left his side for Rhode Island); defeats (Brandywine Creek and Germantown, 1777); and an honorable draw (Monmouth Courthouse, 1778). These engagements, coupled with Gates's victories at Saratoga, had frustrated Britain's efforts to subdue the northern and middle colonies. Even British patriots wanted to see who had brought this about, while the political opposition, small but vocal, wished to see the man they admired. America's ally France offered another market for Washington's image. An engraving of John's painting by Valentine Green, mezzotint engraver to the king, went round Europe.[16]

John had ventured into modern history painting with a single image of two figures. His ambitions, and his cast of characters, would expand exponentially.

Before that could happen, his studies were cut short in a manner as dramatic as it was unexpected: in November 1780 he was arrested on suspicion of being a spy.

John's ordeal began with a midnight knock at the door. His housemate, Tyler, was out, presumably partying: "some of his merry companions" were looking to extend the evening, John told their landlady. Instead the caller was a middle-aged police official with a warrant for Tyler's arrest for treason, and additional orders to pick up John and his papers. After a night in a lockup, John was sent to Bridewell, a sixteenth-century prison (the Gordon rioters had burned most of the city's jails).

John's first reactions were astonishment and lethargy, twin symptoms of shock. At a stroke he had been transformed from an art student living under a special dispensation of the government to a prisoner, he knew not why. In a burst of indignation during his first interrogation, he declared that he was the son of an American governor and a former aide to the American commander in chief. "Treat me as you please, always remembering, that as I may be treated, so will your friends in America"—British prisoners of war—"be treated by mine."[17] His captors became more polite after that, although on John's first night in Bridewell he was made to sleep in the same bed with a highwayman.

Soon enough he became habituated to his new situation. Bridewell had a garden and a taproom, where the prisoners could order meals. (The government allowed prisoners two pence a day for their maintenance. Anything more expensive had to be paid for out of pocket.) The warden, who had been butler to a duke, was well-mannered. John rented the parlor room of his lodging, which, except for the bars on the windows and the bolts on the doors, was pleasant enough.

John had fallen afoul of a change in the political climate since John Temple had first proposed he study with West. Britain's peace offers had long since been rejected. The government had settled on a strategy of retaking the American South, which it believed harbored Loyalists waiting to welcome them. The successful siege of Charleston in the spring of 1780 was the first step in the new plan. A smashing victory at Camden, South Carolina, that August seemingly put the entire region at Britain's mercy.

An even greater victory had been narrowly forestalled in September when the treason of General Benedict Arnold was exposed. Arnold, whom the British had turned months before, offered to surrender West Point and control of the Hudson valley, effectively knocking New York out of the war. What Burgoyne failed to achieve by arms was nearly won by a plot. As a bonus, Arnold hoped to bag George Washington, who was due to come to West Point for an inspection. Arnold managed to flee to British lines, but his handler, Major John André, was caught by the Americans and hanged as a spy.

The opposition and the public were tiring of the long war, but the government seemed desperate to win. Among the war's most zealous supporters were exiled American Loyalists, yearning to return to their homes, and yearning even more to punish their American enemies. They had complained of the extraordinary leniency shown John's art studies; the instructions for his arrest had been written out by Lord Germain's undersecretary, a Massachusetts Loyalist.

John believed that he had been seized as a tit for tat for the unfortunate André. André had been an aide to the British commander in occupied New York; John had been an aide to George Washington. As André had suffered, so might John.

Had he been guilty of anything more substantial than his American patriotism and his former rank? The British, in examining his papers, found three letters that they claimed were suspicious: one, not yet sent, to his father; one from Benjamin Franklin's grandson in Paris, whom he had met months earlier; and a third from a Mr. William White. The first two letters were routine communications. The letter from White, seemingly about a commercial venture in the West Indies, was puzzling if not compromising.

White's letter had been addressed to John, care of a Mr. Waters, at an address near John's lodgings. It is both wordy and vague, which could suggest the presence of a code. "William White" is also the sort of bland alias favored by spies. John told the officials who examined him that he barely knew White, having met him casually at a public park. He also said the man who had forwarded it to him was named not Waters but Digges.

One of John's thoughts in going abroad had been to oversee his family's merchant business. He had put that idea aside after he first arrived in Europe, but the letter from White could refer to a newly hatched

venture. Thomas Digges was a Marylander living in London who dab-
bled in transatlantic trade. He had also been involved in helping American prisoners of war held in England, providing them publicly with
money for jailhouse expenses—and helping them, on the sly, escape.[18]

However romantic it might be to think of John springing Americans from enemy jails, there are obvious difficulties with the idea. If he
had been involved with Digges in something treacherous, why had he
volunteered Digges's name under examination? Why would someone as
conspicuous as John be taken into a secret operation at all? In a lifetime
that stretched sixty years after the Revolution, John never alluded to any
mission he may have had.

Silence comes naturally to spies. John Jay ran American spies and
hunted down enemy ones in the lower Hudson valley, and the tales he
told of his operations inspired his son-in-law James Fenimore Cooper's
first bestseller, *The Spy*. But even decades after the fact, Jay concealed the
names of his agents.

Still the absence of proof cannot be offered as proof. Most likely
John fell victim, as he believed, to the malice of American Loyalists.

His arrest was the talk of the town. Horace Walpole, aesthete and
busybody, noted in his journal that "Mr. Turnbull [*sic*]" had been taken
up as a spy. Walpole thought the government was trying to pin the Gordon Riots on American agents.[19] The newspapers carried longer, and
correctly spelled, accounts. One described John as "a genteel looking
man, about thirty five years of age" (off by eleven years), who had "behaved much like a gentleman" at the time of his arrest, "making no attempt to escape."[20] Tyler, who had been tipped off by a knowledgeable
friend, had escaped to the continent.

As soon as West learned what had happened, he hastened to the
king, not only to see what might be done for his student, but to ensure
that he remained in his patron's good graces. George III assured West
that he did not doubt his loyalty. As for the prisoner, he said the law must
take its course, though he promised that if the American were sentenced
to death, a royal pardon would spare his life.

John consulted a lawyer, hoping to be tried in a court of law, an
indication that he believed the government's suspicions of him were
baseless. He was advised that political influence might be more effectual

in freeing him. Charles James Fox, leader of the opposition in Parliament, and Edmund Burke, Fox's political mentor, visited John in Bridewell. Fox, a wealthy, silver-tongued rake, admitted that he had no influence to wield (the king detested him). Burke, who was a shade less flamboyant, promised to do what he could.

John kept painting in prison. It was both a pastime and a way to maintain his identity in enforced confinement. Stuart visited him, to bestow a nickname—"Bridewell Jack"—and to paint his portrait. John himself added the bars on the window that Stuart showed behind his head. West loaned his copy of Correggio's *Madonna with St. Jerome*, which John copied in turn.

Winter passed, then spring. Although the British continued to win victories in the American South, the condition of their army there only seemed to worsen. Walpole noted that Lord Cornwallis, the commander on the spot, lacked supplies, clothing, and information. He could not "get intelligence from a single person, nor could ever learn where the enemy was till he met them."[21] Through some combination of war weariness and Burke's efforts, John was released in June 1781, provided he leave England in thirty days and post £400 in bail. He put up £200 of his own money; West and Copley contributed £100 each.

John left promptly for Amsterdam. There he tried to raise a loan for the state of Connecticut, to no avail. His journey to America was prolonged by quarrels with the captain, bad weather, and a change of ships after a detour to Spain. Not until January 1782 was he in America once more, a year and a half after leaving it.

FOUR

John returned to Lebanon, and fell ill—not an unnatural reaction to his situation.

He had spent a year and a half abroad, hoping to learn his art. He had met talented painters and seen a life-changing painting, but the progress he had made had been shadowed, almost swallowed up, by imprisonment. The time seemed "thrown away."[1] He took to his bed, and did not fully recover until the fall of 1782. More time thrown away, but at least he had thrown it away himself, not lost it to uncontrollable jailers.

When he reemerged he helped his brother David supply Washington's army, which was camped near Newburgh, New York, seventy miles north of New York City.

John's months in London and in transit had seen tremendous military and political changes in America. Four months after John got out of Bridewell, Lord Cornwallis, would-be conqueror of the South, had surrendered his army to a Franco-American siege at Yorktown, Virginia. While John lay sick in Lebanon, Britain's antiwar opposition was finally able to form a government, compelling the king to admit defeat. Until a peace treaty was signed, however, the British still occupied New York City. While Franklin, Adams, and other American diplomats dickered in Paris with their British opposite numbers, Washington and his army had to stay under arms, observing the enemy from the Hudson River corridor.

In this period of enforced idleness, officers whose pay was long in arrears almost mutinied. It took all of Washington's charisma to restore them to good discipline.

John was not privy to these maneuvers. He did his jobs—helping his brother fulfill his contracts; helping himself by observing Washington, his once and future subject. Historians, biographers, and historical painters cover the big moments. But the big moments are informed and illuminated by the little ones: how people walk, stand, gesture; how they sit a horse, how they look about them. John would be exaggerating when, as an old man, he called Washington his "master and friend."[2] Washington was gracious with everyone, intimate with almost none. Supplying troops did not give John daily contact with their commander, as he had experienced during his brief time as an aide. But every encounter or glimpse he managed to have passed, consciously and unconsciously, into his visual mind, for later use.

The Treaty of Paris was signed September 3, 1783. American patriots could travel safely to Britain without fear of midnight knocks. Before John returned to resume his studies, he had a last discussion about his future with his father. By this time Governor Trumbull must have recognized that the claims of art had an unshakable hold on his youngest son. Both men knew it, and knew each other knew it. Yet they argued the point one more time.

The governor "urged the law, as the profession which in a republic leads to all emolument and distinction." Lawyers make money; some lawyers go on to win elections. John countered by abusing his father's option—lawyers spend their days contending in court with the vices that make lawyers and courts necessary—and praising his own, dwelling "upon the honors paid to artists in the glorious days of Greece and Athens."

"My father," John recalled, "listened patiently, and when I had finished, he complimented me on the manner in which I had defended what still appeared to him to be a bad cause." Just like a lawyer, his father added.

"But," the old man went on, "... you appear to have overlooked, or forgotten, one very important point in your case."

"Pray, sir," said John, "what was that?"

"You appear to forget, sir, that *Connecticut is not Athens.*"[3]

The governor bowed, and, according to his son, never said anything more on the matter.

He had said enough. Connecticut was not Athens, nor was it London. No artist could make a career there, still less learn. John was back at West's in January 1784.

He had brought with him a letter from his father to Edmund Burke, thanking the great parliamentarian for his efforts on John's behalf. John delivered it personally, which gave Burke the occasion for offering some advice: the American should study architecture as well as painting. "You belong to a young nation," Burke explained, "which will soon want public buildings; these must be erected before the decorations of painting and sculpture will be required."[4] John did not follow Burke's advice, though years later he would, via his paintings, become involved in the design of a great public building.

Burke was an intimate of Sir Joshua Reynolds. West knew Reynolds too, of course, but they were fellow artists (i.e., rivals), whereas Burke and Reynolds enjoyed the repartee of a weekly dining club presided over by Samuel Johnson. Johnson had prized Reynolds as an independent spirit since they first met, at the home of a pair of sisters who were mourning the death of a benefactor. Reynolds told them that, after all, they had "the comfort of being relieved from a burthen of gratitude."[5] Reynolds, Johnson decided, was a man who thought for himself. Thought, and spoke: Gilbert Stuart was not the only sharp-tongued painter in London.

John threw himself into his painting—"I am fixed a painter," he wrote to his brother Jonathan, Jr., in March; "I study night and day," he wrote to David three months later—and he took one of the first paintings he finished in 1784 to Reynolds for his opinion.[6] John's offering was a portrait of Jeremiah Wadsworth, a merchant and Trumbull family friend, and his young son. It evoked a tender feeling between the two: Wadsworth, sitting at his desk, turns toward the boy, who leans on his shoulder. But the picture had problems: Wadsworth's legs are spindly as dowels and twist at an unlikely angle.

Reynolds lighted upon Wadsworth's gray coat. "That coat is bad, sir, very bad," he scolded. "It is not cloth—it is tin, bent tin."

John replied that he knew his work had defects, but he hoped that Reynolds "would kindly have pointed out to me how to correct my errors."[7] He took his painting, and himself, away.

John also did a history painting, a second image of George Washington. This time he inserted Washington into an ancient scene: Cincinnatus, a Roman farmer of the fifth century BC, taking command of the city's troops to defeat an invasion of Gauls. According to the semilegendary account of his life, Cincinnatus saved the day, then earned immortality by returning to his plow. Washington seemed like a modern Cincinnatus because of his behavior at war's end. Even after the treaty of peace had been signed in August 1783, he still had four months of work to do: sending his soldiers home, dismantling the Newburgh encampment, taking possession of a broken New York City on the heels of the departing British, then finally, in December, surrendering his commission as commander in chief to Congress, the body that had conferred it on him eight and a half years earlier. That first ceremony had occurred in Philadelphia. The second unfolded in Annapolis, Maryland, where Congress had relocated. "Having now finished the work assigned me," Washington told the assembled delegates, "I now retire from the great theater of action."[8] Washington had reenacted one of history's most glorious moments. Like Cincinnatus, he knew the proper, and obedient, place of the military in a free state. Even Britons admired his gesture; it "excites the astonishment and admiration of this part of the world," John wrote at the time.[9] By putting Washington's face on Cincinnatus's body, John made the reenactment literal.

This painting is lost, which is just as well. It was a conceptual dead end, taking John back to the classical paraphernalia of his youth. He found better models close to hand.

At the end of 1784 West commissioned John to copy two of his modern history paintings: *The Death of General Wolfe* and *The Battle of La Hogue*. The second painting, which West produced in 1778, showed a 1692 naval battle off the French coast between a British and a French fleet. The British sunk twelve enemy ships in the engagement, scotching plans for a French invasion. But, unlike *The Death of General Wolfe*, in which the fighting is relegated to the background, *The Battle of La Hogue* is a scene of maritime mayhem. Ships burn at close quarters; sailors and marines swing cutlasses and muskets; a floundering man in the water cocks an arm to slug a struggling enemy. Here was history in action, in contemporary—or at least, contemporary as of the last century—garb.

By commissioning John to copy his history paintings, West, ever the generous teacher, wanted to give a student a leg up. Ever the self-promoter, he wanted to put these works once more before the public eye.

In May 1784 John Singleton Copley exhibited a dramatic history painting of his own, about very recent history indeed. In 1781, while John was languishing in Bridewell, France had raided Jersey, an island remnant of the duchy of Normandy which, though lying only a dozen miles off the French coast, remained a possession of the British crown. The invaders reached St. Helier, Jersey's capital, where they were repelled by a party of British soldiers. In the course of the counterattack Francis Peirson, the twenty-three-year-old major who led it, was killed by a French sniper. *The Death of Major Peirson* dispatches the hero—and his killer: a black man, servant of another British officer, fires back at the sniper, finishing him off (figure 4). The composition is schematic: three groups of figures—marching soldiers, fighting soldiers, fleeing civilians—are lined in a row from left to right. But the fighting group in the middle twists and turns, and the colorful uniforms and flag—red coats and a huge, billowing Union Jack—are bolder than anything in West's palette.

Meanwhile West had thought of a new subject. In the summer of 1783, while John was still in Connecticut, West wrote to Charles Willson Peale, an American former student of his then living in Philadelphia, asking him to send descriptions and drawings of the uniforms of American troops in the Revolutionary War. (West was always particular about what the people in his canvases wore; Peale, himself a veteran, could have honestly told him that the American fighting man commonly wore very little, and that was ragged.) West wanted the information, he wrote, because the Revolution "has engaged all the powers of Europe. All will be interested in seeing the event ... portrayed."[10] West planned a series of paintings of the major events, and a spin-off series of engravings based on them. He had already begun a group portrait of the diplomats who signed the Treaty of Paris, for which all the American negotiators—Franklin, Adams, and three others—obligingly posed.

Then West's project hit a snag. The British diplomats who had negotiated the document refused to sit for him. Why should they be memorialized for ceding half an empire? West was left with five men

Figure 4. John Singleton Copley, *The Death of Major Peirson, 6 January 1781,*
1783. Copley created this work to commemorate a British victory in a
losing war. His black marksman makes a polemical point about Britain's
(supposedly) enlightened attitudes.

arranged at one end of a table, facing a beige void. West began to consider that he was known for painting British triumphs (Quebec, La
Hogue). Perhaps it would be less than politic for George III's American-
born history painter to begin painting American triumphs. Similar con-
siderations forestalled Copley, the other artistic émigré, from pursuing
such a subject.

The subject was perfect for John. He had been thinking about it for
years. His standing portrait of Washington had been his first tryout.
Shortly after his second arrival in London, he wrote to his brother Jonathan, Jr., that "the late war opens a new and noble field for painting."[11] He
was seeing, and copying, modern history paintings by adepts of the

genre. He was acquainted with some of the most important characters in the history of the late war, Franklin and Adams, Washington and Horatio Gates. He had seen battles and their aftermaths, bullets had been shot at him. He would not need to ask anyone for descriptions of American uniforms; he had worn one himself.

West's abandoned project gave John a focus, and a project of his own. When he wrote to Jonathan, Jr., again at the end of 1784, the noble field of painting had a path through it. "The plan I have in view" was "painting a series of pictures of our country, particularly the great events of the revolution."[12] The series would occupy him, on and off, for the next forty-five years.

In order to fulfill such a plan, he needed to work his skills up to highest pitch. That meant studying drawing, something he had hitherto neglected. According to the prevailing notions of how art was made, drawing supplied the structure of every image. The term that signified as the generic tool of the painter's art was "the pencil," not "the brush." Lessons in drawing focused on the human body—a new thing for Americans abroad, since drawing nude models was as yet unknown back home. John labored away, alongside budding artists who were by now years younger than he was (he turned twenty-eight his first June back in Britain). If he learned his lessons, there would be no more scarecrow arms or spindle legs in his paintings.

He also needed to support himself. Youthful experience of material comfort had accustomed him to a style of living that he would never give up. He was not profligate. He never blew fortunes on the turf or at the gaming table, as British noblemen spectacularly did. But he thought of himself as a gentleman, and a gentleman's son. Starving in a garret for art's sake, like a Grub Street poet, would never be his way either. So how could a painter turn a decent profit?

The obvious recourse was portrait painting. The wealthy in America liked to see themselves replicated over their mantels; the wealthy in Britain liked it too, and there were more of them, with more money. John would paint many portraits in his life, in both countries, charging the upper end of the going rate, but he often chafed at the task. Pleasing a customer seemed like gratifying vanity.

An aspiring history painter needed a dependable backer. West's was George III (out of the question). John turned to his brothers Jonathan, Jr., and David, asking for an advance of £200 or £300.[13] The Trumbull siblings had been helping each other out for years, John's brothers giving him advice and work, he giving them necessary assistance in return. Now, however, they pleaded poverty. "To tell you the truth," wrote Jonathan, Jr., "our abilities are not increasing."[14]

John found a backer in an acquaintance from the war, a man he had known as John Carter, who, like his brothers, was a supplier for the American army. Carter's business was lucrative, and he augmented it by also supplying the French. He had "riches enough," wrote one of his American acquaintances, "to make the longest life comfortable."[15] After the war Carter moved back to Britain, his homeland, where he resumed his real name, John Barker Church. (Helping his country's enemies, he must have thought, was best done under an alias.) Church commissioned John to paint a portrait of his wife and son, and offered to be his banker, providing loans that, he assured John, needed only his personal receipt, and a promise to pay back at five percent interest.[16] Their relationship would continue for a decade.

Across the ocean, meanwhile, a chapter in John's life was closing. His father had concluded his last term as governor in May 1784. He had held the job for sixteen years. He had steered Connecticut out of the empire, into independence and statehood. He had been the provisioner of the American army, supplying everything from cattle to cannons. In the last days of the war his state had become a battleground as Benedict Arnold, native son turned traitor, raided the coast. The governor himself had been the target of death threats (Connecticut's Loyalists were few, but bitter).

He had been true to the principles of the Revolution, according to his lights, and his temperament. When the General Assembly decided that the proper title for Connecticut's governor should be "His Excellency," he tried it for a year, then balked. "High sounding titles," he told the legislature, "intoxicate the mind, ingenerate envy, breed disorders in a commonwealth, and therefore ought to be avoided . . . . may it not honorably be repealed?"[17] At the end of his tenure, the General Assembly passed an act for the gradual abolition of slavery in the state (very gradual: children born to slaves after March 1, 1784, would be freed when they turned twenty-five).[18] Slaveholder though he was, the governor signed it.

He was weary. In another address to the General Assembly, he spoke, truthfully, of "a life worn out almost in the constant cares of office."[19] He had lost his wife, the mother of his six children, four years earlier.

He missed John. "His mind dwells much on his absent son," Jonathan, Jr., wrote to the wanderer at the end of 1784.[20] Jonathan, Sr., himself wrote to John in April 1785, "You will never return to Europe after leaving it."[21] It was the last echo of their long-running dispute about John's future, shorn finally of squabbling over his career choices. What the old man was saying, silently, was *I want you to put Europe behind you, so that I may see you*. It was not to be. The governor died in August 1785.

That fall Trumbull—I will now call him by his surname—began painting the project of his life. Over the years he would list the scenes he intended to paint, in prospectuses or letters. Most of these scenes made it to canvas, some not. He carefully collected portraits of persons meant to populate works that he never started; entire categories of topics, meant to be covered by more than one work—the war in the South, diplomacy—would fall by the wayside.

Trumbull began with subjects that he had been studying as a painter—battle scenes—and the battles he depicted were two in which he had participated, even if only at secondhand, as a soldier: Bunker's Hill (the name historically assigned to the battle, even though the Americans were entrenched on Breed's Hill, an elevation just below Bunker's) and Quebec. He had seen the smoke and heard the gunfire of the first from across Boston Harbor; he had tallied the sick survivors of the second in upstate New York.

These, and his subsequent Revolutionary War paintings, will be described when the series is finally finished, and displayed in the gallery Trumbull designed for it. An artist's great project deserves to be judged when it is complete. Until then it will be enough to give some details about how the paintings were done, and the impression they made on first viewers.

Trumbull began his Bunker's Hill painting in the fall of 1785, finishing it at the end of January 1786 (plate 3). He began his Quebec painting in February; by March it was well along (plate 4). Each painting is named after the death of a prominent American: General Joseph Warren, a Boston doctor and patriot leader, shot during the last British charge at Bunker's Hill; General Richard Montgomery, the Irish-born patriot commander, killed by a blast of grape shot in the failed assault on the citadel of Quebec.

The paintings are not large: twenty by thirty inches. West's *Death of General Wolfe,* by contrast, was five by seven feet, Copley's *Death of Major Peirson,* eight by twelve feet. Trumbull's predecessors made grand presentations; Trumbull focused the viewer's gaze. West's and Copley's work required you to stand back; Trumbull's pulled you in.

His paintings were immediate successes, especially *The Death of General Warren at the Battle of Bunker's Hill,* the busier of the two canvases. West praised it warmly: Trumbull wrote to his brother David that his teacher had called it the "best picture of a modern battle."[22] Since the most famous picture of a modern battle in the English-speaking world at that time was by West himself, this was warm praise indeed. Ordinary viewers echoed West's judgment. "Mr. Trumbull has made a painting of ... the death of General Warren," wrote Abigail Adams, who had accompanied her husband to London on a new diplomatic assignment. "To speak of its merit I can only say that in looking at it my whole frame contracted, my blood shivered, and I felt a faintness at my heart."[23] William Dunlap, yet another American student of West's, ten years younger than Trumbull, was inspired by it to poetry.

> In firm array the Britons onward bend,
> Treading in blood of father, son, or friend.
> Striding o'er kindred slain they gain the field;
> Our yeoman slow, to numbers only, yield.[24]

Goethe, the German Renaissance man, saw *Bunker's Hill* when Trumbull took it to the continent to be engraved, and praised its composition: "For a picture in which so many red uniforms must be introduced, it is very judiciously colored."[25]

Most gratifying to Trumbull was the reaction of Sir Joshua Reynolds. One winter night early in 1786 West hosted a dinner party for artists. *Bunker's Hill,* which was well along, was displayed on an easel in a prominent place. Reynolds noticed it as soon as he arrived.

"Why, West," he said, "what have you got here?—this is better colored than your works are generally."

"You mistake," West answered, "that is not mine—it is the work of this young gentleman, Mr. Trumbull; permit me to introduce him to you."[26]

Trumbull recorded this story decades later, as payback for the pressed tin coat that had excited Reynolds's derision, but it sounds accurate: Reynolds's rudeness, and his good judgment, both ring true.

Trumbull began sketching two other history paintings at this time. One belonged to his American revolutionary series, and memorialized another heroic casualty—*The Death of General Mercer at the Battle of Princeton.* The battles of Trenton and Princeton in central New Jersey arrested the tide of defeat in which the American cause had been floundering throughout the second half of 1776. Trumbull had not seen them, or their aftermaths. But he had been briefly with Washington's army just before they were fought, when fortune was at its ebb; he would have recalled the desperate need to do something, anything.

The second history painting Trumbull began planning was a suggestion of West's, in the nature of a career boost. It would help Trumbull's standing in the London art market, West thought, if he were to paint a British victory. Bunker's Hill and Quebec were British victories, of course, but the American theater in which they occurred had been a catastrophic loss. Britain, however, had scored important successes against other enemies in the world war that the American Revolution became. One of the most stirring had been the defense of Gibraltar. Britain had taken the strategic Spanish promontory at the mouth of the Mediterranean in 1704, and one of Spain's primary reasons for entering the Revolutionary War as an ally of France was to get it back. But Britain had broken a years' long Spanish siege in 1782: a perfect subject for Trumbull, flattering for the British, but no loss for America.

West was doing some career boosting of his own. He had lost a commission from the city of London to memorialize the lifting of the siege to Copley. Now his pupil could compete with his rival. Trumbull, who admired both painters, chose to depict an earlier incident in the siege, rather than go head-to-head with Copley. He wanted to paint battles, not engage in them.

West gave some career advice that was potentially far more consequential. Painters could make good money selling individual works; they could make better money from engravings. There was a public unable to buy original art who nevertheless wanted to see it; printed engravings satisfied that slice of the market. For *The Battle of La Hogue*, West had earned 500 guineas; the engravings of it earned him 1,500 more. The engraver had to be paid up front, but a good sale could easily cover that expense.

Trumbull was initially reluctant to spend the time it would take to find and supervise an engraver. Happily, London offered a convenient middleman, Antonio di Poggi, a transplanted Florentine who dealt in paintings, made and sold printed fans, and, most important for Trumbull, published artists' prints. Poggi was a protégé of Reynolds, and also well known to West. When Trumbull approached him, he advised that there were no engravers in Britain capable of executing "a work of the first class."[27] (None capable, or none willing: British engravers probably shared British painters' reservations about celebrating American independence.) Poggi offered to look for some in Paris on a trip he planned to take in the summer of 1786.

Trumbull followed him, taking his two completed paintings, first installments of his lifework.

FIVE

Trumbull arrived in Paris with a letter of introduction, and a residence already awaiting him.

The letter, from a London art dealer, was to Jean-Baptiste Pierre LeBrun, a portraitist, a restorer of old paintings, and a fellow dealer, who knew everyone in the Paris art world, beginning with his wife, Élisabeth Vigée-LeBrun, a better painter than he was (he acted as her agent). Through LeBrun and his contacts, Trumbull would meet Jean-Antoine Houdon, a sculptor who had traveled to the United States to take a life mask of George Washington; Jacques-Louis David, an upcoming painter still in his twenties; and Richard Cosway, an English miniaturist who was in Paris to depict the family of the duc d'Orléans, a cousin of the king.

Trumbull's host was Thomas Jefferson. The Virginian, who had been serving as minister to France since 1785, had met Trumbull on a visit to London. Always on the lookout for talented younger men, he had invited Trumbull to stay with him at the nobleman's house he rented in the western suburb of Chaillot.

Jefferson, then forty-three years old, had served as a congressman and governor of his state before going abroad. Tall and sandy-haired, he was graceful on horseback, shy and almost physically awkward in person; "He sits in a lounging manner on one hip," wrote one observer, "... and with one of his shoulders elevated much above the other."[1] But his manners were impeccable, and his conversation, when he was among intimates, sparkled.

Intellectually Jefferson was both a visionary and a magpie. He could conceive ideas with the force and clarity of eternal truths, without neglecting a learner's roving curiosity about how things in the world around him looked and worked. Among his many interests were the arts, especially architecture; back home he had already begun designing a plantation house on a small summit (*monticello* in Italian) that would be the project of his life. It was natural that he would be drawn to a patriot, and a painter like Trumbull.

And natural for Trumbull to be drawn to his host. He would call George Washington his "master and friend," but here was a man who could truly be the latter—a dozen years older, not a quarter century; amiable, once one got to know him, not remote through very nobility; interested in Trumbull's lifework. Jefferson, finally, was a fellow American abroad.

Paris was the second-largest city in Europe, after London, with two-thirds of a million inhabitants. French kings, distrusting Parisians as insufficiently docile, had lived for over a century safely distant at the palace of Versailles, where ceremony and intrigue consumed the attention of those engaged in them. But liveliness was to be found in the city: plays, concerts, coffeehouses, and salons—gatherings in the homes of the wealthy where everything from gossip to philosophy might be discussed, under the direction of aristocratic hostesses. The poor worked or begged; when harvests failed, they starved.

The Paris art scene was on the cusp of a change. The prevailing style of the last half century, which still echoed in the work of Vigée-LeBrun, was rococo, a softening and sweetening of the baroque. One of her more ambitious efforts was *Peace, Bringing Back Abundance,* in which one allegorical woman, dark-haired, casts an arm and a sheltering cloak over another, a ripe blonde showing a bare breast and pouring the harvest out of a cornucopia. Trumbull called the coloring "very brilliant and pleasing."[2]

For young David, the way ahead was a leap back into the classical past—and into manly conflict. His *Oath of the Horatii* showed three noble Romans swearing before their father to fight the enemies of the city (figure 5). Their womenfolk—mother, sister, and wife—mourn, because they are related by marriage to the enemies in question. Whoever wins, they will lose. The figures—warriors, father, women—form three parallel units, rigid as planks. But this arrangement, rather than draining

Figure 5. Jacques-Louis David, *Oath of the Horatii,* 1784. This painting prefigured the spirit of the French Revolution. Trumbull called David naturally kind, but "ardent . . . even violent" in his political opinions. (Scala / Art Resource, NY.)

the painting of life, as in Trumbull's youthful classical exercises, acts as a launching pad for flinging lines of force across the canvass—outthrust legs, saluting arms, swords. The *Oath* was a blockbuster, bursting with energy. All it lacked was humanity. When Trumbull saw it in David's studio, he called it a "story well told, drawing pretty good, coloring cold."[3]

The main object of Trumbull's gaze was the art of generations past. Paris offered royal and noble collections, made available to him by his new acquaintances, into which he plunged with the enthusiasm of a tourist, and the eye of a practitioner. A journal of his sightseeing during the month of August records his judgments. Not all were favorable. Although he admired the dome of the Hôtel des Invalides, a hospital and old age home for veterans, he found the paintings hung there "intolerably bad."[4] The cathedral of Notre Dame struck him as "not grand" (Trumbull's century did not appreciate the gothic).[5] The figures of the Venetian master Veronese seemed "cut out in pasteboard, and stuck upon the canvass."[6] But when he liked what he saw, which was often, his delight was unbounded. The Palais Royal, owned by the duc d'Orléans, offered the "best works of every great man"; the Paris home of the comte d'Orsay had the "most beautiful collection of perfect little things."[7] He esteemed works by Correggio, Carracci, Van Dyck, Rembrandt, Poussin. But the painter he praised over and over was Rubens. He marveled at his "grandeur in composition" and "splendor of coloring"; "the richness, the glow . . . the truth of color and effect is wonderful."[8] "For color, composition, and expression, nothing can excel a Rubens."[9] He was hailing traits—bravura hues, and the dramatic placement of light, shadow, and people—he hoped to impart to his own historical paintings.

He spent one August day at Versailles, in an ecstasy of observation, marveling at the buildings, the collections within them, and the layout of the grounds. "Magnificent in the highest degree . . . . the view from the windows, magnificently beautiful . . . . a collection of the most precious things I have yet seen. . . . I had no imagination of ever seeing such works in existence." The visit ended with a late afternoon walk through the gardens. "I had expected to see immense monuments of labor and bad taste, where nature was overwhelmed in art; but I was disappointed." Delightfully disappointed; nature and art—trees and gardens, statues and fountains—collaborated to bewitch. "The evening was advancing, and the growing obscurity of twilight left the imagination at liberty to vary and veil the forms of objects." Trumbull lingered until half past eight; it was ten o'clock when, exhilarated and exhausted, he finally got back to Paris. "I had indeed seen too much."[10]

Trumbull did not make such expeditions alone. His companions might include Houdon the sculptor; Antonio di Poggi, the man who was supposed to be finding him an engraver; Richard Cosway and his wife, Maria; or Jefferson. One day Jefferson and the Cosways accompanied him together (Trumbull introduced them). Jefferson wanted to visit a pair of architects, from whom he sought tips on how to design a public market for Virginia's new capital, Richmond. But his attention was drawn far from architecture.

Maria Cosway was twenty-six years old. She had been born and raised in Florence, daughter of an English innkeeper who hosted gentlemen making the grand tour of the continent and artists come to learn from Italian masters. After he died, she and her Italian mother moved to London, where she married Richard Cosway. She was herself a talented painter and musician, and spoke half a dozen languages with ease, and with little errors that only enhanced her charm. She had a slender figure and a sweet face under a mass of golden curls. Her husband was nineteen years older than she was, foppish, and described by everyone as looking like a monkey. Jefferson fell hard.

The consultation with the architects concluded, the two Americans and the Cosways spent the rest of the day sightseeing along the Seine west of Paris, dining in the village of St. Cloud, stopping in the hilltop suburb of Montmartre to see a show of fireworks, calling finally on Jean-Baptiste Krumpholz, a composer for the harp, one of the instruments Maria played. "The wheels of time," Jefferson wrote, recalling the day later, "moved on with a rapidity of which those of our carriage gave but a faint idea, and yet in the evening, when one took a retrospect . . . what a mass of happiness had we travelled over!"[11]

Jefferson and Mrs. Cosway met again and again, sometimes with Trumbull, sometimes *tête-à-tête*. Jefferson's beloved wife, Martha, had died in 1782; his relationship with his slave Sally Hemings had not yet begun. Maria was filling an emotional void in his life, and Trumbull served as a friendly go-between. When he and the Cosways returned to London in the fall, Trumbull was the conduit for Jefferson's communications with his newfound love. (Jefferson explained the necessity of an intermediary thus: his own letters, as those of a diplomat, "are read both in the post offices of London and Paris.")[12]

Jefferson's correspondence with and via Trumbull continued for the three years the Virginian remained at his post in Paris. The two friends wrote about many things—harpsichords, musical glasses, and carriages, all to be ordered by Trumbull for Jefferson in London—but always there was Maria. She was angry with her admirer, Trumbull reported in one letter, "yet teases me every day for a copy of your little portrait"—a painting he had done of Jefferson in Paris—"that she may scold it, no doubt."[13] Maria herself wrote to Jefferson asking if he would "give Mr. Trumbull leave to make a coppy of a certain portrait he painted at Paris? It is a person who hates you that requests this favor."[14] A month later, Maria was still waiting for her copy. "Trumbull puts me out of all patience. I always thought painting slow work, 'tis dreadful now."[15] Finally, the copy was done. "Wish me joy," Maria wrote to its subject, "for I possess your picture. Trumbull has procured me this happiness for which I shall ever be grateful for."[16] Jefferson, for his part, told Trumbull to "kneel to Mrs. Cosway for me, and lay my soul in her lap."[17] So the *billets doux* went back and forth, slackening only after Jefferson returned finally to the United States. "If you ever see Mr. Trumbull," Maria wrote to him there wistfully, "I hope you will speak of me together."[18]

Trumbull was enmeshed in Jefferson's erotic life. What of his own? He turned thirty in the summer of 1786. Over the years he had recalled the "demoiselles" of Lebanon and learned French from the Robichaud family, which included daughters. In the journal that he kept of this, his first trip to Paris, and of a cruise down the Rhine he added on before heading back to London, he regularly noted the presence of pretty women: one in Brussels had "the precise style of beauty which Van Dyck so loved to paint."[19] He left sketches of some of the women he admired. Did he do more than sketch? His letters written at the time, and his autobiography written years later, keep the secret, if there was any.

More important to Trumbull than Jefferson's flirting was his advice, political and artistic. Jefferson encouraged Trumbull to include the Declaration of Independence in his revolutionary project.

Fifteen months of combat (and most of Trumbull's military career) had preceded America's formal exit from the British empire. The deed was finally done on July 2, 1776, when Congress resolved that the thirteen united colonies "are, and of right ought to be, free and independent states." But in a country so verbal, with an unusually high number of preachers, lawyers, and newspaper readers, it was thought necessary to present a longer justification to the public, and to the world. Congress assigned the task to a five-man committee, including John Adams, Congress's most eloquent orator, and Benjamin Franklin, thanks to his almanacs and journalism the most widely read American then living. But the committee gave the job to young Jefferson, already famous for his revolutionary polemics. Adams and Franklin made a few small changes to his draft, which Congress then cut and rewrote more heavily. Jefferson, like any sensitive author, resented the alterations to his handiwork. Like a proud author, he believed in its importance for the country, and for his own reputation.

Trumbull's father had promulgated a declaration of Connecticut's independence a month before Congress debuted Jefferson's. The governor's declaration looked to "preserve our precious rights and liberties." But it wove the political struggle into a Calvinist account of the Fall of man into sin, the consequent need for just governments, and the hope that Americans might be "blessed of the LORD, as long as the Sun and Moon shall endure."[20] Jefferson's declaration pared theology to a minimum, but what remained was compelling nonetheless: men were endowed with rights "by their Creator"; America was entitled to nationhood by "the Laws of Nature and of Nature's God." Many men had already fought and died for the cause, and more struggle and bloodshed were to come. When you ask men to pledge their lives, fortunes, and sacred honor, you must tell them why, and say so as clearly and stirringly as possible.

Jefferson gave Trumbull a sketch of the room in the State House in Philadelphia where Congress had met. (He misremembered the number of doors.) The oval-backed Louis XVI chairs of his Paris house provided the model for the chair in which Trumbull would place the president of Congress. Trumbull's thoughts for his revolutionary series had so far run to battles, the most vivid experiences he had had. Now, inspired by his new friend, he would add a painting of a political event (plate 5).

He returned to London in the fall, via the Rhine and the low countries. He was back at his easel and his efforts to make a mark in the British art market by November 1786.

In addition to the *Declaration,* he was planning four more compositions in his revolutionary series. Two featured Washington—*The Capture of the Hessians at Trenton* (plate 6) and *The Death of General Mercer at the Battle of Princeton* (plate 7; he had already begun the latter before visiting Paris). One projected painting would celebrate the triumph of his other commander, Horatio Gates—*The Surrender of General Burgoyne at Saratoga* (plate 8). *The Surrender of Lord Cornwallis at York-*

town (plate 9) would show the end of the fighting. If he finished them all, he would have, including *Bunker's Hill* and *Quebec,* three battles, three surrenders, and one document. Trumbull learned additional details about the Philadelphia State House from John Adams, posted now in London, and painted his portrait: "the color and natural curl" of Adams's hair, he wrote, "were beautiful."[21] Late in 1787 he traveled briefly to Paris—"become a part of our family again," Jefferson had written, wooing him—where he painted the portrait that Maria Cosway coveted.[22]

Trumbull also worked on his painting of the siege of Gibraltar, the theme West had suggested to please the British public. It was Poggi who offered a usable episode, which the Italian had learned of when he visited Gibraltar himself after the war ended. In 1781, two years into the siege, the British had made a nighttime sortie against the enemy's lines. Surprise was complete and the operation a terrific success. The British burned Spanish fortifications, destroyed their ammunition, and spiked their siege guns. Trumbull envisioned a night piece, with clambering, almost jubilant soldiers scaling enemy positions on the left and a party of senior officers surveying the action on the right. In the center he placed a Spanish artillery officer, deserted by his men and mortally wounded, who lies where he has fallen, refusing the help the British are offering him. Devotion in extremis and magnanimity extended even to gallant foes were important themes for Trumbull; they would appear twice in his revolutionary series.

He worked hard at this painting, producing three different versions, increasing the size of his canvas from his preferred small scale and altering the gaze of the wounded Spaniard. The weak element of his composition is the group of British officers on the right. Compassion at a distance is hard to pull off, in art as in life. They look as if they are waiting to board some public conveyance, a coach or a packet boat. The soldiers on the left, by contrast, vibrate with an emotion that is sometimes true to combat, the delirium of success: *we caught those Spaniards napping!* Trumbull's own battles had been far from successful; he must have recalled momentary bursts of elation, and projected them onto a longer action and a mass of men. In painting the Spanish artillery officer, he imitated a work of art: *The Dying Gaul,* a decadent Roman sculpture of an expiring enemy, twisting on the ground. But Trumbull has made the pose his own, infusing it with pride and pain, despair and disdain. Or maybe his Spanish officer simply embodies duty: *I have done my job, let me die doing it.* Horace Walpole, the busybody aesthete, called *The Sortie Made by the Garrison of Gibraltar* the finest picture painted north of the Alps.[23] Patriotism warped Walpole's judgment. But the *Sortie* is a fine painting.

While Trumbull worked, traveled, and wrestled with the Revolution, he followed current events. Late in 1786 overtaxed farmers in Massachusetts seized an armory and shut courts that were foreclosing mortgages. Shays's Rebellion, as it was called, after one of its leaders, disturbed Trumbull, yet he trusted that the "decrees of Providence" would secure America's "greatness."[24] Although order was restored in Connecticut's neighboring state, the episode prompted American politicians already concerned with the feebleness of their postrevolutionary government to design another. Trumbull kept abreast of the struggle to ratify the new Constitution, writing that the president, a new executive office, ought to be term-limited, and reading a defense of American constitutionalism by John Adams.[25] Liberals in Europe (and some in America) thought popularly elected legislatures should rule; Adams praised separation of powers.[26]

Even more dramatic changes occurred in France. In 1789 the king convened an antique forum, a meeting of the three estates of the realm (nobility, clergy, commoners), to address France's debts. The assembly coincided with a year of wretched weather and dearth. Most Americans, Trumbull included, were initially sympathetic with the revolutionary energies that were unleashed, seeing in them an emulation of their own struggle. "America [has] given the great example," Trumbull wrote.[27] Trumbull went to Paris yet again in the summer of 1789 to collect materials for a painting of the fall of the Bastille, the Paris prison and armory looted and demolished by a mob. While there, he had a cautionary conversation with the marquis de Lafayette. The young liberal nobleman had been the foreign hero of America's revolution, suffering at Valley Forge, leading a charge at Yorktown. He seemed now to be the leader of France's, consulting with Jefferson on a declaration of the rights of man, commanding a newly formed citizen militia, the National Guard, and designing a new national color scheme: blue and red from the arms of the city of Paris, flanking white, the color of the royal family. Lafayette warned Trumbull that all was not well: the duc d'Orléans, Richard Cosway's sometime client, was subsidizing radical agitators in order to snatch the crown for himself. The king's cousin was indeed behaving as Lafayette described, but the roots of France's unrest went deeper than the duke's machinations, even as its effects would surpass his wildest schemes.

It is not clear how serious Trumbull was about painting the French Revolution, for he had already decided that he must return to America.

He had a number of reasons for going. After three years Poggi had found an engraver in Stuttgart, Johann Gotthard von Müller, who was willing to engrave *Bunker's Hill* for £1,000—a significant sum, the going rate for a top artist—but he had yet to run a proof.[28] The delay seemed fatal, as far as European sales went: French events made America old news.

Trumbull's British career had not taken wing. He was offered a handsome sum for the *Sortie,* but had turned it down, hoping (mistakenly, it turned out) to make even more money from it later on. Many still held his rebel past against him. Although several British officers had posed for the *Sortie,* Lord Rawdon, a veteran of Bunker's Hill, among other American engagements, had condemned Trumbull at a public dinner, saying "nothing done by that man ought ever to be patronized by officers of the British army."[29]

His best prospects for monetizing his revolutionary paintings seemed to be in America. The new Constitution presaged a fresh start; his former master, George Washington, had been unanimously elected first president and inaugurated in April 1789. America had turned to its revolutionary hero; Americans might be willing to revisit their revolutionary glories.

Death was already winnowing his subjects. The career of Nathanael Greene epitomized the social and professional mobility encouraged by the Revolution. A Rhode Island Quaker who ran his family's foundry, Greene turned out to be a military genius. Sent south by Washington to retrieve the disasters of Charleston and Camden, Greene's maneuvering drove Lord Cornwallis out of the Carolinas, to his rendezvous with defeat at Yorktown. In the summer of 1786 Greene had died of sunstroke, not yet forty-four years old. Trumbull believed his project required him to depict more than panoramic views of events; he must include the likenesses of the actors involved. West and Copley had done the same in their historical pictures, sometimes transporting a subject hundreds of miles to bring him into the event. Trumbull took the responsibility seriously. Greene had died young. But many of his comrades were older—Washington turned fifty-seven in 1789—and illness struck young and old alike. Trumbull had captured Jefferson and Adams abroad, as well as a clutch of French officers for *The Surrender of Lord Cornwallis at Yorktown*. But most of the faces he needed resided in America.

He reviewed some of these reasons in a mid-summer correspondence with Jefferson. Trumbull's new friend made him a tempting offer. The American minister was planning a trip home, which he expected to be temporary; meanwhile, his secretary, another young protégé named William Short, seemed eager to return to America himself, for good. If Jefferson had to go back to Paris without Short, might Trumbull take Short's place? Jefferson described the duties of a diplomatic secretary with the airiness he always used when speaking of scut work: sometimes there was "a squall of work," copying documents, "but it can be hired [out], and comes very rarely." Trumbull would live as Jefferson's houseguest, hence paying no room and board. A long sojourn in France "may even," Jefferson added, "give you an opportunity of going to Italy"—and, he did not need to add, of completing his artistic education there. Paris brimmed with riches, but the source of so many, ancient and modern, was Italy. West had gone there to study them, so had Copley. The Protestant world had broken with the Roman church, but the Rome of culture still cast its spell.[30]

Trumbull answered with a long letter dated June 11. He began with a report on friendly errands: in his role as personal shopper he had sent Jefferson some new editions of *Tristram Shandy* and other whimsical works by Laurence Sterne.

The body of his letter was taken up with his reasons for declining to become Jefferson's secretary, however "flattering to my pride" was the offer. He complained about Poggi's slowness in finding an engraver: "I expected him to use the utmost energy and dispatch; instead of which, three years have been suffered to elapse, without almost the smallest progress having been made." He noted the change in European taste occasioned by the change in European politics: "The warm attention which the nations of Europe once paid to us begins to be diverted to objects more nearly and immediately interesting to themselves … France, in particular, from which country I entertained peculiar hopes of patronage, is beginning to be too much occupied by her own approaching revolution, to think so much of us." He even acknowledged the possibility that the *Sortie* might not be a hit with the British public, which felt "no partiality for me, or for my country."

So much for his problems ("I am ashamed to trouble you with such details," he protested). But he also explained, in a noteworthy passage, his hopes. "The greatest motive I had or have for engaging in, or for continuing, the pursuit of painting has been my wish of commemorating the great events of our country's revolution. … To preserve and diffuse the memory of the noblest series of actions which have ever presented themselves in the history of man; to give to the present and future sons of misfortune, such glorious lessons of their rights, and of the spirit with which they should assert and support them, and even to transmit to their descendants, the personal resemblance of those who have been the great actors in those illustrious scenes, were objects which gave a dignity to [my] profession."

Trumbull packed a lot in here. He was asserting that the American Revolution was the most important political subject a painter could have: more important than noble Romans; more important than the siege of Gibraltar, the raid on Jersey, or the battle of La Hogue. The death in defeat of General Montgomery at Quebec was more important than the death in victory of General Wolfe at Quebec.

The American Revolution was more important than any of these events, ancient or modern, because it was more than an imperial struggle, or even a defense of the homeland. It was a struggle for rights, and a demonstration of how to assert and support them, on the battlefield and in political deliberation. Nor was the Revolution a one-time exercise. It offered a model, for men of all times and places—Americans of the future; French, British, foreigners everywhere—of what they could, what they must do, when under an unbearable yoke.

Trumbull had been meeting men of liberal views in Britain and France: Fox, Burke, Lafayette. Such contacts may have broadened his own views, even unconsciously. But the universalist sentiments of this passage needed no foreign prompting; they were all-American. Jefferson, his recipient, no doubt stimulated and sharpened them, inducing Trumbull to include the Declaration in his artistic drama, and to take its sentiments to heart. The Declaration's sentiments, however, were common American currency. That was why Congress, which cut and rewrote so much of the document, left its opening fanfare untouched. Americans believed they had embarked on something that was simultaneously new and eternal: a revolution in the distribution of power designed to nurture and secure human liberty. Jefferson had put it in writing; Trumbull would put it in paint.

Trumbull himself—aide, eight months' colonel—had not been one of the great actors. But he would be the preserver of them all: of Jefferson, Adams, Washington the greatest, and French allies, whom he had already painted; of the many others he would track down in America. More than that: he had, however small his role, shared the drama with them. His letter explained: "[I have] borne personally a humble part in the great events which I [am] to describe. No one lives with me possessing this advantage, and no one can come after me to divide the honor of truth and authenticity, however easily I may hereafter be exceeded in elegance." *I was in the struggle myself; no other painter was; the future may see American Rubenses, but they will not have marched where I marched, seen what I saw.* Trumbull was stretching the truth here: Charles Willson Peale, from whom West had gotten American uniforms for his contemplated paintings, had served in the Pennsylvania militia, fought in more battles than Trumbull had, and filled a museum in Philadelphia with portraits of revolutionary heroes. But Trumbull's boast was true of the American and American-born painters he knew—West, Copley, Stuart.

He concluded: he would return to America to seek "the warm patronage of my countrymen." He would offer a subscription for prints of his paintings, and he would seek the patronage of Congress. He knew that public money had already been spent on commemorative statuary: the state of Virginia had, at Jefferson's recommendation, commissioned Houdon to sculpt a statue of Washington, and Houdon had already been to Mount Vernon to take the hero's life mask and measurements. "Why then," Trumbull asked, "should I doubt a readiness in our country to encourage me in producing monuments, not of heroes only, but of those events on which title to the gratitude of the nation is founded, and which by being multiplied and little expensive, may be diffused over the world?"[31]

So Trumbull would be going back to America, where he hoped to meet Jefferson on his own brief visit. This letter of regret was a show-piece: showing off for Jefferson, showing off probably for himself. But he meant it. He sailed from Gravesend on the Thames at the end of October 1789, arriving in New York a month later.

S I X

When Trumbull arrived at the end of 1789, New York was, at thirty-three thousand souls, the second-most populous city in America, having surpassed Boston (only Philadelphia was larger). It had had a rough war; the British occupied it for over seven years, a fire destroyed a third of its buildings, and every tree in it or nearby had been felled for fuel. But the spirit of commerce was in its genes, and it had bounced back.

The old Congress, threatened by a mob of unpaid soldiers at war's end, had abandoned Philadelphia for a series of cities and towns in the mid-Atlantic states, landing finally in New York City, where it met in a tavern. The town fathers determined to give the new government under the Constitution grander accommodations. City Hall on Wall Street was redesigned by Pierre L'Enfant, a French engineer, and christened "Federal Hall." The House of Representatives met on the ground floor, the Senate on the second. Legislators had to shut the windows to drown out the racket of carriages in the streets outside. George Washington took the oath of office as president from the balcony. He settled finally in a rented mansion, around the corner on Broadway. Thomas Jefferson would join him, in the city and the government, when he accepted Washington's request to serve as secretary of state. His trip home from Paris would be lifelong.

Trumbull's brother Jonathan, Jr., and Jeremiah Wadsworth, whose coat had provoked Joshua Reynolds's scorn, had both been elected congressmen from Connecticut. Trumbull boarded with them, and set to work.

In January 1790 an announcement of his Revolutionary War series ran in the *Gazette of the United States,* a newspaper launched to support the new government. Trumbull proposed to offer prints of thirteen paintings, patriotically matching the number of states. Two—*The Death of General Warren at the Battle of Bunker's Hill* and *The Death of General Montgomery in the Attack on Quebec*—were completed; four—*The Declaration of Independence, The Capture of the Hessians at Trenton, The Death of General Mercer at the Battle of Princeton,* and *The Surrender of Lord Cornwallis at Yorktown*—were described as "far advanced."[1] Still to come were five scenes of the Revolution itself: *The Surrender of General Burgoyne at Saratoga* (already conceived, though Trumbull had made only a sketch or two); the signing of the treaty with France, which brought America its great ally; the signing of the Treaty of Paris, which ended the fighting; the British evacuation of New York (not accomplished until November 1783); and General George Washington resigning his commission (which occurred a month later) (plate 10). Two proposed canvases would depict postwar scenes: George Washington's welcome by the ladies of Trenton in April 1789 as he rode north to his inauguration, and the inauguration itself later that month. Trumbull was proposing an expansive narrative, geographic and political. France was to be recognized, not only by its officers at Yorktown, but by two scenes set in Paris. Victory in war would be linked to renewal in peacetime: the surrender at Trenton, echoed by the inaugural celebration there; the enemy's evacuation of New York at war's end, making possible the establishment of the newly ratified federal government. Trumbull's prospective additional canvases recalled his own experiences: even as he had begun his series with the battles to which he had some connection, so he was now reflecting his time in France, and in the nation's new capital.

In a prospectus published in April, Trumbull proposed to add one more scene, depicting the Battle of Eutaw Springs in September 1781— Nathanael Greene's last major engagement in the Carolinas. Like most of Greene's battles, it had been a tactical victory for the British, a strategic victory for him. The enemy could fight Greene, but not prevent him from retiring in good order and attacking them again. Trumbull would memorialize the dead hero, and give due attention to the war in the American South, which had been the vital theater of the endgame.

He offered subscribers prints of *Bunker's Hill* and *Quebec*, the two paintings that were already finished, at three guineas each, half to be paid in advance, the remainder on delivery.

The broadside containing the prospectus included some verses in praise of Trumbull by Joel Barlow, one of a group of Connecticut versifiers known as the Hartford Wits, which included several Trumbull family friends (such were the advantages of living in a small state). Barlow had published a four-thousand-line opus, *The Vision of Columbus,* in which the explorer at the end of his life foresaw the future of what he had discovered. Book VII (out of nine) described the progress of the arts in America, from the fur trade and fisheries, to painting and poetry.

> Fired with the martial toils that bathed in gore
> His brave companions on his native shore
> Trumbull with daring hand the scene recalls,
> He shades with night Quebec's beleagur'd walls. . . .
> On Charlestown's height, thro' floods of rolling fire,
> Brave Warren falls, and sullen hosts retire.[2]

Patriotic Americans thought well of Barlow, though the talent gap between his cut-and-dried couplets and Trumbull's brushwork was considerable.

The connecting personal thread in Trumbull's series, it was becoming clear, was his "master and friend," George Washington. He was in three of the paintings Trumbull had already done, and would be the star of three more to come: a battle and two surrenders, plus three civilian ceremonies. He would win the war, and the peace. Trumbull began to paint him from life in January 1790.

Washington came from a short-lived family. His father had died in his late forties, his favorite half-brother in his early thirties. In the summer after his inauguration as president, he had been plagued by a tumor on his thigh. He was more deeply plagued by worry about the job he had taken on. He had won the applause of the world by winning a war against a superpower, and the wonder of it by going home into retirement afterward. Now he had returned to public life, in a role—head of state of a republic—with few precedents. No wonder he wrote to Henry Knox, his old artillery commander, that he took it up "with feelings not unlike those of a culprit who is going to the place of his execution."[3]

Whatever his anxieties or his ailments, Washington was still in full possession of his manly charisma. America's adoring citizens would have seen it in him whether he possessed it or not. Trumbull's paintings would help them see what they needed to see.

Washington recorded his sittings with Trumbull in laconic diary entries (his terseness reflected no lack of interest in the artist: Washington's entries were almost all brief). On January 10 Trumbull met Washington at one of his periodic dinners with congressmen (his brother Jonathan and Jeremiah Wadsworth were also of the party, and probably procured the invitation). On January 23 the president went "with Mrs. Washington" to see Trumbull's paintings; on February 10 he sat for two hours "for Mr. Trumbull to draw my picture in his historical pieces."[4]

Washington had been sitting for painters for years. His first portrait had been taken in 1772, when he was forty, by Charles Willson Peale, the student of Benjamin West. Washington had worn his old French and Indian War uniform for this painting, perhaps as an intimation of the coming imperial crisis. Peale gave him a round, bland face, made interesting only by the tough line of a mouth; Washington had lifelong dental problems, which affected his appearance in person and in paint, though here the set of his mouth signaled determination. Since his sitting with Peale, he had been painted by Americans and foreigners, men and women, mature artists and beginners (William Dunlap, Trumbull's fellow student at West's, had painted him when he was only seventeen). In a 1785 letter, Washington mused on the pictorial burdens of celebrity. At first, sitting made him "as restive under the operation, as a colt is of the saddle—The next time, I submitted very reluctantly, but with less flouncing. Now, no dray [horse] moves more readily . . . than I do to the painter's chair."[5]

Trumbull put him through his paces. The president posed for him eight more times, once on horseback so that Trumbull could "see me mounted."[6]

The painting that resulted shows Washington standing alongside a white mount, his right arm resting on the saddle and the horse's neck. The image is delightful, almost lighthearted. In the far distance, French and American troops, fresh from victory at Yorktown, are assembling at Verplanck's Point, a camp on the Hudson River. The highlights on Washington's epaulettes and boots gleam; his neckcloth, a cloud behind his head, and his horse's coat shine with different shades of white. Washington's pose is relaxed; so is the horse's, bending to nuzzle the knee of a foreleg. Trumbull made Washington's face blockier and ruddier, and thus truer to life, than he had when drawing him from memory. This painting was given to Martha Washington; New York's town fathers were so impressed with it that the mayor asked Trumbull to do a larger version for City Hall.

In designing his picture, Trumbull was influenced by a Van Dyck he had admired at the Louvre, showing Charles I of England standing in front of his mount during a break on a hunt. Both paintings share an air of ease. King and general each rests his left hand casually on his left hip, and the necks of both their horses droop down. Still there is a difference: Charles seems to be saying, *how good it is to be a king;* Washington, *how good that this war has ended well.* Charles's horse is held for him by a groom; Washington manages his own (no black attendant in an imaginary turban this time).

Trumbull also drew the representatives of another nation—Creek Indians come to New York to sign a treaty with the United States. The Creeks lived in the backcountry of Georgia, which then stretched to the Mississippi River. A vigorous tribe, able to send hundreds of warriors into battle, they had sided with Britain during the Revolution, and were prepared to ally with Spain, which owned Florida and the Gulf Coast, or the Americans on their eastern flank, whichever made them the better deal.

How to approach them had preoccupied Washington and his secretary of war, Henry Knox, since the preceding summer. President and secretary had gone in person to the Senate to seek its approval of a draft treaty (the Constitution stipulated that treaties be made "by and with" the Senate's "advice and consent"). Senators raised both substantive and procedural difficulties, as legislators are wont to do; after two days of discussion, Washington, who had expected a brief meeting, left with the advice he had sought, though the Senate doorkeeper overheard him say he would be damned before he ever came there for advice again. Negotiations with the Creeks' astute leader, Alexander McGillivray, were equally intricate. (McGillivray's father was Scottish and his paternal grandfather French, but chieftainship in the Creeks was matrilineal, hence his position.) Finally a treaty was ready to be inked, and the Creeks arrived in New York.

Trumbull would reproduce the pencil portraits he made of five of them in his autobiography, prefaced by an account of a deception. Washington, he said, "was curious to see the effect" of painting "on their untutored minds." He had Trumbull mount the larger-than-life-size version of his new portrait in a room of the presidential mansion. After dinner, the president led his guests there. "When the door was thrown open, they started at seeing another 'Great Father' standing in the room. . . . At length one of the chiefs advanced towards the picture, and slowly stretched out his hand to touch it, and was still more astonished to feel, instead of a round object, a flat surface, cold to the touch. He started back with an exclamation of astonishment—'Ugh!'" Trumbull went on to write that he very much wanted to paint the Creeks, to capture their "dignity of manner, form, countenance and expression, worthy of Roman senators." The experience with Washington's portrait convinced them, however, that "there must be magic" in the art, and they were not willing to pose. Trumbull concluded by saying that he managed to make several drawings "by stealth" (plate 12).[7]

Alexander McGillivray had been educated in Charleston, where he learned Latin and Greek. His people, while they did not share his literacy, had been trading with white men, French, Spanish, British, and American, for decades. This delegation of Creeks had traveled north from their homes through towns and cities, feted along the way. How likely is it that they would have been startled by pictorial realism? Perhaps they behaved as they imagined their hosts expected them to.[8]

Trumbull's pencil drawings show men poised between cultures, wearing gorgets and officers' coats given to them by white men, and turbans, egret feathers, and nose rings characteristic of a traditional wardrobe. Their expressions are variously thoughtful, assertive, amused, or indifferent. They are not an anonymous exotic mass, but subjects, each with a different mood or personality. Trumbull the writer remembered them as noble savages—Roman senators who did not know what a painting was. Trumbull the artist showed them as individuals.

Trumbull spent much of the next three years traveling up and down the East Coast, collecting faces for what Washington called his "historical pieces." He went as far north as New Hampshire, as far south as South Carolina. If a subject was dead—General Hugh Mercer is killed in the center of Trumbull's painting of the Battle of Princeton—Trumbull drew a son as a substitute.

His travels kept bringing him to Philadelphia, where the federal capital itself traveled at the end of 1790, as a result of a three-way deal between Pennsylvanians who hoped to keep it there, Virginians who were promised that it would move on after ten years to a site on the Potomac, and Treasury Secretary Alexander Hamilton, who, New Yorker though he was, shortchanged his hometown in order to win enough congressional support for his financial program. Philadelphia and its suburbs held forty-four thousand people, making it the largest urban area in the country. It had enough sophisticated citizens to have sent West to Europe and to patronize Peale now.

The artistic mementos of Trumbull's travels, besides the faces he painted into his thirty-by-twenty-inch canvases, were a collection of oval portraits, all about three by four inches, each showing its subject's head and shoulders. These were not miniatures on ivory, meant to be worn, such as Richard Cosway produced, but small paintings on mahogany. They were Trumbull's notes, his *aides-mémoire*. His father is there; so is John Adams; so is Ebenezer Stevens, who helped him arrange the cannon shot demonstration at Fort Ticonderoga. One man, physician Lemuel Hopkins, appears seemingly because of the spectacle of his extraordinary bulging eyes (he was also a Trumbull family friend and a Hartford Wit). There are three Indians, members of a delegation of Senecas who came to Philadelphia to negotiate a treaty with Congress in 1792. There are a number of women, old and young. Despite the barriers of another century's styles in hair and head bands, several of them are attractive, and seem intent on attracting.

One young woman in particular attracted Trumbull. Harriet Wadsworth was the daughter of Jeremiah, his early subject. She had been a girlhood friend of one of Trumbull's nieces. Before Trumbull went to Europe, Harriet had sat on his lap. In 1788, while he was still in England, she wrote him a brief note on a letter from his niece. Trumbull replied that Harriet must now be an "elegant, accomplished, amiable woman."[9]

For two years Trumbull had been the confidante and go-between of Thomas Jefferson and his twenty-something inamorata, Maria Cosway. Wondering perhaps when his time would come, he had been contacted by a family friend, almost a former neighbor—the Wadsworths lived in Hartford—who was nineteen years old. Trumbull was stirred, sight unseen.

Meeting Harriet again in person, which he did when rejoining his own family in Lebanon soon after arriving in New York, he was not disappointed. No letters of hers survive, but we know, thanks to Trumbull's brush, that she had blue eyes, brunette curls, and delicate features. His courtship showed all the clumsiness of a much younger man. He sent her a book about the South Seas (one would think that telling her about Paris would be more likely to pique her interest, though that might have required silences about Jefferson and Mrs. Cosway). He complained that business kept him in New York, and that other men, not so occupied, enjoyed opportunities to see her. In the desperation of ardor, he asked her to make him feel better: "You … will not I hope refuse your assistance in reconciling me to the world."[10] Her father, for his part, assured her that her suitor—if that was indeed what her anxious correspondent was—"intends to be more explicit."[11]

It was December 1790—over a year into their renewed acquaintance—before Trumbull declared himself. "You have seen and cannot have misunderstood my attentions … but may I not hope, Harriet, from the candor and kindness of your character, that had you disapproved those attentions you would have discouraged them without disguise." *I haven't said enough, but since you haven't said anything to discourage me, you must welcome what I haven't said.* "I know I am not worthy of the happiness I solicit, but be you my instructress—exert the power you possess over my mind, and teach me how to merit your kindness."[12] Trumbull was like a runner collapsing in the home stretch, begging to be pulled over the finish line.

Trumbull had a competitor, whom we know only through Harriet's father's letters, where he appears by the initials "I.M." Jeremiah Wadsworth assured his daughter that he would let her choose for herself—"your happiness will be mine"—so long as her husband could maintain her "as you have been used to live." Trumbull's career seemed well launched, but there were warning signs with regard to I.M. "Mr. I.M.," Jeremiah wrote, "is personally as agreeable to me as JT—but his connections are less so—not one of his brothers do I like, two of them I detest. His father is not very respectable."[13]

Harriet fell ill the winter Trumbull proposed. He tried to enliven her by sending her a book on drawing and offering to teach her himself.[14] In all his anxious letter writing, this was the most poignant moment. Trumbull offered to open his world to her. Maybe she would have been uninterested in it, or unsuited to it, but in this he hoped to treat her as someone like him, not as an object of admiration nor as a savior.

Harriet's ill health continued through the following winter. In February 1792 she wrote to both Trumbull and I.M., telling them that courtship must wait until she recovered; her father delivered the letter directed to Trumbull in person. She had what her century called consumption, what we call tuberculosis. In November, she went to Bermuda; mild sea air was thought to have curative powers. They failed Harriet. She died there in April 1793, and was buried in a local Anglican churchyard. Trumbull's only surviving comment on her passing was the posthumous portrait he added to his collection of small ovals that year.

While Trumbull yearned for Harriet, he slept with another young woman. We know this because she bore his child some time in 1792. Her name was Temperance Ray. She came from Haddam, a town south of Hartford. Trumbull met her when she worked as a servant in his brother Jonathan's house in Lebanon. Trumbull wrote of their encounter in a letter seven years after the fact: "An accident befell me, to which young men are often exposed;—I was a little too intimate with a girl who lived at my brother's, and who had at the same time some other particular friends;—the natural consequence followed, and in due course a fine boy was born;—the number of fellow laborers rendered it a little difficult to ascertain precisely who was the father." If the boy was now living with his mother, Trumbull went on, he feared that his son might be growing up in a "blackguard [contemptible] family."[15] Blame-shifting, incompletely masked by jocularity: *I was just one of the boys, and she was a slut anyway.*

Trumbull asked James Wadsworth, a cousin of Jeremiah's, to report on the status of his former partner, and their offspring. Wadsworth, free from the embarrassment that animated Trumbull, wrote that at the time he investigated, Temperance was married to a seafaring man, that they had several children together, and that they lived "comfortably."[16] Her encounter with her gentleman lover over, she seems to have done all right for herself.

The laws of Connecticut required the father of an illegitimate child, as identified by the mother, to support their offspring.[17] In writing about the affair, Trumbull strove to maintain an image of public responsibility and personal blamelessness: "As I was best able to pay the bill, the mother using her legal right, judiciously chose me."[18] *I take my punishment, though I probably wasn't even guilty.*

Trumbull's affair with Temperance Ray was a consequence of his courtship of Harriet Wadsworth, a product of wounded ego and frustrated desire. He must have felt Harriet's failure to accept his proposal as a rejection; Temperance, his brother's servant girl, was in no position to reject him. Trumbull would have a long, fraught relationship with his son, but after his belated letters about his affair with Temperance, she drops from Trumbull's story, and from history. He never painted her portrait.

Trumbull's picture-taking took him back to Philadelphia in 1792, where he painted Washington once more. He had gotten a commission to portray "the *great man*" from the city of Charleston.[19] The sittings would have been held in the three-story mansion on Market Street that Washington occupied during his years in Philadelphia. No presidential diary survives for the period in which the sittings occurred, but Trumbull described them years later. Trumbull made this portrait a history painting, showing Washington in the interval between the battles of Trenton and Princeton, "the most sublime moment" of his military career. Other battles Washington fought were more consequential; no battles were more daring. Washington took up Trumbull's idea "warmly, and as the work advanced, we talked of the scene, its dangers, its almost desperation. He *looked* the scene again."[20]

Since Trumbull would later hang this painting with those of his historical series, it will be described along with them, but the effect of painting it on Trumbull can be described here. His second sittings with Washington bound him ever more closely to his subject. It was sublime to have fought and prevailed at Trenton and Princeton; it was only one degree less sublime to hear of it from the commander in chief himself. Trumbull, who had been posted hundreds of miles away in Rhode Island at that moment in the war, could relive the moment with Washington years later. By capturing Washington in paint, he could bring his viewers into the moment too.

When the portrait was finished, it did not please its purchasers: Charleston wanted an image representing the fruits of peace, not the dangers of war. So Trumbull produced another for them, with the city reposing in the background. Washington wrote a letter to a brother officer there blessing the new painting: "The merit of this artist cannot fail to give much pleasure to those of his countrymen, who possess a taste for the fine arts."[21] Trumbull kept his first essay for himself (plate 11).

Even as Trumbull traveled and painted, he had been soliciting subscriptions for his proposed series of engravings. His prospectus, issued in 1790, had been a combination history lesson and sales pitch. "No period of the history of man is more interesting than that in which we have lived. . . . Americans have a right to glory in giving to the world an example whose influence is rapidly spreading." Historians would tell the story in words, but artists could tell it better: "the language of painting is universal and intelligible in all nations, and in every age."[22]

Washington signed up for four sets of engravings, and acted almost as Trumbull's agent. He sent a letter of praise to Lafayette. "His pieces . . . meet the applause of all who have seen them; the greatness of the design, and the masterly execution of the work, equally interest the man of capacious mind [and] the approving eye of the connoisseur." This combination of grandeur and modesty was characteristically Washingtonian: *I am the world-famous hero of these paintings, but don't take my word for their excellence; everybody likes them.*

"To you, my dear sir, who know Mr. Trumbull as a man and as an artist, it would perhaps have been hardly necessary to say so much as I have done on this occasion; but I could not in justice say less of him."[23] Washington concluded by invoking, not just vox populi, but justice itself.

The stars in the constellation of the American elite joined the president in subscribing. Thomas Jefferson and Alexander Hamilton, secretaries of state and treasury, each signed up for two sets, as did Trumbull's congressman brother. Vice President John Adams and Representative James Madison each bought one. Andrew Craigie, an apothecary who had made a fortune speculating in land, signed up for six. There were sales in London, ideological sympathy or simple curiosity overcoming losers' resentment.

Yet the subscription, however glittering, did not match Trumbull's expectations. After all his travels, and despite Washington's enthusiasm, he managed to sell 344 sets. At three guineas each up front, this represented a return of about $5,000, which, although it would cover the engraver's fees, could not support the artist. In his June 1789 letter to Jefferson, Trumbull had mentioned the possibility of direct congressional support, but although thirty-eight members of Congress decorated his subscription list, a direct congressional subsidy was out of the question. The advice Trumbull had gotten from Edmund Burke in England proved prescient: the new country's attention was first directed to its public buildings: cornerstones for a presidential mansion, permanent not rented, and for Congress had been laid at the new Potomac site in 1791 and 1792. Official America would turn to government-sponsored painting later, if at all.

Trumbull and his engravers were partly to blame for their weak showing: them, for being slow; him, for not pushing them harder. When Trumbull first arrived in the United States at the end of 1789, the battles of Bunker's Hill and Quebec were already fourteen years old. Every intervening commission he accepted, every trip he took to collect portraits, pushed the completion of his project farther into the future, and its subject deeper into the past.

Not just the passage of time but the breeding of new events worked against him. Current history made even recent history fade. The Washington administration, which began as a reunion of revolutionary figures—generals Washington and Knox, Colonel Hamilton, Continental Congressmen Adams and Jefferson—began to split into factions before two years had passed.

Hamilton's agenda at the Treasury was one source of conflict. The New Yorker envisioned a mixed economy, fueled by a national bank. Jefferson, the Virginia planter, trusted only the political instincts of his yeoman neighbors and feared a powerful federal government. Their dispute about the future shape of the economy would burn through American politics for another hundred years. In Trumbull's lifetime, his brother Jonathan voted consistently for Hamilton's program in Congress, as did his father-in-law manqué, Jeremiah Wadsworth, a wealthy merchant made wealthier by government jobs—just the sort of man that Jefferson distrusted.

But the great accelerant of political turmoil was the progress of the French Revolution.

Trumbull, and most Americans, initially viewed it as a reenactment of their own. As his prospectus put it, America had "giv[en] to the world an example whose influence is rapidly spreading." But he had also heard Lafayette's warnings of possible difficulties, which he had shared, at Lafayette's request, with Washington. French politics swiftly spiraled beyond Lafayette's, or anyone's, control. By January 1793 Lafayette had fled the country, in danger of his life; the king whom he and other moderates had hoped might become a constitutional monarch had been deposed, tried, and executed.

France went to war with most of its neighbors, Britain included. Every prudent American wanted to stay out of this superpower conflict, but political Americans (the prudent ones included) adopted pro- or anti-revolutionary European language and symbols to ramp up domestic political rhetoric. Jefferson's followers sang bloodthirsty French ditties and displayed toy guillotines at their public dinners. Hamilton and his allies attacked Jefferson in the press as a dangerous radical, toying with atheism and French nostrums.

Trumbull and Jefferson had been intimate in Europe. As secretary of state, Jefferson continued to think well enough of Trumbull's abilities to offer to send him on a mission to the Barbary States, which lined the Mediterranean coast of Africa. These piratical Muslim countries preyed on the shipping of infidels, collecting ransoms for their crews and passengers, and enslaving those who could not buy their liberty. Most European powers paid protection money to keep the pirates at bay, but America had lost Britain's protection when it gained independence. How then to deal with their depredations was a problem that had occupied Jefferson from his days as a diplomat. Trumbull declined the offer of a mission. He had not left Paris to relocate to Algiers or Tunis, and he had his project to promote.

As time passed, politics came between him and his friend. Washington sustained Hamilton and his policies; Jefferson opposed them. Washington resisted pressures to support revolutionary France; Jefferson fomented them, at least for domestic political purposes. Jefferson was a hero of one of Trumbull's revolutionary paintings, and the subject of a portrait for his lady friend; Washington was the hero of Trumbull's revolutionary series, and of public portraits besides. Jefferson had been the engaging, worldly older brother; Washington was the conquering father. If it came to a choice of heroes, there was no question which one Trumbull would pick.

Late in his life, he crystallized his break with Jefferson in an anecdote about a bad dinner party. Jefferson was the host; the villain of the occasion, in Trumbull's telling, was another guest, William Branch Giles. Giles, six years younger than Trumbull, was a Virginian, a congressman, and a blowhard, even by the standards of his state and his office. One colleague recorded his conversation thus: "Canvas-back ducks, ham and chickens, old Madeira, the glories of the Ancient Dominion, all fine, were his constant themes. [He] boasted of personal prowess; [he got] *more manual exercise than any man in New England.*"[24]

Giles and New Englander Trumbull had already had one run-in, at a Philadelphia tea. Giles was abusing John Adams's *Defense of the Constitutions of Government of the United States of America* to a young lady. Trumbull suspected him of not having actually read the tome, and said so. So the young Virginian had a score to settle.

No sooner had Trumbull arrived chez Jefferson than Giles began to mock "the puritanical ancestry and character" of New England. "Although conscious that I was in no degree qualified to manage a religious discussion," Trumbull stuck up for the faith of his fathers.

Giles kept at it, from the drawing room to the dining table, condemning "the character, conduct and doctrines" of Jesus Christ. No one of the party would defend Trumbull or Christ except David Franks, a Jew from Montreal who had sided with the Americans during the Revolution. Trumbull, vexed, noted the irony of this to Jefferson, who was attending silently to the conversation. Giles fired one more shot, denying an afterlife in which misdeeds were punished: "I do not believe one word of a Supreme Being who takes cognizance of the paltry affairs of this world, and to whom we are responsible for what we do."

Trumbull claimed never to have heard or seen "such a broad and unqualified avowal of atheism." If this was the first time Trumbull had encountered such ideas, he had not paid attention to the philosophical talk in the most advanced salons of Paris. Perhaps he hadn't; he was involved with paintings. He concluded his account of the dinner with the delivery of an eloquent reproof. "Sir," he told his tormentor, "in my opinion, the man who can with sincerity make the declaration which you have just made, is perfectly prepared for the commission of every atrocious action, by which he can promise himself the advancement of his own interest, or the gratification of his impure passions, provided he can commit it secretly.... I would not trust such a man with the honor of a wife, a sister, or a daughter—with my own purse or reputation, or with anything that I thought valuable. Our acquaintance, sir, is at an end."

The story of the dinner had not become any less dramatic by the time it appeared in Trumbull's memoirs. One obvious "improvement" is that Trumbull identified Giles as a senator, a job he would not hold until years after the Washington administration had ended.

But Giles was not the point. Trumbull's righteous wrath was displaced onto him from Jefferson who, though silent, allowed the baiting of him and his family's beliefs to go on—even, according to Trumbull, "smiling and nodding approbation" while Giles railed. It was an attack by proxy—and a betrayal: Jefferson in Europe had been happy to use Trumbull as a go-between; in America he preferred Virginian acolytes.[25]

But there was another object of Trumbull's wrath (no doubt unconscious)—Trumbull himself. He had courted Harriet Wadsworth as a wife, and turned from her to a handy servant. And Temperance Ray was someone's daughter, yet he had caused her to give birth to an unwanted child. Who was he to rebuke the morals of the Virginia atheist?

His country had turned from its revolution to partisan wrangles. His fiancée was dead, the son his lover had saddled on him growing up he knew not where. His subscription was failing. His father had been right—America, never mind Connecticut, was not Athens. It was time for Trumbull to do something else.

SEVEN

T rumbull escaped into diplomacy.

His opportunity was provided by America's efforts to tie up the loose ends of the Revolutionary War. Trumbull had told the world he would do a painting of the Treaty of Paris, which was already a decade old; meanwhile the signatory nations, slow as the artist, had yet to fulfill a number of its provisions. Although the British had ceded the new United States their holdings in the trans-Appalachian west, they still manned forts in the American frontier, from which they maintained alliances with local Indians and controlled the fur trade. American debtors had not repaid prewar British creditors; Britain harbored thousands of escaped American slaves.

The wars of the French Revolution added a new cause of discord. Britain had seized hundreds of American ships for the offense of trading with her enemy, France.

President Washington, now in his second term, tapped John Jay to undertake a special mission to London to resolve these matters. Since 1790 Jay had been serving as chief justice of the Supreme Court. But his career before the Constitution included stints as a diplomat; he was one of the five Americans who had negotiated the Treaty of Paris in the first place (and sat for West's unfinished painting). The Court's duties in those days were light. In May 1794 Jay left New York for Britain.

Trumbull accompanied him as secretary. He may have got the assignment thanks to the suggestion of his brother Jonathan, Jr., still a congressman. The pay was adequate—twenty-five pounds a month—and the disappointed artist would have the satisfaction of playing a role, however small, in an important negotiation.

At first his role was small indeed. Jay and his opposite number, the secretary of state, Lord Grenville, agreed to lay the groundwork for their discussions by talking informally without committing anything to paper. As a result Trumbull and Grenville's secretary "had a real holiday for a month."[1] Once negotiating began in earnest, they had paperwork to copy and manage; a treaty was finished by November.

Behind the reserved demeanor of his Calvinist forbears, Jay had both a sly wit and a hard head. Treaties, he believed, were parchment securities, which did nothing more than incarnate the interests and the power of the nations that signed them at the moment they were made. Because America's power on the world stage in 1794 was slight, Jay lowered his sights accordingly. His biggest accomplishment was getting the British out of their frontier forts. He did not press for the return of escaped American slaves (he was the president of an antislavery society in his home state, New York). The compensation owed American merchants was to be decided by a binational commission.

A copy of the treaty would not arrive in America until March 1795 (transatlantic travel could be as slow as painting or diplomacy). While it was still en route, Trumbull was dispatched to Paris to communicate its terms to the new American minister there, James Monroe.

Monroe, two years Trumbull's junior, was, like him, a veteran and a colonel. He had been shot in the shoulder at the Battle of Trenton, and would appear, wounded, in Trumbull's painting of the event. Monroe's experiences as a diplomat, occurring at intervals over the next two decades, would ultimately make him a realpolitiker like Jay, yet at this point in his career he was an earnest and ardent Francophile. One reason president Washington had sent him to Paris was to please American friends of France, and France itself.

When he first arrived at his post, Monroe had assured the French government that he would keep them informed of Jay's negotiations with their British enemy. Jay, resenting this interference in his labors, had refused to tell Monroe anything of his progress. Even now that the treaty was done, he would not send Monroe a copy. Trumbull was directed to memorize it and repeat it to Monroe, if Monroe promised not to divulge what he learned.

Monroe refused the condition, and the French began to consider Jay's tight-lipped secretary persona non grata. Trumbull heard from Benjamin Hichborn, a Massachusetts merchant then living in Paris, that persons in the government had hinted that he should leave the country. Trumbull, irked, said he would obey orders to leave, not hints.[2] At the same time, Trumbull assured Hichborn that France had nothing to fear from the Jay Treaty, which made no alliance between America and its former mother country, merely clearing up long-standing points of contention.[3] Hichborn passed this information to Monroe, who passed it to the French, but they remained doubtful.

Trumbull's salary as secretary ended when the mission did. To keep himself in funds, he tried his hand as an investor. Élisabeth Vigée-LeBrun had left France as a monarchist, but her art dealer husband stayed to help the new regime build the collection of the Louvre. Paintings formerly owned by exiled nobility could be bought for a song, and Trumbull, acting on LeBrun's advice, snapped up eighty-seven Old Master works, with the intention of reselling them in London. The haul included works by Rubens, Rembrandt, Van Dyck, Raphael—this last painting was, in fact, a copy—and a crowd of Dutch genre and Italian religious artists. Trumbull had an investment partner, Daniel Parker, an American speculator who had formerly done business with his brother David; LeBrun got a consultant's cut. Trumbull and Parker spent $4,700, and expected to double that.

Disaster befell the scheme when the paintings arrived in London in August. The customshouse was closed, in honor of a birthday in the royal family, so the art was left overnight in a ship-to-shore barge, chained to the quay. The chain was not long enough, however, to let the vessel rise with the tide; she swamped, and the paintings in their cases floated away. A watchman saw, and saved them, but the canvases were soaked. Trumbull took his investments to West's, where he spent months restoring them. "Inferior to what I expected," wrote one English artist when he saw the collection offered for sale.[4] In the end, Trumbull bought some of the best paintings, including the "Raphael," for himself; he and Parker realized a small profit.

When Trumbull returned to London in August 1796, another diplomatic job came his way. The Anglo-American commission that the

Jay Treaty had established to review the claims for damages of American merchants was to have five members. Each nation picked two (one of the Americans was Christopher Gore, a Massachusetts lawyer and Harvard alum whom Trumbull had met when they were young together in Boston). The four commissioners were then to pick a fifth. Trumbull, the patriot with so many British connections, was the man they picked.[5] When he wrote to Jay to announce his new assignment, he acknowledged his "imperfect preparation" for such a subject, but hoped that the relevant law was "neither so voluminous nor so intricate" that he could not master it.[6] The pay was $2,500 a year.

The legal conundrums that arose were intricate enough. Trumbull's records of his labors show him throwing himself into the details (the need to keep pace with four professional lawyers seems to have spurred him on). On one occasion he showed real political savvy. Foreseeing a 2–2 national split on an important question on which he thought the Americans were in the right, rather than decide it himself, he asked the opinion of Lord Loughborough, the lord chancellor, Britain's highest judge. This authority agreed with the Americans; Trumbull escaped the onus of partisanship.

The commission adjourned for three months at the end of July 1797, allowing Trumbull to make another trip to Paris, which involved him in yet another episode in the mazes of America's European diplomacy.

Trumbull's and Monroe's assurances that the Jay Treaty did no harm to France had persuaded no one. Any rapprochement with Britain was considered by France a hostile act. War made her suspicious, and success in war made her arrogant. France's armies had overrun the Austrian Netherlands, the Rhine valley, and northern Italy. France's leaders were not minded to consider the sensibilities of a weak transatlantic republic.

Trumbull's master and friend, George Washington, had been succeeded as president by Vice President John Adams, in March 1797. (Trumbull's former friend, Thomas Jefferson, had run against Adams in the first contested presidential election; according to the rules that governed the Electoral College at the time, finishing second had made him vice president.) The new president's first priority was to repair relations with France.

Adams sent three commissioners to treat with America's angry sometime ally: Elbridge Gerry, an old friend of his from Massachusetts; Charles C. Pinckney, a veteran and planter; and John Marshall, a young lawyer. Trumbull had painted two of them—Gerry, as a signer of the Declaration of Independence; and Pinckney, in a small portrait taken in Charleston. Their French interlocutor was the minister for foreign affairs, Charles-Maurice de Talleyrand-Périgord, an excommunicated Catholic bishop who had turned to revolution and statecraft. When the revolution had become too violent for his tastes and his safety, he had spent a few years in the United States, where he enjoyed the hospitality of a number of Americans, including Trumbull's brother Jonathan, Jr. Talleyrand had also socialized with Gerry, with Christopher Gore, Trumbull's partner on the claims commission, and with Rufus King, another Trumbull friend from long-ago Boston, now minister to Britain. These personal connections might make Talleyrand approachable, if not sympathetic.

Trumbull's role was minor, but useful. He was to brief Gerry, Pinckney, and Marshall on the progress of the claims commission: they could rebut French suspicions most effectively if they knew exactly where matters stood between Britain and America. When he returned to London in the fall, he could brief King on the progress of negotiations in Paris.

Trumbull arrived in Calais at the end of August, and wrote directly to Talleyrand for a passport. For three weeks, however, he heard nothing. Was this a sign of official coolness, to him, and to his country? "Straws," he wrote to King, may "indicate the direction of the current."[7] He was forced to move on by a case of mistaken identity. Leaving his inn one morning, dressed in a gray cloak with a black cape, he heard a crowd shouting, in French, "Down with the black collars!" After he had hurried back to his room to change, he learned that black was a royalist color; revolutionary authorities had suppressed an incipient royalist coup in Paris, and provincial republicans were rallying to the government.

Trumbull left Calais as fast as possible. Gerry, Pinckney, and Marshall were due to land in Holland before presenting their credentials in Paris. Trumbull met them in Rotterdam, writing to King that they "had such conversation as was necessary."[8] He managed to get to Paris himself by a roundabout route, asking the French minister in The Hague for permission to enter France from the Rhine frontier to the east.

Entry made, he went to Paris and applied to the police for a residence permit (a legal formality that continues into the twenty-first century). The police were not pleased to see him. "How in the devil's name
did you get here?" they demanded. Trumbull showed his passport issued
in The Hague. It was accepted, with a mutter that the blockhead in Holland was always making mistakes.[9]

Trumbull met again with the three American diplomats. Their
mission was not going well. After a brief interview with Talleyrand, they
had seen nothing of him. But they had been approached by intermediaries, friends of Talleyrand speaking unofficially, who told them that negotiations could begin after a payment to France, and a bribe to Talleyrand
personally.

Talleyrand also sent out a feeler to Trumbull. Perhaps the amateur
diplomat could bring his countrymen around. The man who had not
deigned to answer Trumbull's letter from Calais now invited him to dinner. Trumbull accepted and found himself in a small but select company
that included Madame de Staël, a noted bluestocking, and Lucien
Bonaparte, younger brother of France's most successful young general.
When Madame de Staël asked Trumbull about American affairs, Talleyrand grandly announced that politics was not discussed at his table.

The time for politics came later. Trumbull's commission was due to
meet again in London at the beginning of November; when he applied
to the police for a passport to leave France, he was shuttled from office
to office in a manner that suggested deliberate unwillingness to help,
beyond the ordinary delay of routine. He decided to call for assistance
on his new friend Talleyrand, who received him promptly. The minister
for foreign affairs treated him as privy to the American negotiation, and
demanded "the employment of money." Trumbull, playing the innocent
abroad, said he could not imagine that the Americans expected they
would have to pay to talk. "But they must!" Talleyrand declared, striking
the table. When Trumbull continued to be uncooperative, Talleyrand
showed him out.[10]

In this impasse, Trumbull was saved by his art. He applied to his
old acquaintance, Jacques-Louis David, who had gone from painting
scenes of ancient virtue to serving the republican revolution. The saluting arms of *The Oath of the Horatii* had reappeared in his sketch of *The*

Oath of the Tennis Court, the moment when the delegates of the Third Estate had sworn allegiance to themselves as a new National Assembly. After the revolutionary politician Jean-Paul Marat was assassinated, David painted the dead man as a republican Christ. One turn of politics found David imprisoned, perhaps at risk of being guillotined. But the danger passed, and he had already attached himself to the rising star of Lucien Bonaparte's brother.

David immediately agreed to accompany Trumbull to the police. "I have known Mr. Trumbull these ten years," he lectured the astonished functionaries. "I answer for him, he is as good a revolutionist as we are. ... He is a great artist, and it is wrong to interrupt him in his present peaceful occupation of the arts." This outburst of zeal and aestheticism produced the necessary document, though the minister of police joked that he had half a mind to keep "so talented an artist" in France, to serve its republic.[11] Trumbull made a beeline for Calais and the Channel, not knowing when David's protective endorsement might be overridden.

By the second week of November he was in London, where he gave King the first account, from the American negotiators themselves, of Talleyrand's machinations. Their dispatch identified the corrupt intermediaries who bedeviled them with the letters *X, Y,* and *Z.* When Americans learned how their diplomats had been treated, there was an explosion of insulted patriotism.

In the waning years of the century, Trumbull was drawn, via his old friend King, into one more diplomatic venture, more grandiose than anything he had yet been involved in.

King had begun his political career twenty years earlier as a friend of indebted Massachusetts farmers. Once they took up arms to support their grievances, however, he became a proponent of constitutionalism and order. From his post as minister to Britain he looked for opportunities to contain revolutionary France.

France's European enemies were not faring well. Prussia and Austria had been driven from the field; Spain had switched sides to become a French ally. Perhaps Britain, fighting almost alone, could change the global equation by widening the field of conflict.

An opportunity appeared in the person of Francisco de Miranda, a Venezuelan patriot who had been wandering the world for fifteen years looking for allies in an effort to liberate Latin America. He had met George Washington in the United States, fought as a general for revolutionary France, and won the affection of Catherine the Great. A boy who saw him when he was in America recalled him "commenting ... with great vehemence of enthusiasm and severity of denunciation ... with his whole frame in motion, and pacing the room with giant strides."[12] Now he was in Britain, where he laid his hopes before the government, and before Rufus King.

Spain had become France's ally. If it were to become its vassal, as so many other European states had already become, its New World empire, stretching from California to Buenos Aires, would be opened to French ideas, garrisons, and fleets. But with the help of a British navy and an American army, Miranda and like-minded patriots could liberate Spain's empire and rule it themselves. As a side benefit, Britain and the United States would be able to trade with a free Latin America, a privilege the Spaniards had always jealously withheld.

King, Miranda, and Trumbull were discussing the plan as early as 1797. So enthusiastic did Trumbull become that he designed a house for Miranda (never built). The British government gave the Venezuelan a pension and a hearing, and other highly placed Americans besides King and Trumbull—Henry Knox, Alexander Hamilton, John Adams's son-in-law William Smith—showed interest in his plan. President Adams, however, intent on dealing with the French directly, did not.

In March 1799 Trumbull appealed directly to the man who would always be his model of a president, George Washington. "New scenes," he wrote, "... are bursting upon us at every moment of this eventful period, and I trust, sir, that you are now destined to act a more important part in this great drama than you have done in any former period of your life." The new scene in which Trumbull wanted Washington to take a starring role was Latin America, "where oppression has long since prepared the minds of men for change; where liberty and independence are the objects of all men's wishes; and where they who shall first offer those blessings, will be received with rapture." If liberation came via France, the United States "shall have fifteen millions of Jacobins at our doors." But if it came from ourselves, "we give to liberty, real and rational liberty, a secure and wide asylum." To effect that happy result, Washington should leave Mount Vernon one more time, "not merely as the father of the United States, but of the united empires of America."[13]

In a much longer letter to his brother Jonathan, Jr., who had by now followed in their father's footsteps as governor of Connecticut, Trumbull outlined the details. Washington should lead the struggle. After Spain had been defeated, there should be two independent countries, Mexico and Peru. Each should have a constitutional monarch, descended from the Aztecs or the Incas, respectively (Trumbull always had a romantic's fondness for indigenous peoples). Lawmaking would be the province of an upper house, chosen by the nobility and the clergy (Catholic—what would Jonathan Trumbull, Sr., have thought?), and a house of representatives, "on the plan of our own." The United States and these new countries should have reciprocal low tariffs, easy naturalization, and "intimately connect[ed]" banks.

"I may be enthusiastic and full of error," he concluded, as if, reading over his missive before sending it, he had second thoughts, "but, living as I do, amidst the wreck of nations ... I look with increasing anxiety to my country."[14]

Washington answered Trumbull's extraordinary proposal in June. The man who had always considered his most successful maneuvers— crossing the Delaware to attack Trenton, converging with the French on Yorktown—as miraculous, said nothing about the logistical problems involved in invading a continent on the far side of the Caribbean, but began, as was his way, with the most immediate problem, which was, in this case, political. "Strange as it may seem, a party, and a powerful one too, among us"—he meant the followers of Thomas Jefferson—trusted France and distrusted any American efforts to spend more on defense. Given those facts, Washington asked Trumbull "to decide on the probability of carrying such an extensive plan of offense as you have suggested in your last letter, into execution."[15] The probability, he did not have to add, was nil. So ended Trumbull's and King's plans for liberating Latin America. (Miranda would labor on for years, before dying, in 1816, in a Spanish prison.)

In July the British members of Trumbull's maritime claims commission abruptly withdrew, in protest over an unrelated dispute between the two countries.[16] Trumbull's long-running diplomatic job, and the salary attached to it, were over.

For five years, he had been marginally involved in successive diplomatic episodes, by turns productive, incendiary, and crackpot—the Jay
Treaty, the XYZ negotiation, and dreams of hemispheric revolution.

In all this time he had not entirely ignored his art. He had moni-
tored the progress of the engraving of *Bunker's Hill.* Both his trips to
Paris had been accompanied by visits to Stuttgart, where Johann von
Müller was bringing the work (slowly) to completion. In 1797 Trumbull
had come to France from the Rhineland with the canvas itself. David
had told him to bring it with them when they went to appeal to the police. "That picture," he told his American friend, "is worth a multitude of
passports," and he displayed it as proof of Trumbull's republican bona
fides. "He saw the Battle of Bunker's Hill," David declaimed, "and he has
painted a fine picture of it. Here it is!"[17] A picture was worth a thousand
words, even David's zealous words.

Bunker's Hill, and its companion piece, *Quebec,* were appreciated by
someone more important to Trumbull than David. When corresponding
with George Washington about the Latin American scheme, Trumbull
had been able to announce the delivery of the four sets of prints that
Washington had ordered a decade ago. Washington responded, with characteristic politeness—simultaneously sincere and elaborate—assuring
Trumbull that he had sent a check for the remainder of the purchase price
to Trumbull's Philadelphia dealer. "I give you the trouble of this detail
because I should feel unpleasant myself if after your marked politeness
and attentions to me in this, as in every other transaction, any tardiness
should have appeared on my part, in return for prints so valuable."[18]

In the fall of 1799, Trumbull was reminded of his art by another
revolutionary comrade, Lafayette. America's favorite Frenchman had had a
bad decade. Steadily losing power and prestige as the French Revolution
unfolded, he had fled his country after the arrest and dethronement of
Louis XVI, only to be imprisoned by its enemies, as a dangerous revolutionary. He had spent years in a small, damp cell in an Austrian fort in what
is now the Czech Republic. American appeals and Napoleon's victories had
finally secured his release, and he wrote to Trumbull from Holland.

Lafayette's letters, no less than Washington's, were as unmistakable
as fingerprints, infused with his personality, as ardent as Washington's
were grave. After inquiring about Trumbull's family and "all friends in

that dear and blessed country," he asked after Trumbull's paintings. "In vain have I endeavored, my dear sir, to have a sight of your fine prints; they are not to be found in this country.... I knew you had [planned] the Declaration of Independence, Saratoga and Princeton; Bunker's Hill also. Did you not intend to make Monmouth?" (a battle in 1778 in which Lafayette had served with distinction). "I much wish it, because in that battle ... I could see several portraits very precious to me.... Have you chosen the ground where Gen. Washington came up to the retreating vanguard [and] honored me with the care to support the attack? ... What are the other performances which complete the collection? Wherever my definitive home is fixed, your works shall be the first, or according to circumstances, the only ornament of my dwelling."[19]

The aging, ingenuous hero—Lafayette was now forty-two—wanted to recall the glory of his youth; wanted to see his own glory memorialized; wanted equally to see depicted the images and deeds of his friends and comrades. Lafayette yearned to see the finished work—and was urging Trumbull, discreetly but unmistakably, to complete it.

Trumbull answered him in November 1799. After congratulating Lafayette on his liberty, he explained what he was thinking about his project, a dozen years after conceiving it. He set it in a geopolitical context. Most of Europe had been indifferent to the American Revolution, and to paintings about it. The country that wasn't indifferent, France, had become anti-American. (Trumbull expressed this as delicately as he could: "By the unaccountable turn of political opinions, [it] had become equally hostile to the men and to the events which formed my subject.") And America itself was now too buffeted by current events to care about its founding, and art generally. "My native country ... is no longer in that state of easy and affluent tranquility which is so indispensably requisite to the prosperity of the fine arts."

He had "persevere[d] ... in collecting materials and advancing several compositions" so long as he had retained any hope of a receptive public. But he had given up: "Convinced at length, that I was sacrificing the most precious part of my life, I have for several years given all my attention to other objects."

This was an account shaped by a combination of political partisanship, depression, and wounded self-esteem. Seeing American patriotic unity riven by political strife, he had chosen one side—the side of his brother, his oldest friends, and George Washington—and sought, with their patronage, work abroad whose activity and complexity would drive artistic aspirations out of his head, at the same time that it paid his bills.

But perhaps Lafayette's letter, even more than Washington's—allowing Trumbull to be the recipient of admiration, rather than the giver—jogged him. "If different prospects should hereafter open, I may perhaps resume the work."

Or perhaps not. "I very much doubt whether I shall ever resume sufficient courage."

His project was an ambitious one, and his skills had lain fallow for five years.

Trumbull ended by telling Lafayette that Washington, at the time of his last letter, "was then very well."[20] In three weeks Washington would be dead, felled by an infection of the throat. His party, deprived of its icon, would sink into internecine quarrels, followed by defeat. John Adams's successor in the newly built White House would be patron of atheists Thomas Jefferson. Trumbull's friends would never be in a position to offer him diplomatic, or any other, work again.

The plates of his life, personal and artistic, were already shifting. He would pick up his brush again, after finding a wife, and acknowledging his son.

EIGHT

All we know of the early life of Trumbull's wife comes from letters he sent in the new century introducing her to family members.

Sarah Hope, he wrote, was born, near London, in April 1771. Her father, William Hope, was a Scotsman; her mother, an English-woman by the name of West.[1] Her parents and her siblings died when she was a child. Until her teens she lived with a woman "in the country" who taught her reading, writing, and "housewifery"; she was then raised in the family of a London merchant who had been a friend of her mother's, where she continued to learn "the business of the family and economy." Accomplishments that were merely "elegant"— Trumbull specifically mentioned music—had formed no part of her education.[2]

Her name first appears on a document in 1799. It was a lease, writ-ten by Trumbull, for a room in a house in Marylebone, then a London suburb. She signed it "Sarah Hope Harvey." How she had acquired that surname, whether from a youthful marriage, or from being taken into the family of one of the persons she had lived with, is unknown. A year later, she married Trumbull in an Anglican ceremony in Hendon, an-other London suburb. The wedding party was tiny: one woman friend of hers, and two men friends—Christopher Gore and Rufus King—of the groom. King seems not to have met, nor even heard of, Sarah before-hand; when he asked Trumbull, "Who is this lady?" he was told only, "Mrs. Trumbull, sir."[3]

Sarah's lack of family, and Trumbull's tight-lipped discretion, would make her a magnet for gossip. A tale that circulated in America in later years identified her as an illegitimate child of an eminent English jurist, Lord Thurlow.[4] ("No man," quipped Charles James Fox, "is as wise as Thurlow looks.")[5] Thurlow's longtime mistress was named Harvey, and the coincidence of names must have generated the story, but it is incredible; Thurlow's daughters by his mistress are known and accounted for, and none of them was Sarah.[6]

Another story held that she had been the wife of an English army officer; that she and Trumbull had become lovers; and that the husband, discovering it, had offered to let Sarah have Trumbull and an annuity so long as they married quietly. (The agreeable husband was named Williams, not Harvey.)[7] This story appears in the diary of William Dunlap, the artist who had been inspired to poetry by *Bunker's Hill* (we shall encounter more of Dunlap later); he heard it a decade after Sarah's death from the novelist James Fenimore Cooper. It may have as firm a foundation as the story of her birth.

A first marriage at age forty-four is a serious change in midlife; a man who undertakes it is likely (unless he is merely desperate) to take the relationship seriously. Another relationship Trumbull began to take seriously, at his wife's urging, was with the boy he had fathered in America.[8] He had been paying the town of Haddam for the child's sustenance, but had taken no other interest in him. Sarah insisted he provide for his son's education as well as his mere livelihood. The woman whose own youth had been so uncertain wished to spare her husband's child a fate she had—barely—escaped.

In 1799, the same year that Trumbull rented the room for Sarah in Marylebone, he made his first inquiries after his son. His agent in these efforts was James Wadsworth, the cousin of his Hartford friends whom he had also asked to report on the status of the mother, Temperance Ray. "What is past is folly," Trumbull wrote to Wadsworth, "but to neglect the poor little wretch (who at all events is not here by any fault of his own) would deserve a much severer name."[9] Wadsworth found that the boy had been settled by Haddam's town fathers on a family named Smith, who had taken him with them to the Military Tract of western New York, a slice of land recently made over to Revolutionary War veterans.

Wadsworth was himself a prominent landowner in the tract. When he called on the Smiths, they were living in the brand-new township of

Scipio, named, in hifalutin American style, after the Roman general Scipio Africanus. The boy, Wadsworth wrote to Trumbull, had been named John Ray, after his parents. He was out tending the cows when the visitor arrived, but when he came back, Wadsworth "viewed him with much attention.— His clothes were dirty and ragged and his hair in every direction. I perceived however a fine countenance, hazel eyes, with ruby cheeks. ... John with some interest asked me if I knew his father. I waived the question."

Since the Smiths were clearly unable or unwilling to give John any education, Wadsworth proposed to take him to a family that could. The Smiths wanted a bonus payment of fifty dollars for the expenses they had spent maintaining him. "His apparel," Wadsworth scoffed, "was not worth sixpence." When he offered to submit the question to third-party arbitrators, the Smiths agreed to let the boy go for nothing.

Acquaintances of Trumbull's in the Military Tract who now saw young John "pronounced him yours without question. [One] in particular thought him quite your counterpart. ... I have no doubt," Wadsworth added, with almost painterly exactitude, "but he is your son—his forehead in particular and the upper part of his face resembles yours." So much for Trumbull's assertion that the mother's promiscuity made paternity unknowable.

John jumped at the idea of being educated, and Wadsworth lodged him with a Mr. Whally, a broken-down English merchant living in Geneseo, another Military Tract town. Whally, Wadsworth reported, would make "a very excellent schoolmaster," though he was "a little inclined to drink." Wadsworth gave the boy books, paper, and "decent clothing," and left him in his new home.[10]

Trumbull had righted the wrong of almost complete neglect, though his ongoing relations with John Ray would continue to be marred by shame. He could not see fathering a child out of wedlock as anything but an embarrassing mistake; John Ray was like a milestone erected to proclaim his indiscretion. For years, he tried to conceal the truth by maintaining the pretense that the boy was his nephew. The relationship provoked all that was proud and self-involved in his character.

His feelings toward his wife, by contrast, were ardent, affectionate, admiring. He expressed them in the way that was most meaningful to him, by painting her. Sarah stimulated him to take up his brush again.

His skills had suffered from their long sleep. He was mortified, he wrote to his brother Jonathan, Jr., to discover "in how great a degree I had lost the powers I once possessed."[11] To retrieve them, he turned to portraiture.

Trumbull had a complicated attitude toward portrait painting. He labored to fill his historical canvases with exact likenesses: hence his travels up and down America's coast capturing faces; his collection of four-inch painted notes to himself; even his efforts to paint a famous man's son if the man himself had died, genes supplying at one remove what no sitting any longer could. But his subjects, with a few exceptions, were chosen because they had played a role in great deeds. Memorializing the deeds and the persons who had taken part in them was what Trumbull's early reading, confirmed by his life experience, had taught him was the task of art.

Painting portraits for money could sustain a career. But it made the artist, as Trumbull had written in the mid 1780s, "the servant ... of vanity," obedient to the whims of sitters and the fashions of the day. It was "trumpery and caprice and nonsense."[12]

Sarah Trumbull, however, was no paying client, but his wife. Early in the new century, and in their marriage, he began painting her image.

The first portrait he did of her, which he may have sent across the Atlantic to introduce her to his kin, shows her in a white dress, arms crossed in front. Her left hand holds a billowy fold of fabric, her right fingers the cross she wears around her neck—a sign, along with their Anglican church wedding, of a drift from Trumbull's religious roots: the children of Calvin carried the cross in their thoughts and their prayers, not on their persons. Sarah wears her hair up in a fashionable topknot; she has a long nose, a small, puckered mouth, and wide eyes that look straight at the viewer.

There is more color in a second portrait—a dark background, red, satiny trim on her gathered bust—but the overall effect is still light and bright (plate 15). A dog gazes at her, a traditional symbol of devotion. Most striking perhaps in this painting is Sarah's lovely long neck, visible here because she turns slightly to the side.

Trumbull also put her in Biblical compositions, inspired by his supposed Raphael. Sarah becomes the Madonna, bending toward the

Christ child, with an infant St. John the Baptist kneeling at her feet. These paintings show her in half profile, a more attractive angle, rendering her nose less prominent.

Christopher Gore and Rufus King, Trumbull's two guests at his own wedding, sat for portraits. So did the artist himself. Trumbull's youthful self-portrait had shown him leaning eagerly forward, as if about to plunge into life. Now in middle age he sits in profile, straight, with a still-military bearing, and turns slightly to the viewer (plate 14). The pose and the expression are proud, serious, and thoughtful. His artist's palette is by his side, but his right hand, closer to the viewer, clasps the hilt of his sword. He remains a colonel, after two decades.

These paintings, efforts to get back into stride, show how much ground Trumbull had lost. Christopher Gore's head looks like a large white pumpkin. King's shows more character—which, of course, may reflect a difference in the sitters. But Trumbull had known and liked both men since their days together in Boston; he ought to have done better by one of them. Sarah, in her portraits, appears empty-headed, an impression enforced by the loyal dog, which is a spaniel: dogs symbolized devotion, but spaniels were notorious for servility. Shakespeare uses them so.[13] Sensitive, like all artists of his time, to the traditional symbolism of things, persons, and poses, Trumbull here blundered into an iconographic crack-up.

On the canvas these paintings lack the little accents and strokes that had made Trumbull's best earlier work blaze and shimmer. From now on he has to be judged on the basis of design, arrangement, and narrative meaning. At his best he will master some or all of those features; panache of execution, with rare exceptions, will be beyond him.

In 1804 Trumbull and his wife left England for the United States. He must have wanted his family to meet her (a traveling nephew had already seen her in London, and written back home that she was "a fine woman").[14] He may have wanted to see the son he was still unwilling to acknowledge. Whatever his reservations about painting portraits, he must have calculated that he would find more customers in his native country, however long he had been away from it. He thought at first of settling once more in Boston, but his old friend Gilbert Stuart had lately moved there. American cities could not sustain more than one first-rate painter apiece. (Philadelphia was out, as the home base of Charles Will-son Peale.) So the Trumbulls established themselves in New York City, on Broadway, a block above Wall Street.

He was witness, initially unawares, to a dramatic moment of American history. On July 4, 1804, the New York members of the Society of the Cincinnati held a banquet in honor of the holiday. The Society was a fraternal organization of men who had served as officers in the Revolution. Its first president general had been their former commander in chief, George Washington. After his death the honor passed to his wartime aide and peacetime Treasury secretary, Alexander Hamilton, who naturally attended the New York gathering. Also present was Aaron Burr, a New York lawyer and politician who was currently serving as Thomas Jefferson's vice president.

Trumbull had painted a standing portrait of Hamilton in 1792, which is a monument to his intellectual activity: Hamilton's gloved left hand holds the glove he has just removed from his right, which rests on a piece of paper on a nearby table. It is as if he cannot wait to sit down and get back to work, writing one of the reports, essays, or political letters that poured from him. Trumbull also painted him in the still-unfinished *Yorktown;* Colonel Hamilton had led an attack on a British redoubt during the siege, and was present at the surrender. Captain Aaron Burr (later promoted to colonel) had fought gallantly in the doomed attack on Quebec, though Trumbull had not included him in his painting of it. The best portrait of Burr had been done by Gilbert Stuart in the early 1790s. Stuart, like Trumbull with Hamilton, emphasized his subject's intelligence, highlighting his balding, egg-shaped forehead. There are no writing implements to be seen, however. Public expression was not Burr's métier, in politics or in business; as he warned his law clerks, "Things written remain."[15]

What no one aside from a handful of intimates knew on that July 4 was that the two men were already engaged to fight a duel. They had been political enemies for years, but Burr believed that Hamilton had recently crossed a line, referring to him, in an after-dinner conversation, as "despicable." An offense to honor could only be resolved on the field of honor. The gentlemen had chosen seconds, who had negotiated a time—the morning of July 11—and a place—a ledge along the Hudson

River below Weehawken—to meet. Trumbull's recollection in his memoirs of the Cincinnati's dinner is the best account we have of the antagonists' last pre-duel encounter. "Burr, contrary to his wont, was silent, gloomy, sour; while Hamilton entered with glee into all the gaiety of a convivial party, and even sung an old military song."[16] Hamilton's song, "How Stands the Glass Around," was a sentimental ballad about the hard life of a soldier, who either dies in battle, or in some rented room nursing a bottle. Hamilton would die, after thirty hours of agony, from Burr's bullet, lodged in his spine.

Hamilton and Burr's fatal interview was more than personal. Ten years earlier Trumbull had left America in the throes of partisanship. He had returned to a country that was, if possible, even more shrilly divided. Thomas Jefferson, who had narrowly won the presidential election of 1800, had delivered peace, low taxes, and the Louisiana Purchase, and was headed for a smashing reelection in 1804. His political party, called the Republicans (ancestors of today's Democrats, not the GOP), commanded large margins in both houses of Congress. Die-hards in the Federalist Party, to which Hamilton belonged, were so embittered by Jefferson's success that they plotted a secession of Federalist-dominated New England states. Aaron Burr, whose party was himself, schemed with them to take New York along, should he win the governorship in that fall's election. Hamilton had learned of these plots, which he opposed vehemently—yet another reason for him to dislike Burr. (His death smirched Burr, and caused the Federalist plotters to stand down, for the present.) What Trumbull called "the demon of discord" still held sway in American public life.[17] In this atmosphere portraiture, the art of the personal, would be Trumbull's sole painterly outlet.

He found many customers. He charged $500 for a full-length portrait, $250 for a half-length; $150 for a bust with hands, $100 for a bust without. In a good year—and his first years in New York were all good—he could earn $4,000.

The works he produced varied in quality. The City of New York paid him to supplement the full-length Washington it had commissioned a dozen years earlier with paintings of great New Yorkers, living and dead; the collection still hangs in City Hall. He did a posthumous Hamilton, using a white marble bust by the Italian republican Giuseppe

Ceracchi to model the head. Hamilton's standing figure in this portrait is as stiff as marble, more suited to a billboard than a painting. His right hand, instead of resting on his desk, as it had in 1792, is flung out in a gesture as if he were hawking merchandise. New York City mayor De-Witt Clinton, depicted in a half-length portrait, has an even more awkward pose. His left arm (farthest from the viewer) slides out of the picture frame to the right, then curls back as a hand that looks as if it belonged to somebody else, clasping a book.

Trumbull's portraits of women are better. Mrs. John Murray was the wife of a wealthy merchant (Murray Hill, now a Manhattan neighborhood, is named for the family). Trumbull captures a face that is shrewd, slightly amused, not to be trifled with. Thomas Sully, an artist in his early twenties, paid Trumbull $100 to paint his wife, so that he might watch the older man at work. He learned from the experience how best to arrange his paints and brushes, the tools of the trade, and developed a lifelong respect for Trumbull and his talent. The portrait of Mrs. Sully that Trumbull produced is sweet, and rather sad (reasonably enough: her first husband, Sully's elder brother, had just died).

New York was moving ahead of Philadelphia as the nation's largest city—each now had a population of about sixty thousand—and wealthy New Yorkers, proud of their urban energy, wished to set up cultural and learned societies. A proposal to establish a Literary and Philosophical Society brought from one caustic New Yorker the question, where would they find philosophers enough to join it?[18] New Yorkers went on organizing regardless, confident that if they built the societies, members would come. Among the organizations they founded was a New York (later American) Academy of the Fine Arts. Its backers and officers included the city's best and brightest: Mayor Clinton; Robert Livingston, returned from negotiating the Louisiana Purchase; Trumbull's friend Rufus King, retired finally from diplomatic service. The purpose of the Academy, like that of the Royal Academy in London, was threefold: to raise the status of artists, to exhibit their works to the general public, and to provide models for budding artists to study and copy. There was no king in New York to confer prestige, but the support of a republican elite might be enough.

Trumbull was informed of the Academy's gestation before he left London. It planned, he was told, to import "from Paris the best possible copies of the best originals in statuary."[19] Trumbull put the Academy's agent in touch with his old friend David, for advice on the ground. When the statuary arrived in New York, fig leaves were placed over the pudenda, in consideration of ladies who were allowed to visit the Academy on Saturdays. Trumbull was elected to the Board of Directors in 1805. He would remain connected with the institution through many ups and downs of its and his reputation.

Edmund Burke had told young Trumbull to study architecture since a new nation needed new public buildings. In 1804 he designed the most important public building in Lebanon, his hometown: a new First Congregational Church (figure 6). During the previous century, Lebanon's worshippers had met first in a barn, then in successively larger wooden meetinghouses. The one that Trumbull and his family knew was built in the 1730s. For the new century Trumbull designed a brick church with a rectangular sanctuary, a white steeple, and four embedded columns supporting a pediment—a clean, simplified imitation of St. Martin-in-the-Fields, London, which had become the model for Protestant churches worldwide. In 1938 a hurricane that devastated Long Island and New England ripped Trumbull's church apart. It was rebuilt according to his specifications in the 1950s. The dimensions of the sanctuary are thirty-seven by forty-eight feet—a bit of architectural numerology that yields a patriotic result, since thirty-seven times forty-eight equals 1776.[20]

During his New York sojourn, Trumbull had letters from his son, who had just become a teenager. Young John reported on geometry lessons, dancing lessons, and the fit of a military-style jacket, the gift of his "Uncle and Aunt" (so Trumbull's deception was maintained).[21] So long as the growing boy was safely distant, all went well.

Once Trumbull and his wife came to know Trumbull's family, all did not go well. Sarah was a foreigner, without family or connections—apart from her husband—to explain and situate her. The nephew who had called her a "fine woman" in his letter home had added that she "has neither Father, Mother, Sister, Brother, Uncle, Aunt, and [I] may almost say Friend."[22] The Trumbulls, by contrast, lived in an oyster bed of siblings, spouses, and in-laws, all small-state gentry. Differences between her and them were unavoidable. They broke out painfully in 1805 when

Figure 6. The First Congregational Church, in
Lebanon, Connecticut, just up the village green
from Trumbull's childhood home, is the only
building designed by him that survives.

Trumbull and his wife joined a family expedition to James Wadsworth's
properties in western New York. Trumbull planned to buy a tract of his
own, as an investment, with a portion set aside to be a future homestead
for his "nephew." The traveling party included Jonathan Trumbull, Jr.,
and his wife, and two Trumbull nieces and their husbands. During the
journey Sarah and a Trumbull niece had some sort of tiff that left Sarah
in tears. Whatever it was that upset her, no one apologized for it, for
more than a year later Trumbull wrote a chiding letter to his niece: "from
that day to this not a word has been said to heal the wound."[23] A year

after that Jonathan, Jr., wrote Trumbull a chiding letter of his own: "May your returning good sense tranquilize the scenes of distress which seem to have taken unhappy possession of your mind."[24] Trumbulls were equally incapable of retracting, or forgetting, slights.

American public life, meanwhile, took a turn for the worse. Britain's ongoing war with Napoleonic France put the shipping of neutral America at risk as each belligerent seized ships bound for its enemy; Britain, with the world's greatest navy, seized the most. President Jefferson's solution, at the end of 1807, was to forbid American ships from sailing to any foreign port. If they stayed home, Jefferson reasoned, they could not be seized; and once the dueling superpowers felt the loss of American trade, they would come to their senses and annoy America no more.

The superpowers instead raged on as before, while America's commercial cities withered under the lockdown. One visitor described grass growing on New York's unused wharfs; "not a box, bale, cask, barrel, or package was to be seen."[25] Trumbull was a secondary victim, as merchants who could not do business became unable to commission portraits. Jefferson had gone from insulting his religion to picking his pocket.

In Britain there would be an ocean between him and the havoc Jefferson had wrought. In January 1809 Trumbull and his wife, accompanied now by John Ray, returned to London.

NINE

The move to Britain turned out to be unfortunate in almost every way.

The Trumbulls settled in Argyle Street, in a middling neighborhood that was neither fashionable nor artistic. Trumbull found his market for portraits as limited in London as it had been in New York, for potential patrons on both sides of the Atlantic had economic hardships to contend with. Political prejudice also told against him, as many Britons, locked in their death struggle with Napoleon, were simply contemptuous of neutrals, especially Americans.

He turned his hand to historical paintings, literary paintings, religious paintings. The history was not the history he knew firsthand, but events he gleaned from reading—episodes in the lives of Edward III or Peter the Great of Russia—and his productions based on them seem, not surprisingly, stagy and remote. He painted scenes from the poems of Walter Scott and James Macpherson. Scott is unjustly unread today. It is a mystery that Macpherson was ever read at all. The Scottish antiquary claimed to have discovered ancient Gaelic epics, homegrown Homer, supposedly written by a bard named Ossian; he had collected some authentic bits and pieces of poetry, but all the stitching together was his own. When Samuel Johnson was asked if any modern man could have written such poems, he answered, "Many men, many women and many children."[1] Yet almost everyone else in Trumbull's world loved them. Napoleon was a fan; so was Thomas Jefferson, who called Ossian "the greatest poet that has ever existed."[2] Now we pass by Trumbull's Ossian paintings in embarrassment, as if he had rendered scenes from *Star Wars*.

Plate 1. Faith Trumbull, *Milking Scene Needlework,* 1754. John copied his sister Faith's needlework on the parlor floor.

Plate 2. John Trumbull, *Self-Portrait,* 1777. The young artist, ready to show the world his skills. (Photograph © 2024 Museum of Fine Arts, Boston.)

Plate 3. John Trumbull, *The Death of General Warren at the Battle of Bunker's Hill, June 17, 1775,* 1786. A wave, breaking.

Plate 4. John Trumbull, *The Death of General Montgomery in the Attack on Quebec, December 31, 1775,* 1786. Death at midnight.

Plate 5. John Trumbull, *The Declaration of Independence, July 4, 1776*, 1787–1820. The reasons why.

Plate 6. John Trumbull, *The Capture of the Hessians at Trenton, December 26, 1776*, 1786–1828. At last, a victory.

Plate 7. John Trumbull, *The Death of General Mercer at the Battle of Princeton, January 3, 1777*, c. 1789–c. 1831. Victory is hard.

Plate 8. John Trumbull, *The Surrender of General Burgoyne at Saratoga, October 16, 1777*, c. 1822–32. The surrender in the wilderness.

Plate 9. John Trumbull, *The Surrender of Lord Cornwallis at Yorktown, October 19, 1781*, 1787–c. 1828. Triumphant allies.

Plate 10. John Trumbull, *The Resignation of General Washington, December 23, 1783*, 1824–28. Principles obeyed.

Plate 11. John Trumbull, *General George Washington at Trenton*, 1792.
Trumbull asked to be buried beneath this portrait.

Plate 12. John Trumbull, *Hopothle-Mico,* or
The Talasee King of the Creeks, 1790. Trumbull
sketched this Creek chieftain by stealth.

Plate 13. John Trumbull, *Reclining Nude,* late 18th–early 19th century.
The pose is after Velázquez, the model may be Trumbull's wife.

Plate 14. John Trumbull, *Self-Portrait*, c. 1802. Colonel Trumbull shows himself near his palette, holding his sword.

Plate 15. John Trumbull, *Sarah Trumbull with a Spaniel*, c. 1802. Trumbull called his wife "beautiful beyond the usual beauty of women!"

Plate 16. Andrew Robertson, *Lieutenant John Trumbull Ray*, 1814. Trumbull's illegitimate son in uniform, pleasing his father at last.

Trumbull's *Woman Taken in Adultery* faces the problem encountered by all naturalistic art in depicting Christ: Is He a man? Is He God? How can He be shown as both? Trumbull's sleek dude is not a good answer. The pose of the woman kneeling before Him was suggested, to Trumbull, by Sarah when she bent to pick up a pair of scissors she had dropped while sewing. Trumbull told her not to move and quickly sketched the position on his canvas.[3] By painting her in this character, was Trumbull refuting the gossip that swirled around her, or unconsciously endorsing it? The most effective features of the painting are the crabbed faces of the woman's accusers, dark and bunched together like bad fruit. Perhaps they represent art critics.

Trumbull's best painting from his time in Britain is *Maternal Tenderness*, in which Sarah bares her right breast to suckle a baby (figure 7). The pose is that of the Madonna and the Christ child. It took Renaissance artists a long time before they managed to paint babies that looked like babies, rather than ugly homunculi. Maybe the lag was due to the fact that actual infants are unable, except when sleeping, to hold a pose. Yet painters finally learned to represent children as well as mothers. "The Madonnas of Italy," Trumbull wrote, "are among the most interesting and beautiful of their pictures."[4] Trumbull had done a quick pencil sketch of a Madonna and child twenty years earlier while he was soaking up art in Paris. Now he moved the scene into the present, into his own life—or into what he wished his own life to be. Outside of this painting, he and Sarah never had a child of their own.

Early in the Trumbulls' British sojourn, Sarah received a blow as humiliating as the coldness of her husband's family. Before leaving the country, Trumbull had drawn up a will (he was fifty-two, the age for thinking of such things), assigning almost everything he owned to Sarah. But New York law forbade foreigners from inheriting property in the state—a serious loss to her in the event she became a widow, since Trumbull's upstate land was his only asset, apart from his paintings (his own and those he had collected). DeWitt Clinton had assured Trumbull before he left New York that the legislature could pass a special bill granting an exemption to Sarah, and such a bill was offered in the 1810 session. But Clinton, now reversing himself, delivered a patriotic philippic against it. Britain's bullying of American ships and sailors had driven

Figure 7. John Trumbull, *Maternal Affection, Tenderness,
or Love,* 1809–after 1815. This secularized Madonna
and child shows a situation that Trumbull and his
wife were never able to experience.

the two countries to the brink of war; how could New York allow its land
to pass into the hands of enemy aliens? The bill for Sarah lost 25–1 in the
state senate, with only the Federalist who had moved it voting in favor.
Clinton had his eye on the presidency, and his rhetoric was a way to appeal to Jeffersonian Republicans; Rufus King, who understood both
Clinton's ambition, and the cutthroat ways of New York politics, advised
his friends in Britain to discount it. Sarah, however, was outraged at the
slight.

Difficulties of a different kind arose concerning John Ray. Trumbull had planned for some time to set his "nephew" up as a farmer in

New York, and had set aside a portion of his western lands to be his homestead. Farming on a small scale was not a gentlemanly occupation, but it could be respectable. Although snobbish Emma Woodhouse disdains to associate with Robert Martin, the neighborhood farmer, Mr. Knightley, her friend and social equal, does so without embarrassment or loss of caste. As soon as Trumbull arrived in London, he asked Sir John Sinclair, a Scottish agronomist, to recommend "a thorough practical farmer" who was also "a moral and respectable man" with whom his "nephew" could live and learn.[5] Sir John placed young John with a farmer in Fenton, a hamlet in the far north of England.

But the young man had other ideas. "I am now going to mention something to you," he wrote to Trumbull in the summer of 1811, "which I am doubtful whether it will please you or not, but I thought the best way was to tell you honestly at once what I wish, that is to go into the army."[6]

Trumbull was not pleased. His reply scolded Ray for succumbing to "the charms of a red coat." He pointed out that military service was not free. Officers' commissions in the British army could be purchased, but the price of a commission for an ensign—the lowest officer's rank, equivalent to a second lieutenant—was £400, no small sum. In addition, an ensign's pay was "not sufficient to live upon with decency."

Beyond all that, Ray's scheme was unpatriotic: "You have chosen, of all times, to enter the British Army at the moment when a war with America is almost inevitable." The British might be suspicious of him; Americans would certainly be angry with him.

Trumbull himself was angry. Partly on Sarah's behalf: consider, he wrote, "those accusations which Mr. Clinton and his worthless friends will not fail to ground upon such a step." Sarah would become, in their telling, not only an enemy alien, but the aunt of an enemy soldier.

But Trumbull was most upset by Ray's proposed reversal of the trajectory of his own life. Trumbull and his comrades had fought Britain; he had painted their defeats and their victories. What they had done—he, Washington, young Jefferson—was more important than what Clinton and old Jefferson were doing now. "America with all her follies and vices is still my country and yours." Do not "abandon America because the ruling party of the day is composed of worthless and unjust men."[7]

Ray did not give up. "Did you not enter into the army when you was young [as] I am . . .? Did you not follow your own inclination in the choice of your profession?"[8] This was a hit. Trumbull replied petulantly that he had not in fact followed his own earliest inclination, since his had been to study with Copley rather than go to Harvard. Yet he had been "overruled."[9] So the older man and the young one fought with each other, and with the ghost of Jonathan Trumbull, Sr.

It ended with Trumbull bowing to Ray's wishes, and even writing letters to the War Office on the young man's behalf. (Foreigner though he was, Trumbull was well-connected.) Ray enlisted in the Forty-Fifth Nottinghamshire, an infantry regiment, and early in 1812 he saw action in two bloody British victories in Spain, the Siege of Badajoz and the Battle of Salamanca. He was lightly wounded in both; his tone in a letter to Sarah brims with the confidence of an old soldier (newly hatched): "You would have thought some times that a mouse could not have [escaped] from the balls, they were flying so thick."

Ray concluded, "Make my best respects to Uncle."[10] "Uncle," for all his reservations, was proud of the young man's exploits. "To have been wounded," he wrote to Rufus King, ". . . secures him the respect of his comrades through life and from such a beginning I cannot but hope that he will make a distinguished officer."[11]

The United States declared war on Britain in June 1812. For a second time Trumbull found himself in a hostile country during wartime. He and Sarah lingered in London, their uncertainty about what to do augmented by the uncertainty of the war itself. Long thought to be inevitable, it seemed almost half-hearted once it came. Congress's vote to declare war had been divided, with every Federalist and one quarter of the dominant Republicans voting nay, or abstaining. President James Madison was divided in his own mind, sending out peace feelers as soon as the fighting began. And Britain, although it clashed with American armies on the frontier and American frigates at sea, was preoccupied with its climactic struggle against Napoleon.

Trumbull finally booked passage on a ship sailing home in August 1813. Too late. That month, the British government forbade all Americans living in Britain to leave. For their enforced stay, the Trumbulls shifted their lodgings to Bath, in order to save money.

They needed to save, for Trumbull was running up an enormous debt to his London banker, Samuel Williams, who had assumed the role once occupied by John Baker Church. Williams's many creditors included revolutionaries in Greece and opium traders in China. By 1815 Trumbull owed him over $38,000. Like many a man in debt, Trumbull was hoping for something to turn up: peace, prosperity, new commissions. Meanwhile he fretted, marooned in a resort town where the nobility and the gentry paraded their ailments and their marriageable daughters. "I am heartily weary of this waste of Life," he wrote to Williams.[12]

He did a favor for John Ray, recommending that he have a miniature portrait painted by Andrew Robertson, a Scottish protégé of Benjamin West's (plate 16). Robertson brought more color and verve to his works than the typical miniaturist—he dismissed Richard Cosway's productions as "pretty things, but not pictures."[13] Robertson's miniatures, in their painterly freedom, indeed resembled Trumbull's own small oils. "Beg to have the picture in your uniform," Trumbull reminded Ray.[14] Robertson did a fine job, showing a dashing young officer with fashionable side whiskers and a curling lock of hair.

These years in Britain—the last Trumbull would spend abroad—were not an entire waste of his talent. His skill at drawing had not diminished, and one of his works, a reclining female nude, is the most seductive he ever made (plate 13).

His inspiration was that erotic masterpiece, Velázquez's *Toilet of Venus*. This painting had been bought in Spain, in the wake of British victories there, by George Augustus Wallis, an Anglo-Italian painter sent out as an art scout by a British dealer. Wallis brought the Velázquez to Britain in 1809, where it was bought four years later by J.B.S. Morritt, a gentleman classicist, who installed it in his home, Rokeby Park, whence its more widely used name, *The Rokeby Venus*. (There is no account of Trumbull seeing it, but he had painter friends in common with both Wallis and Morritt; a Velázquez for sale in London would have been big artistic news.)

Velázquez's naked Venus lies, back to us, stretched sinuously on a couch. Her son Cupid hovers in front of her, holding a mirror in which we glimpse the reflection of her hidden face. The painting is a web of gazes: ours at her back; Cupid's at her front; hers, via the mirror, at herself, and back at us. Velázquez himself is the master gazer, orchestrating it all. So much looking; so much to look at. Small wonder that an early twentieth-century English feminist would slash the canvas, hung by then in the National Gallery in London. It celebrates beauty, and voyeurism.

Trumbull's drawing, chalk and crayon on blue paper, flips the pose right to left, and dispenses with Cupid. All we see is the female form, almost hovering in space (her couch is barely sketched). Losing the mythological trappings, Trumbull seems to give us a real woman, intimately viewed. Is she aware of our presence? Indifferent? Expecting us? And who was she? It was possible to hire female nude models in Britain then, but they were expensive, charging as much as a guinea per sitting (not that Trumbull ever stinted himself). One modern art historian thinks the model may have been Sarah.[15] Trumbull never exhibited this drawing.

Another creation of his was never exhibited because it was never commissioned, though the idea would bear fruit after he returned to America. On Trumbull's trips to western New York he had visited and sketched Niagara Falls. The triple waterfall had first been seen by white men's eyes in the seventeenth century. By the end of the eighteenth it had become a symbol of the sublimity of nature, and of America. It became a pilgrimage site for honeymooners (Aaron Burr's daughter Theodosia among them) and artists. When Trumbull arrived in Britain in 1809 he brought with him four paintings of the falls—two of ordinary size, and two fourteen-foot-long monsters. He hoped the last two would generate sufficient interest to allow him to paint one larger yet: a 360-degree image, known as a panorama.

Artists have ever pushed the bounds of scale. Miniaturists like Cosway and Robertson went small. Other painters went big—bigger than West's and Copley's history paintings, filling the walls and ceilings of churches, mansions, and palaces. Panoramas were a late eighteenth-century invention, immense images designed to be shown in specially built spaces, encircling the viewer. So painters reached for the immersive effects of cinema even before the invention of still photography. Panoramas would be a new reach for Trumbull, who had preferred to work relatively small.

The London entrepreneur of panoramas was Robert Barker (he coined the word, from two Greek words: *pan*, meaning "all," and *horama*, meaning "view"). Customers paid three shillings to enter his establishment near Leicester Square and walk down a darkened corridor to a raised observation deck, where the painted view surrounded them, lit from above by a hidden skylight. Barker's ads quoted a plug from Benjamin West, who supposedly called his panorama "the greatest improvement to the art of painting that has ever yet been discovered."[16]

Shortly after he arrived in London, Trumbull approached Barker with the idea of displaying a panorama of Niagara Falls, and asked West to put in a good word. The only result of this proposal was a rupture in Trumbull's and West's friendship, for Trumbull believed, based on a hearsay account, that West had disparaged his paintings to Barker instead of praising them.[17] It was a dubious bit of hearsay, for West had always been generous to his former student. But Trumbull could be a touchy man.

Whatever the reason, Trumbull's panorama of the great falls never got made. He would soon hope to do a panorama of revolutionary history instead.

Napoleon's defeat and banishment to Elba in the summer of 1814 allowed Britain to concentrate its resources on the war with America. Even so the British were turned back at every point. Americans, for their part, realized that the gaudiest hopes of the war's supporters—conquering Canada, forcing Britain to change its maritime practices—were impossible. A peace restoring the status quo ante was negotiated at the end of 1814. Wandering Trumbull returned with his wife to America in August 1815.

TEN

The Trumbulls settled once again in New York City. After a brief time on Broadway near Trinity Church, they occupied a series of residences in what was then the northern part of town.

Trumbull threw himself into the cultural life of the city, now clearly the most populous in the country. The American Academy of the Fine Arts, which had elected him as a director during his last period in New York, had found new quarters in a building on Chambers Street, north of City Hall, grandly named the New York Institution of Learned and Scientific Societies. The structure was intended by the city fathers "to give a greater impulse and elevation to our intellectual character."[1] The American Academy featured Trumbull's paintings at a gala exhibition in 1816. He was tapped to serve as president the following year.

The city had been untouched by the War of 1812. Washington, the nation's capital, had not been so lucky. In the summer of 1814 a British expeditionary force arrived in Chesapeake Bay, with the intention of taking Baltimore, the country's third-largest city and a booming port. On the way, the enemy made a detour to Washington. The American defense was routed; the federal government, including President Madison, evacuated, leaving the enemy a free hand. The British burned the White House and the Capitol; the retreating Americans had themselves torched the Navy Yard. When night fell, towering columns of flame and smoke lit the sky. A diplomat who witnessed the spectacle wrote, "I never saw a scene at once more terrible and more magnificent."[2] A hurricane on the following day completed the destruction.

It had been a humiliating defeat. But the enemy had suffered defeats of his own, in his efforts to take Baltimore, and at other points on the American periphery. However much the American people yearned for peace, and welcomed it when it came, they felt proud of having concluded their war with an honorable draw. America was a young nation; it would rebuild its federal public buildings where they had stood. It was to them that Trumbull now turned his attention.

He proposed to decorate the rotunda of the restored Capitol with his own history paintings. Now that Burke's long-ago prophecy was about to be fulfilled, with new buildings, Trumbull could surpass it by adding his works to them. The concept of the panorama would be revived, not to depict natural wonders, but to display the actions of men.

Trumbull had friends who could lobby Congress on his behalf from the inside: Rufus King, now a senator from New York; Timothy Pitkin, a congressman from Connecticut (Pitkin's grandfather had preceded Trumbull's father in the colonial-era governorship). For outside help Trumbull turned to two of his subjects from the revolutionary era.

In December 1816 he wrote to former presidents John Adams and Thomas Jefferson. Since the federal government's destroyed buildings were to be restored "to more than their original splendor," he wanted them to display "the paintings which have employed so many years of my life," and he asked his famous acquaintances to help make that happen.[3] The arguments he used with them were similar to those he had used when soliciting subscriptions for engravings at the dawn of the Washington administration: he alone had both the talent and the personal experience to memorialize the Revolution. One argument he deployed was new: time was running short for him. "I who was one of the youngest actors in the early scenes of the war have passed the age of sixty."[4]

John Adams, now eighty-one, had spent his post-presidential years in Quincy (formerly Braintree), his native town in Massachusetts, reading voraciously and deluging a host of correspondents with letters that were by turns pert, eloquent, and disputatious. He answered Trumbull with one such.

Adams began, none too courteously, with a vigorous denunciation of the arts. "You will please to remember that the burin and the pencil, the chisel and the trowel, have in all ages and countries of which we have information, been enlisted on the side of despotism and superstition. I should have said of superstition and despotism, for superstition is the first and universal cause of despotism." No Puritan could have been more contemptuous of the arts; William Branch Giles had said nothing more censorious about organized religion.

Adams pivoted, however, as he often did, to a tone that was personal and sympathetic (ideas often alarmed him, people frequently warmed him): "Your country ought to acknowledge itself more indebted to you than to any other artist who ever existed." America was indebted to Trumbull for his depictions of its founders, including John Adams.

Adams then pivoted again: "I must beg pardon of my country when I say that I see no disposition to celebrate, or remember, or even curiosity to inquire into the characters, actions or events of the Revolution." Here Adams, as he so often did, was projecting: the country, which had been run by his political rivals for sixteen years, had shown little disposition to celebrate him. His own banishment from the public mind must, he assumed, be shared by his entire generation.

He concluded by wishing Trumbull success "with all my heart."[5] With all his heart, if with none of his help.

Trumbull had more luck with his old friend turned enemy Thomas Jefferson. The Virginian, now seventy-three, had been living, since leaving the White House in 1809, at his aesthete's aerie, Monticello, endlessly building and rebuilding it, and corresponding with his own wide circle of friends, which included outgoing president James Madison, and incoming president James Monroe.

Trumbull's appeal came to the old Virginian like a voice from the past. The lapse of years "since our first intimacies," he answered, "has diminished in nothing my affection for you. We learn, as we grow old, to value early friendships, because the new-made do not fit us so closely." Jefferson recalled one friendship in particular. "I think I learned from some quarter that Mrs. Cosway was retired to a religious house somewhere." Maria, by now married in name only to her husband, had founded a convent school for girls at Lodi in northern Italy. "Thus you see how your letter calls up recollections of our charming coterie of Paris, now scattered and estranged but not so in either my memory or affections."

Jefferson turned from his memories to Trumbull's appeal for help. "You think you need a borrowed patronage at Washington. No, my dear sir, your own reputation, your talent known to all, is a patronage with all; to which any addition offered [by me] would be impertinent, if you did not ask it."[6]

But Trumbull had asked for Jefferson's patronage, and Jefferson gave it, writing on his behalf to president-elect Monroe—"He asks my notice of him to my friends, as if his talents had not already distinguished him to their notice."[7] (Trumbull's and Monroe's altercation over the text of the Jay Treaty seemed as forgotten as Jefferson's encouragement of Giles.)

More to the point, Jefferson wrote to Virginia senator James Barbour, since it was Congress that held the power to commission Trumbull or not.

> I have been very long and intimately acquainted with Col. Trumbull, have had the best opportunities of knowing him thoroughly, and can therefore bear witness of my own knowledge to his high degree of worth as a man. For his merit as a painter I can quote higher authorities, and assure you that on the continent of Europe, when I was there, he was considered as superior to West. . . .
>
> You know how averse I am to be quoted on any occasion. Yet as far as my testimony to Col. Trumbull's worth and talent can be of any avail, by using it in private circles, you are entirely free to do so, as a just tribute to truth and worth.[8]

Jefferson's just tribute was not free of self-interest, for he well knew that among Trumbull's most prominent subjects was a political painting, celebrating Jefferson's greatest literary and intellectual performance.

Still, after many years of silence, Jefferson made a generous gesture, in honor of old friendship and in the cause of patriotism.

Congress was favorable to Trumbull's proposal, commissioning four paintings to hang in the rebuilt Capitol. Trumbull called on President Madison, in the waning days of his administration, to settle the size and subjects of the pictures.

The Capitol building had been unfinished before the British had reduced it to a charred shell; hence Trumbull's language about rebuilding it in more than original splendor. Two wings had accommodated the House and the Senate (the Supreme Court had huddled in a basement room); a covered walkway connected them. There was now to rise between the restored wings a rotunda surmounted by a dome.

Trumbull had so far completed three of his revolutionary paintings—*Bunker's Hill, Quebec,* and the *Declaration*—with three more well advanced—*Trenton, Princeton,* and *Yorktown.* At their present size, two feet tall by three feet long, they would vanish in the vastness of a rotunda. Trumbull would have to surmount his inclinations and (possibly, given his monocular vision) his natural abilities and go big.

He suggested to Madison paintings that would measure six by nine feet, whose figures would be half life-size. Madison insisted they be four times as large; in such a space only life-size figures would register.

They turned next to the subjects. Madison suggested Bunker's Hill, but Trumbull demurred. Since he was to produce only four paintings, he wanted two military victories—the surrenders of the British at Saratoga and Yorktown. One had brought France into the war, the other had won it. They would also honor both of the commanders, Gates and Washington, whom Trumbull had served personally.

Madison then asked, "What for the civil subjects?"

Trumbull offered the Declaration. He had brought his small painting of the event to Washington, and displayed it in the temporary quarters of the House, for congressmen to examine as a preview of coming attractions.

"What would you have for the fourth?" asked Madison.

"I have thought," Trumbull answered, "one of the highest moral lessons ever given to the world, was that presented by the conduct of the commander-in-chief, in resigning his power and commission" to Congress at the end of 1783. Washington had not behaved like so many other generals: Cromwell before him, Napoleon after him. When his job was done, he had gone home.

Madison agreed. "It was a glorious action."[9]

So the sizes and the subjects were set. Congress would pay Trumbull $32,000: $8,000 up front, $6,000 for each painting upon delivery.

Why, after so many years of official indifference, had Congress acted with such speed and munificence?

There was a need. America's progress on its federal public buildings had been slow enough; the British added the stimulus of destruction. Once the buildings at Washington were to be (re)built, it seemed only right to decorate them.

One of the great drags on Trumbull's project had been removed. The partisanship of the early republic had for a moment dissipated. The War of 1812, like a thunderstorm, had cleared the mephitic air. Trumbull's own party, the Federalists, had all but disappeared, disgraced by their own passionate antiwar polemics. (In 1816 his friend Rufus King, their last candidate for president, had carried only three states in a vain campaign against James Monroe.) The Republicans, the victorious party of Jefferson, Madison, and Monroe, had meanwhile modified several of their most rigid orthodoxies under the pressure of events: the federal government, it turned out, needed to be at least somewhat stronger than they had imagined; with the final defeat of Napoleon at Waterloo, the French Revolution, and their support of it, were no longer issues. In the new era of good feelings (a phrase coined by a Boston newspaper), Americans could look back with shared patriotic pride.

What Trumbull contributed to his own success was focus, and urgency. He had spent two decades on diplomacy, business, and finally on painting portraits in London, New York, and London again, to little enduring result. It seemed at last as if what he should do was what he had first wanted to do—what he had once believed most needed doing. Now was the time—and time, past age sixty, did not stretch endlessly before him.

He set about preparing his materials. He considered a Philadelphia cloth-maker as a source for his linen canvases, but turned instead to a Londoner who had supplied both West and Copley.

He had much more ado in prepping the Rotunda itself. Benjamin Latrobe, an English-born architect, was in charge of finishing the Capitol after the War of 1812. He had somewhat sniffish opinions of America (he called Mount Vernon, George Washington's home, a "neat little country gentleman's house").[10] He wanted Trumbull's paintings set in elaborate niches, which Trumbull feared would overwhelm them. But Latrobe

quit his Washington job at the end of 1817. He was replaced by Charles
Bulfinch, a New England Yankee who had first met Trumbull in Paris in
the 1780s when making his grand tour of continental architecture. After
Bulfinch returned to America, he had designed, among other buildings,
the Connecticut State House in Hartford. He and Trumbull should
have made a better match. Yet one of the new architect's ideas for the
Rotunda—anchoring it with a grand staircase, and shunting the paintings to a side gallery—filled Trumbull with alarm.

"I feel the deepest regret at the idea of abandoning the great circu-
lar room and dome," Trumbull wrote. Galleries were bad spaces for
art, cramped and ill-lit. "The boasted gallery of the Louvre is execrable
for paintings—windows on each side ... and the pictures hanging
not only between them, but opposite to them. ... I should feel deeply
mortified if, after having devoted my life to recording the great events
of the Revolution, my paintings, when finished, should be placed in a
disadvantageous light." A spacious Rotunda, on the other hand, combining "vastness of dimensions" with "simplicity of form," would be "pecu-
liarly grand and imposing. ... Forgive the earnestness with which I
write," he concluded, "for I consider my future fame involved in this
question."[11]

Congress nixed the idea of a staircase and a gallery. The Rotunda
would be built without them, but also without Latrobe's niches. Trumbull got the space, both vast and simple, he wanted. The Rotunda would
be his wraparound easel. When finished, it would be able to accommodate the paintings he had been commissioned to do, with space for four
more. He would be creating half a historical panorama.[12]

It was well for him that he had a job of work to occupy him, for his
family offered little solace. His relationship with John Ray, never close,
broke beyond repair.

The young officer had given some offense, nature unknown, to
Sarah before the Trumbulls had left Britain in 1815 (one letter of Trumbull's mentions "your unkind conduct to her").[13]

Ray soon offended Trumbull in a manner that we know precisely,
since Trumbull deplored it at length in their correspondence. Ray, no
longer in active service in the British army, had gotten work in Calcutta
with the East India Company, which then ran Britain's possessions on

the subcontinent. But in the summer of 1817 he wrote to the Trumbulls to say that he had quit that job, returned to Britain, and married.

Trumbull answered with a mixture of sarcasm, scorn, and self-pity. "We are not much surprised that you have taken the most important step in human life without asking our opinion, for it is not the first instance of your independence."

Ray, newly married, had asked Trumbull for financial help, but Trumbull was having none of it. "What has induced you ... to throw yourself upon the world, with increased expenses? ... It is true that I am employed to paint pictures, but I shall not be paid for them until they are finished. I cannot therefore assist you, *even if I thought it to be my duty.*"

Meanwhile, Ray should respect his elders. "You"—meaning the newlyweds—"are both young, and better able to struggle with the world, than I who am old."[14]

A year later Trumbull wrote again, angrier yet, for the Rays had had a daughter and Trumbull had done the math. Ray had returned to Britain from India in March 1817; he had married in May; the child was born in November. "Now," Trumbull wrote, "as it is only *eight* months from the day of your arrival, and only six from your marriage to the birth of your child, while the ordinary period of pregnancy is *nine,* the inference is obvious and unfavorable."

Trumbull showed no inkling that his own conduct was not a platform from which to deliver moral lectures. Indeed, in this letter Trumbull for the first time acknowledged the circumstances of his son's birth—"your mother was Temperance Ray of East Haddam, a servant in my brother's house"—while still maintaining the possibility that he had nothing to do with it—"the looseness of her conduct left it uncertain who might be your father, but she swore ... that I was."

Trumbull railed on. He had spent over £500 training Ray to be a farmer, the career the young man never wanted. "You have despised my advice, and you now feel the consequences, yet you still seem to think it proper that a man of sixty three should labor to support ... a youth of twenty six."

He ended this sulfurous epistle by signing it, "a Real Friend."[15]

There is no excuse for Trumbull's tone, though there are two possible explanations for it, apart from his own temperament. The first is that his son was in fact a ne'er-do-well, habitually at loose ends, cadging money from him or from his banker, Samuel Williams. Ray's assumption that Trumbull, like the Lord, would provide, was especially galling given Trumbull's own debt to Williams, hanging over him like a comber. Was the old artist as feckless as his scapegrace offspring?

The second explanation is that Trumbull had troubles closer to home, afflicting someone he loved dearly.

It is impossible to say when Sarah Trumbull became an alcoholic. No letters of hers survive; Trumbull wrote sparingly about her (except when blaming family members for offending her). Had drinking played any role in her tiff with Trumbull's niece in upstate New York? Did she turn to the bottle, or turn to it more heavily, after returning to the United States, the country where in-laws scolded her and politicians insulted her?

Accounts of her being intoxicated in public appear in the letters of American friends and acquaintances, none more detailed or more pained than in an 1817 letter from Rufus King to Christopher Gore, the two men who had been guests at the Trumbulls' wedding in London eighteen years earlier.[16] King at that time was in Washington, serving as a senator from New York; Gore had recently gone home to Massachusetts after resigning a Senate seat, on account of ill health. In February the French ambassador, Jean-Guillaume, Baron Hyde de Neuville, threw a party. The capital was in a festive mood: James Madison was leaving the White House in a blaze of glory, his old friend James Monroe was president-elect. Hyde de Neuville had occupied two houses on F Street and joined them at the first floor, creating a double venue. Three hundred people came to his party; most of Congress, the diplomatic corps, and Dolley Madison, First Lady still, and first socialite always.

King painted the scene for his absent friend. "Supper tables, covered with a profusion of good things, were placed in all the rooms; of course everything was cold but very well arranged. After standing and walking from room to room till I was tired, I saw a vacant chair in a corner, where I placed myself" next to the Portuguese ambassador. "We were engaged in conversation when of a sudden I observed Colonel and Mrs. T coming towards me."

Sarah Trumbull was already in the effusive stage of intoxication. She "quitted her husband's arm, and sallying towards me, almost tumbled into an empty chair on my right. She immediately began in expressions of joy on having found me; told me how much she esteemed me, hoped I was her friend and her husband's friend; and under pretense of a low conversation put her mouth to my ear.... All who passed halted to observe our tête-à-tête."

King, embarrassed, escaped. Sarah then fastened on Harrison Gray Otis, senator-elect from Massachusetts. King reported, "She made out to rise and take hold of him, beginning, as with me, to declare her esteem for him." She asked after Christopher Gore. "'Is he any better? ... he is one of my best friends, he is my father, he gave me to my husband [referring to their wedding], Oh, how much I love him; he is my husband's friend, and I love him even more for that, than for anything else.'"

Otis in turn escaped. Sarah ventured further into the room, where she encountered Elizabeth Fromentin, wife of Senator Eligius Fromentin of Louisiana, and her mood suddenly changed. According to King, "They stood face to face, and Mrs. F, looking at Mrs. T, the latter exclaimed, pretty audibly, 'What do you see, what do you look at me for; what are you staring at?'" Mrs. Fromentin turned aside to Treasury Secretary William Crawford, who asked her who the belligerent woman was. "Instead of answering, Mrs. F replied, 'There is her husband,' pointing to Col. T. Like a tigress [Sarah] immediately turned on Crawford ... 'What business have you with my husband, what are you looking at him for? What is it to you that he is my husband?'" Crawford and the senator's wife turned their backs on her and walked away.

Scene from a marriage to a drunkard: the sufferer, making a spectacle, too loud, too friendly, finally too angry; the sober mate, missing in action, endeavoring not to see or hear what had been done and said so many times before.

The sequel on the following day, as King recounted it to Gore, was equally typical of such stricken situations. King had not seen the Trumbulls at supper, and concluded that the colonel, acknowledging his wife's condition at last, had taken her home. But when King ran into him the next morning, he behaved as if nothing had happened. Trumbull "looked as usual without any expression of mortification on his countenance. I had thought I would muster up fortitude to tell him freely how much his own character suffered by this scandalous conduct of his wife." Not character in the modern sense of one's inherent nature, but in the older sense of one's image in the world. But King could not speak. Trumbull's "amiable countenance and polite manners, joined to the uncertainty of how such a communication would be received, discouraged me; and we parted as usual, except that I could not bring myself to make the usual enquiry concerning his wife."

Sarah was not a mean drunk, at least not until she felt reproved. She genuinely liked King and Gore, and must have wondered why the world did not share her enthusiasm. But drunk she was, and although the early republic was an era of hard drinking, genteel women were not supposed to indulge.

Sarah's behavior did not damage her husband's character sufficiently to imperil his commission. His public indifference to it may have shielded him from any taint, besides being an all-too-human strategy for coping with a loved one's distress.

Sarah would not be so lucky. King ended his letter to Gore by saying that her performance at the French ambassador's "will be certain to exclude her from all further civilities here."[17]

Trumbull turned from his woes to his task, painting his life-size canvases in New York. The first he produced was of the earliest scene to be depicted, *The Declaration of Independence.* He finished it by September 1818, and then exhibited it in East Coast cities, as a trailer for the entire project, and as a way of raising extra money for himself (admission was twenty-five cents). The tour was a success. In one month, over six thousand people saw it in New York City. In Boston equal numbers came to see it at Faneuil Hall. Gilbert Stuart took the opportunity of Trumbull's triumphal visit to paint his old friend; the slightly spiky gray hair Stuart gave him strikes us, two centuries later, as almost punk. Eighty-three-year-old John Adams, who had been so discouraging to Trumbull's proposal, felt transported back in time upon seeing the life-size *Declaration.* "There!" he exclaimed, pointing to a painted door, "that is the door out of which Washington rushed when I first alluded to him as the man best qualified for Commander in Chief."[18] This double episode of elevation and modesty had occurred, more than a year before the writing of the Declaration, just as Adams recalled it—combining, on Adams's part, political shrewdness (*We need a Virginian to lead a war in*

New England); on Washington's part, virtuous reluctance (*I am not seeking this job*) and real anxiety (*If they tap me, I will really have to do it*). Yet the door Adams pointed to in Trumbull's painting could not have been the one Washington used, since Jefferson's sketch of the room, on which Trumbull had relied, had been faulty. (Jefferson remembered two doors; in fact there was only one.) As is so often the case with memory, emotion supplied the place of detail. In Philadelphia, Trumbull showed the *Declaration* in the old State House, in the very room in which the actual Declaration had been received and signed. In ten days it drew five thousand people. Trumbull gave his painting a last show in Baltimore, to a gate of three thousand, before delivering it to Washington.

Yorktown was next to be done, finished in June 1820. Trumbull showed it in New York, Boston, and Baltimore, to fewer viewers—less than seven thousand altogether—than had seen the *Declaration*. The nation's birth was a bigger draw than the war's end.

Saratoga required Trumbull to make an entirely new composition. He had sketched the upstate New York setting of Burgoyne's surrender as long ago as 1791. A distant mountain peak he had drawn then reappeared, mysteriously doubled, in the background of his finished canvas. He relied on his collection of miniatures for the faces of the American officers who were present; his comrade from Fort Ticonderoga, Ebenezer Stevens, stands at the far right. Chastened by the modest success of *Yorktown*, he showed *Saratoga* in New York only.

After delivering that painting to Washington in the spring of 1822, Trumbull went to Annapolis, Maryland, to sketch the setting for *The Resignation of General Washington*, another entirely new work. General Washington had returned his commission to Congress in December 1783 in the building that has served, from 1779 until now, as the Maryland State House; in the last days of 1783 Congress also met there. Among the congressmen witnessing Washington's act, Trumbull placed James Madison, who had been at his Virginia home at the time. "I have taken the liberty," he wrote to the former president, "of placing you among the spectators," so that all Virginia's presidents could be present and accounted for (Jefferson and Monroe had also been congressmen then, and appear in the scene). "It is a painter's license," he admitted.[19] Washington had appeared throughout the series (*Trenton, Princeton, Yorktown*); Jefferson (the *Declaration*) and Monroe (*Trenton*) were also repeaters. Adams, the Massachusetts president, had stood alongside Jefferson in the *Declaration*. Trumbull's paintings represented a visual peace treaty among them all, concluding the political warfare of the first two-party system.

Another way Trumbull chose to publicize (and monetize) his project was to commission an engraving of the *Declaration,* and sell subscriptions for the print. He had tried this with his entire series decades earlier, only to encounter long delays and reap meager results. This time, he had the luck to find a good engraver near at hand. Asher Durand, a young man who hailed from Jefferson Village, New Jersey, came relatively cheap (Trumbull engaged him for $3,000, as opposed to the $7,000 he would have paid an established European). Durand was talented, hardworking, and grateful for the opportunity.

Finding buyers proved to be harder. Trumbull set the price of a print at twenty dollars, half up front, half due on delivery, which was expensive: engraved portraits of famous individuals might go for eight dollars. He got all four living presidents—Adams, Jefferson, Madison, and Monroe—to subscribe, and had a prospectus bearing their endorsements laid on the desk of every member of Congress. No one signed up. Trumbull was mortified. "I confess I do not yet understand my countrymen," he complained to one senator.[20] "We cannot be insensible to our own honor," he complained to a congressman. Benjamin West had sold almost two thousand subscriptions for an engraving of the death of Nelson at Trafalgar. But "what was the death of Nelson [to] the happiness of man, compared with the event which I propose to commemorate?"[21] After years of pushing, Trumbull managed to enlist seven senators, twenty-four representatives, three cabinet secretaries, and over two hundred ordinary citizens, enough to do a little better than break even. He sent a copy, gratis, to Lafayette. "I trust," he wrote, "it will call to your recollection many of those good and eminent men whom you knew in the early days of your acquaintance with this country."[22]

There had been some carping in Congress at Trumbull's traveling exhibitions of his work. "By what authority," one representative demanded, had he been "perambulating the country," hawking views at twenty-five cents per customer?[23] Congress had agreed to pay him for the paintings; charging people to look at them before delivery seemed like double-dipping. Trumbull's allies in Congress responded that he had requested, and received, President Monroe's permission ahead of time.

The attacks of public men nettled Trumbull's pride. Real blows fell at home. Sarah had accompanied him on his trip to Washington to deliver *Saratoga,* and on the return journey through Annapolis. But he had made his other trips solo, leaving her alone and lonely. She was also ailing. In the summer of 1823, Harriet Silliman, one of his brother Jonathan, Jr.'s daughters, wrote after a visit that she looked "very bad."[24] On April 12, 1824, she died.

We do not know what, at age fifty, she died of. Trumbull, who had painted her so often in life, painted her once more on her deathbed. In a dark composition, Sarah tilted her head and lifted her arms toward an unidentified source of light beyond the upper-right corner of the canvas. If this expressed her, and Trumbull's, hope for the next world, other details—her wasted hands, the dead weight of shoulders and torso on the bedding—expressed death's finality in this. Trumbull gave her cheeks that still recalled her physical beauty.

The clergyman who gave her last rites was Episcopalian, rector of Grace Church. Her pallbearers were a collection of New York and Connecticut worthies, including one of Trumbull's nephews, and the British consul. On a slip of paper tucked into the frame of one of his portraits of her, Trumbull left a mournful phrase in Latin: "O how much sweeter, most beloved wife, to remember your excellence than to mingle with others."[25] The language he had learned so early as a boy must have seemed more intimate, more personal. The translation is approximate, for by 1824 his Latin was very rusty. He had left many other tributes in the medium that most counted.

Trumbull found distraction in touring the *Resignation* through half a dozen cities. The Rotunda was not ready to receive it and its fellows until November 1826.

The president of the United States then was John Adams's son, John Quincy. The younger Adams had first seen the life-size *Declaration* in the fall of 1818, when he was secretary of state, in Trumbull's New York studio, getting finishing touches. Unlike his father, who would see it a few months later, he had not been impressed. "I think the old small picture far superior to this large new one."[26] But when he saw it and its companions hung in the Rotunda, he changed his mind. "[They] are placed in such a favorable light, that they appear far better than they ever had before."[27] The huge venue suited Trumbull's diminished skills; the qualities he still commanded—design and narrative—were what most counted.

Trumbull had been commissioned to do his paintings in the postwar unity of the era of good feelings. Other feelings had succeeded, for politics never rests even if parties have, temporarily, lost their meaning. Four men, all nominally Republicans, had sought to follow James Monroe in the White House in the election of 1824. William Crawford, who had turned his back on Sarah Trumbull at the French ambassador's party, had been the frontrunner, until he was disabled by a stroke. Andrew Jackson, who had won the last battle of the War of 1812 at New Orleans, had finished first in the Electoral College. But since no candidate had won a majority there, the choice was thrown to the House, which picked John Quincy Adams. This victory only set Adams up for an acrid rematch with a bitter Jackson.

These political crosscurrents touched Trumbull, who longed to complete the decoration of the Rotunda, which he had done so much to design and promote. "There are four other spaces to be filled with pictures of the same size," noted President Adams in his diary, "for which the colonel is very desirous of being employed."[28] As a visual hint, he displayed the small *Bunker's Hill* and *Quebec* and sketches of *Trenton* and *Princeton* beneath the hoped-for destinations of their larger versions.

But Jackson's partisans in Congress suggested a heroic picture of their man's victory at New Orleans. Adams's supporters pushed back by offering a variety of alternatives, including other subjects besides Trumbull's. Years later the niches would be filled by depictions of Columbus, de Soto, Pocahontas, and the Pilgrims, each by a different artist. The story of the Revolution was interrupted for a series of flash cards of colonial history. Trumbull's grand expression of his great project would be cut short in the home stretch.

He continued to pursue his vision by other means.

ELEVEN

The memorialist of current events is particularly vulnerable to the passage of time. What begins as news becomes yesterday's news. What fades from view fades from recollection, unless captured. Death had begun to winnow Trumbull's subjects even as he began his great project, forcing him to rely on descriptions or family resemblance for some of his portraits. Now death was sweeping the entire revolutionary generation from the stage.

Trumbull turned seventy in June 1826. On July 4 Thomas Jefferson, eighty-three, and John Adams, ninety, died, on the fiftieth anniversary of their declaration. Jefferson's last reported words were, "Is it the fourth?" Adams's were, "Thomas Jefferson still survives."

Younger patriots followed them. Christopher Gore died in March 1827, aged sixty-eight; Rufus King, seventy-two, died in April. The last living witness to Trumbull's wedding was Trumbull himself.

The artists of the revolutionary era were dying along with their subjects. The émigrés, Copley and West, had died in Britain in 1815 and 1820, respectively. In America the elder Peale followed in 1827. Stuart— "eccentric," "dirty," and "entertaining" to the end, as one friend testified— died in 1828.[1] How long might Trumbull be spared?

John Ray, now in his thirties, passed from Trumbull's life, even as a correspondent. In mid-decade he had written a few penitent letters from London, informing Trumbull that he was once again working for the East India Company, and expressing regret for their quarrels, which he hoped his father would attribute to "the folly and heat of youth."[2]

Trumbull congratulated him on his employment, asked after his family, then described his own financial situation. His debt to his banker, Samuel Williams, "has eaten me up. . . . Take a warning, and avoid debt, if you subsist on bread and cheese. . . . Although it is no longer in my power to render you any assistance, I shall always be glad to hear of your success."[3]

There was little success for Ray to report. In March 1829 he wrote to his father one more time. His wife was in "very bad health," and their children appeared, by the manner in which he wrote of them, to have died (they are "better provided for in another world").[4] This is the last letter between father and son of which there is any record.

In this season of death and diminution, Trumbull's life was brightened by a new opportunity. A path to the completion of his great project, four specimens of which were enshrined yet stalled in the Capitol Rotunda, opened unexpectedly before him.

The pathfinder was an admiring in-law, Benjamin Silliman.

Silliman, born in southwestern Connecticut in 1779, was too young to remember the Revolution, though it had had a dramatic effect on him. He was delivered in a tavern where his mother had fled to escape a British raid.

He went to Yale College in New Haven, which named him professor of chemistry in 1802, when he was twenty-three years old. Yale, much younger than Harvard, had only just turned one hundred, and wished to broaden its offerings, hence Silliman's appointment. But since he had never studied chemistry, he went first to Philadelphia, then to Edinburgh to learn it. He was a quick study and had a curious mind. When a meteorite exploded over Connecticut in 1807, he found a fragment and analyzed its composition.

In 1808 he gave a series of lectures on chemistry for interested New Havenites, male and female. (Silliman was noteworthy for encouraging young women to attend his regular classes—far in advance of his college, which would not go coed for a century and a half.) One of the auditors of his popular lecture series, who was then staying with friends in town, was Harriet Trumbull, daughter of Jonathan, Jr., the governor. "It was my province in the proposed course," Silliman recalled years later, "to explain the affinities of matter, and I had not advanced far in my pleasing duties before I discovered that moral affinities . . . were playing an important part."[5]

A portrait of Harriet, not by her uncle Trumbull but by a lesser Lebanon artist, Elkanah Tisdale, shows a serious young woman, perhaps shy. When she spent a season as a teenager living with a family friend in New York City, she had seen the sights—the Invisible Woman, an empty box that supposedly answered questions; the Learned Pig, an animal that did the same—and fretted over her inability to experience more.[6] Chemistry, and the professor of chemistry, were more fulfilling.

Silliman had first met Harriet's uncle at Yale, early in his career there. Trumbull had visited the campus, accompanying his brother, the governor. The pair "were elegant, graceful gentlemen of winning manners," Silliman wrote, recalling the occasion years later, "and their familiarity with each other, manifested in little sallies of wit, was pleasing to me, who regarded them only as grave dignified men." After spotting a portrait of their parents—copied from one of John's paintings—hanging on a nearby college wall, John noted their father's imposing, last-century wig. That, he said, was a true governor's hairpiece, "not like this little queue of yours," clasping Jonathan, Jr.'s pigtail and giving it a playful shake—"much to the governor's amusement," Silliman added, "and to my surprise."

A few years later, when Silliman was preparing to study abroad, Trumbull supplied him with introductions and tips on life in London, "embodying," as Silliman wrote, "the results of his own long experience of twenty years." Silliman's marriage to Harriet Trumbull in 1809 added a layer of intimacy to the acquaintance.[7]

In 1825 Trumbull painted Silliman's portrait (figure 8). The professor had come to New York City to raise money to buy a collection of minerals for Yale. His morning regimen was to have breakfast with the artist, then sit for an hour and a half. The painting that resulted is a creamy, rather bland image; Trumbull seemed more interested in his subject's shirt ruff than in his face. Silliman loyally called it "an elegant work of art," though he admitted that it was "never regarded as a striking likeness."[8]

Trumbull all his life had been a loner. He had worked alongside fellow students—Gilbert Stuart, William Dunlap—when he was studying with Benjamin West. He had made two long-term friends in Boston—

Figure 8. John Trumbull, *Benjamin Silliman*, 1825.
Trumbull painted this portrait of his nephew-by-marriage.
The bland image does not do justice to the younger man's
devotion to his in-law.

King and Gore—and a friend, made in Paris, then lost—Jefferson. He
had his family, though in the years after pulling his brother's queue, their
behavior toward Sarah had alienated him from them. And he had had his
wife. In Silliman he acquired something new, a friend who was also an
acolyte: an intelligent, younger man, impressed with his history and his
accomplishments. No painter, Silliman could never work with him, but
was also unable ever to rival him. Trumbull's actual son, apart from a
brief period of military glory, had been an embarrassment. Silliman, his
nephew by marriage, would be his improved, surrogate son.

In the summer of 1830, Silliman, passing through New York City once again, called on the old man. Trumbull was then living in rented rooms on Broadway and Walker Street. The location was north of the center of town, but his rooms were large, offering a good space for displaying his paintings. Although Silliman "had seen many of them singly before, [he] had never seen them all together." Some had just been finished, or were on the way to it. Trumbull was finally completing the Revolutionary War paintings he had begun in the 1780s but left undone—*Trenton, Princeton, Yorktown*. He was also creating three-by-two-foot versions of the scenes he had depicted, life-size, for the Rotunda—*Saratoga*, Washington's *Resignation*. In his New York rooms his design was coming to fruition. Silliman was "strongly impressed and delighted by this unexpected vision."

Trumbull himself was not delighted. He unfolded for Silliman an account of his financial woes. They had been gathering for a long time. Congress had paid him handsomely for his paintings in the Rotunda. But it was not a clear profit. He had had to supply, from his commission, the price of his materials, and pay Asher Durand, his engraver, up front. In 1823, before his last painting was delivered, his longtime banker in London, Samuel Williams, had gone bankrupt, and called in his outstanding loans. Trumbull had two resources to liquidate: the European paintings he had bought years before, some of them now in New York, others left behind in London, and upstate land. He tried selling the paintings, but fewer were bought than he had hoped. He signed over his land, twelve hundred acres, to Williams; if he could have held it until after the completion of the Erie Canal in 1825, it would have been worth more. Meanwhile, he had continued living in the style of a gentleman. As a result, "he was," as Silliman wrote, "without a sure foundation upon which he might repose in the evening [of] life."[9]

At their interview in Trumbull's rooms, the artist "lamented his poverty in energetic and eloquent language.... It was a painful moment."

Silliman looked at the paintings that surrounded them—Trumbull's own—evidently his last assets.

"And what, Sir, do you intend to do with them?" he asked.

Trumbull had prepared an answer. "I will give them to Yale College to be exhibited forever for the benefit of poor students, if they will pay me a competent annuity for the remainder of my life."

Silliman, who had been feasting his eyes, at first did not believe his ears. "Are you in earnest?" he asked.

When Trumbull assured him he was, Silliman asked if he could propose the deal to Yale. When Trumbull again said yes, Silliman said he would go at once to New Haven.[10]

Silliman's motives for volunteering to act as go-between were obvious: he could help the man he admired, and now also pitied, while simultaneously benefiting his alma mater and employer.

Trumbull's motives for making the offer were layered. He needed the money, obviously. But why not offer his works to Harvard, where he, all but one of his brothers, and his father had gone? And why, if not to Harvard, to Yale?

Years later, he explained that he had first considered Harvard, but picked Yale instead because Harvard was rich, and Yale poor.[11] What Trumbull meant by this was that Harvard was already rich in art. She owned Copleys, which Trumbull had seen as a student. She might therefore esteem Trumbull's offerings less. Yale, less favored, would value them more highly.

Yale was the college of Connecticut, Harvard the college of Massachusetts. Thanks to old partisan affiliations—Federalism having been the creed of all New England—Trumbull knew, or could scrape acquaintance with, anyone who mattered in Massachusetts. But Trumbull was simply better connected in his home state. He had already performed one service for Yale, back in the Washington administration. At the behest of James Hillhouse, a Connecticut congressman who was also treasurer of the school, Trumbull had suggested an arrangement for the buildings on its campus—two parallel brick rows—that Yale more or less followed for a hundred years. Trumbull's care had extended even to its latrines, which he called "Temples of Cloacina . . . I would wish to have [them] concealed as much as possible, by planting of a variety of shrubs."[12]

But his main reason for now offering to dispose of his lifework to a friendly private institution was that he could, for the first time, control the entire project. He had had great luck, lobbying Congress and working with Charles Bulfinch, the Capitol's architect. But luck had run out when it came to filling the Rotunda's four remaining niches. At Yale he could design a space from scratch; his paintings to be displayed there were already painted; and no other artist would contend for placement.

Silliman laid Trumbull's proposal before Yale's administration and senior faculty. They showed, he wrote years later, a "lively interest ... to obtain the prize that was thus, unexpectedly, offered." Four of them—Jeremiah Day, president, Chauncey Goodrich, professor of rhetoric and oratory, Stephen Twining, treasurer, and Silliman himself—plus Daniel Wadsworth, a Trumbull family in-law, collectively pledged $1,000 a year for Trumbull's annuity. They expected to be reimbursed by admission fees—twenty-five cents a head to visit the gallery; they also expected Trumbull to live for six more years (he turned seventy-five in 1831).

Silliman turned next to funding the gallery itself. In the spring and summer of 1831 he was in Hartford, lobbying the legislature. He did not expect to be able to wring a new appropriation from it. But the state was due to collect a dividend from the chartering of a Bridgeport bank. Silliman set his sights on that money and formed an alliance with a lobbyist for the Episcopal Church, which was seeking a subvention of its own. Together they "pulled indeed on different ropes attached to the same machine, but pulled in the same direction, so effectually, that ... we succeeded in moving the carriage of state."[13] Yale's share of their joint efforts was $7,000. "And out of this," Silliman wrote to Trumbull, "I shall make it my business to obtain from our corporation enough to erect the building."[14]

Daniel Wadsworth, one of the guarantors of Trumbull's annuity, added a wrinkle to the plan. He had many connections, both direct and oblique, to Trumbull over the years. He was the young son, standing next to his father, Jeremiah, in the long-ago painting that Joshua Reynolds had disliked so. A more romantic image of him as an adult, with tousled hair and loose collar, was painted by Thomas Sully, the young artist who had learned technique from Trumbull. Wadsworth had married Trumbull's niece Faith. Independently wealthy, he was both a patron of the arts and an amateur artist who had accompanied Trumbull on sketching expeditions to upstate New York, including Niagara Falls. He now suggested that there be a second gallery in Hartford, a few miles from his own estate on Talcott Mountain, and that Trumbull's paintings of the Revolution might rotate between there and New Haven.

Trumbull would not agree. The prospect of packing and unpack-ing his precious images dismayed him. Suppose they were harmed? In the Rotunda some vandal had already cut the right foot of General Dan-iel Morgan in *The Surrender of General Burgoyne at Saratoga*.[15] Trum-bull had repaired that damage, but feet were one thing, faces another. "I myself could not now repair the small heads in the *Declaration* and *Yor-ktown*," he wrote to Silliman in November 1831, "and *no one else ever can*." Here was a new note. Hitherto Trumbull had said, in maintaining his fitness as the Revolution's chronicler, that no one else could match his combination of personal witness and painterly skill. Now, at age seventy-five, he was saying that he himself could not. His abilities at small-scale portraiture had left him. He had done what he could do, and once his work was lost, it would be lost forever. "I regard these things as inestimable—and not to be exposed to unnecessary hazard."[16]

In this period of indecision, Trumbull briefly reconsidered his be-quest. He wrote to Josiah Quincy, an old Federalist hard-liner and for-mer congressman from Massachusetts, who was now president of Harvard, offering to insert a clause in his will directing that his paintings be transferred to her if Yale ever meddled with the terms of his gift. This letter is the foundation of a long-standing collegiate legend that such a clause actually exists.[17]

It never came to that. Wadsworth, wrote Silliman, "had the magna-nimity to acquiesce."[18] Wadsworth knew Trumbull: his pride, and, what accompanied it like a shadow, his anxiety. The Hartford scheme was abandoned; the fruits of Trumbull's great project would have one home only.

Trumbull developed the plans for the building with the help of a pair of New Haven architects, Ithiel Town and Alexander Jackson Davis. It was a time of eclecticism in building. Gothic, almost a swear word to a certain type of Enlightenment mind, was coming back into fashion. But so were Doric columns, simplest of the classical orders.[19] Town and Davis sketched a mini-Parthenon, a two-story-tall rectangular building with four freestanding columns at the entrance and pilasters along the sides. Trumbull flattened the roof, sunk the columns into the walls, and moved the entrance ninety degrees to one of the long sides, with two new, tiny columns flanking the door. There were to be two galleries, lit by skylights, on the top floor, one for Trumbull's paintings, one for those of everybody else whose works might be hung there. The walls of the Trumbull room were covered with red upholstery, the floors with green carpets. At thirty-four by sixty feet, the gallery was a trim, solid little building.

Trumbull brought his paintings from New York City to their new home in October 1832. The steamboat line that conveyed him and them let the revolutionary relics travel for free.

The agreement he had signed with Yale specified that his paintings should be "placed and arranged . . . under the directions and superintendence of the said John Trumbull."[20] He had, Silliman wrote, positioned them all in his mind before they were hung.[21] After the job was done, he stood with Silliman looking at his handiwork and said, "These are my children."[22]

TWELVE

The room at the top of the Trumbull Gallery devoted to his own work contained history paintings, including his earliest, *Paulus Aemilius at the Battle of Cannae*; religious paintings, among them *The Woman Taken in Adultery*, the one Sarah posed for; and a painting inspired by Ossian.

His masterwork, the eight revolutionary paintings and the life-size standing portrait of George Washington, occupied one wall. Now, forty-five years after the project was begun, it is time to look at them, one by one, and all together

The Death of General Warren at the Battle of Bunker's Hill

This is a painting of a wave, breaking (plate 3). The wave is the enemy; it is breaking on the defenders, and on us, the viewers.

The Battle of Bunker's Hill (more accurately, Breed's Hill) is the only action, of all those Trumbull depicted in his series, that he witnessed. He witnessed it, however, from the heights of Roxbury, four miles away, across a loop of Boston Harbor and the city of Boston itself. To make a painting of it, he brings himself closer.

How close? His imaginary viewpoint is some yards from the action he is showing, maybe ten from the closest figures. A shadow on the foreground, cast probably by the smoke we see billowing elsewhere in the sky, acts as a frame.

The earliest proto-photographs were being developed in France in the decade that the Trumbull Gallery opened. Yet it would be years before exposure times became quick enough to allow photographers to freeze moving subjects, and years more before their equipment became mobile enough to be taken to active battlefields. Trumbull, however, is not giving us a snapshot, the kind of image that cameras would later produce. He is presenting an overview, a wide shot both in space and time. He is describing and explaining, relating a barrage of actions that, even though they occur almost simultaneously, could not all be registered, and certainly not all comprehended, by an observer in the moment.

And yet Trumbull's image, in order to compel our attention, has to convey a feeling of immediacy. You are there—and there, and there, and there. You are at Bunker's Hill, or this portion of it, all at once.

The context of the battle has been described in Chapter Two. Trumbull's own reconstruction of it, in the catalogue of his paintings for the gallery, gives a false impression, describing the American troops as a valiant ragtag, brave but undisciplined.[1] In fact the American ranks were sown with veterans of the French and Indian War; it was the British soldiers available in Boston for the clash who were green. They were, besides that, compelled to advance up a slope, on a hot day in heavy gear, without effective artillery support, toward defenders in entrenchments, however hastily dug. The American fire broke two British charges. Trumbull chooses the moment, and the spot, where the British overwhelm the American position at the crest of the hill on the third try.

The scene is compact, but crowded. At least twenty individuals, defenders and attackers, officers and men, living and dead, are clearly seen, most of them identifiable. On the far left stands a blue-coated American commander, General Israel Putnam. Brave and rough-edged, he was the model of a common soldier's favorite officer. In peacetime, he had descended into the den of the last wolf in Connecticut to kill it. In the French and Indian War he had survived capture by French-allied Mohawks. At the onset of this battle he told his men to aim for the officers, targeting their waistbands. Now he raises a sword as a signal of retreat.

The British commander, Major General Sir William Howe, is left of center, leading the last successful assault. He is holding his sword in his right hand, pointing onward with his left; his black tricorn rests atop his head. Although Howe was a distant cousin, via a princely mistress, of

George III, before the war his family had been notably pro-American. The colony of Massachusetts had erected a monument in Westminster Abbey in honor of his eldest brother, George, killed on the American frontier in the French and Indian War. William himself was a member of Parliament representing Nottingham, a pro-American constituency (one of a small but vocal minority). He accepted assignment to America nevertheless, in order to preserve the empire, by negotiation if possible, by force if necessary. His ultimate lack of success would harden him; when Trumbull was painting *Bunker's Hill* in London, Howe refused to sit for him. Benjamin West did Trumbull the favor of supplying Howe's face; as a result, the skin tone, reflecting West's palette, is noticeably darker than that of the other white combatants.

But this is no calm picture gallery, no orderly dramatis personae. A few steps behind Howe, Major John Pitcairn, of the Royal Marines, is falling dead into the arms of Lieutenant William Pitcairn, his son. Closer to us, Lieutenant Colonel James Abercrombie lies dead on his back; a fellow British officer strides over his corpse. On the left, beneath Putnam, a lieutenant colonel in a Massachusetts regiment, Moses Parker, sits slumped on the ground, wounded. He will be captured by the British and die a prisoner of war. A New Hampshire officer, Major Andrew McClary, will be killed soon, but now he stands in a knot of his comrades in the middle left, swinging his musket over his shoulder by the barrel. He is wielding it as a club rather than a firearm because he, like most of his comrades, has run out of ammunition. Up the hill to the right come anonymous British regulars, able finally to wreak vengeance on the rebels who have been slaughtering their comrades. Behind them in the distance are glimpses of water; of peninsular Boston, seemingly no bigger than a beached whaleboat; and, in the sky, masses and tongues of smoke and flame, rising from Charlestown, out of sight on the right, set ablaze by red hot British cannonballs.

The title of the painting, *The Death of General Warren at the Battle of Bunker's Hill,* directs our attention to a dying man in the foreground, left of center. This is Joseph Warren. A Harvard-educated physician, Warren had been active for years in Boston's radical politics, a partner of John Hancock and Samuel Adams. Warren had performed the autopsy on radicalism's first martyr, a young patriot rioter shot and killed by a

Loyalist in 1770, a month before the Boston Massacre. On anniversaries of the massacre itself, Warren delivered commemorative orations. In April 1775 he dispatched Paul Revere from Boston to warn patriots in the countryside that the British planned a sweep of the area. After the battles of Lexington and Concord he organized the rolling firefight that dogged the British on their retreat; during the action a bullet clipped a lock of his hair. On the eve of the Battle of Bunker's Hill he was awarded the rank of major general, though he yielded command to American veterans and chose to serve in the ranks instead. There, at the climax of the last charge, a bullet found his head and killed him instantly. In Trumbull's painting he lies with his head falling to the left, his knees drawn slightly up, death recapitulating the fetal posture. His light-blue clothing shines, as do the light-blue and white outfits of two Americans standing behind and over him, trying to protect his body.

They are protecting it from a British grenadier, poised to spit Warren with a bayonet. But the barrel of the grenadier's musket is being grasped by a British officer, who is stepping over Abercrombie's body to do it. This is Major John Small, a Scotsman who commanded a battalion of Highlanders. Trumbull met Small in London and painted his likeness into the canvas there. Small's gesture of grabbing the musket is meant to arrest the jab, and prevent Warren's body from being desecrated.

This never actually happened. Trumbull told Silliman that the scene was "a pictorial liberty," created by him to honor Small, who "was distinguished for his humanity and kindness to American prisoners and therefore [shown] by the artist to do a deed of mercy."[2]

Magnanimity to foes was a quality that mattered to Trumbull and to the officer class generally. However hard they tried to kill each other, they obeyed gentlemanly rules in doing so. (Enemies in the ranks were treated with less consideration.) The British officers in Trumbull's *Sortie Made by the Garrison of Gibraltar* show concern for the dying Spaniard, and Trumbull painted another such moment later in his revolutionary series. Abigail Adams, seeing *Bunker's Hill* in London when her husband was minister to England, shared Trumbull's concern that such deeds be represented and remembered: "He teaches mankind," she wrote to her sister, "that it is not rank nor titles, but character alone which interests posterity."[3]

Small had been the recipient of an act of gallantry during the battle. In the French and Indian War, he had served in America alongside Israel Putnam. At Bunker's Hill, Putnam, honoring their old acquaintance, struck up the muskets of his men when they were about to shoot Small down.

Warren, on the other hand, was not treated well. John Adams was told, after the battle, that a British naval lieutenant found the spot where Warren had been buried on the field, uncovered the body to stomp and spit on it, and finally cut off the head.[4] This was a patriotic exaggeration, rumor on its way to propaganda. But Warren's corpse had indeed been stripped and tossed in a common grave.

There is one other complication in Trumbull's desire to emphasize Small's humanity toward Warren, and that is that he does not quite manage it. The highlights on Warren and the two Americans defending him (echoed by patches of light blue in the otherwise darkened sky) make them stand out, but not enough. The sweep of the enemy surging up the hill; the smoke and the flags, American and British, that seem to surge along with them; the red of so many uniforms—not, Goethe to the contrary, a monotony, but an excitement—dominate the painting, and the viewer's attention. Trumbull's image is far less static than West's of General Wolfe's death, or even than Copley's of Major Peirson's. Trumbull's predecessors gave us parallel clumps of figures; Trumbull gives us one heaving mass, comprising the force and the resistance that it is about to bear down and sweep away. It is not even clear, at first viewing, what Small at the bottom is doing with his hand; perhaps he means to drive the grenadier's bayonet home.

There is one detached group in Bunker's Hill—two men, one white, one black, standing at the lower right and turning back to view the action. They are Lieutenant Thomas Grosvenor and Asaba. Grosvenor was a lawyer from Pomfret, Connecticut, twenty miles northeast of Lebanon. His right hand is tied with a white bandage; a British bullet has passed through a rail fence, his hand, and the stock of his musket, before finally striking his chest, where it left a bruise.

Trumbull's catalogue calls Asaba, stereotypically, "a faithful negro."[5] At the time of the battle he was Grosvenor's slave, though a later census would list him as a free man. Silliman, describing Trumbull's painting, insisted that he was "a brave man and not a chattel."[6] His disordered left stocking now shows that he has been in the thick of it, along with Grosvenor.

For a time the fighting black man was thought to be Peter Salem, a former slave enlisted in a Massachusetts regiment. Salem was popularly credited with firing the shot that killed Major Pitcairn (there were other claimants). Far back in Trumbull's knot of patriots, to the right of Putnam and behind him, is a second black man, looking, across the canvas, in Pitcairn's direction.

British polemicists harped on the hypocrisy of American rebels, fighting for their freedom while holding slaves. The scoffers were not free of hypocrisy themselves, for while Britain liberated the slaves of American rebels, it kept a tight grip on its many slaves in Jamaica and other sugar islands. The uniformed black slave in Copley's *Death of Major Peirson*, dispatching the French sniper who has killed his commander, could be read as a painterly jibe in this dispute: the Loyalist ex-American shows, *we Britons give blacks arms (in the home islands, if not the Caribbean)* (see figure 4).[7] By showing Asaba, Trumbull is replying, *We did too (in Massachusetts at least)*. It is a moral contest, using black men as counters.

But this painting invites analysis less than it compels reaction. Abigail Adams spoke truly when she began her description of *Bunker's Hill* by saying "my whole frame contracted, my blood shivered, and I felt a faintness at my heart."[8]

Faintness from the drama of the scene, and from the result depicted: the enemy wins.

The Death of General Montgomery in the Attack on Quebec

Trumbull's connection to the American attack on Quebec, though real, was far more attenuated than his connection to the Battle of Bunker's Hill: at Crown Point, in the summer of 1776, he tallied the survivors of the beaten American army. Painting an event that had occurred half a year earlier and 270 miles away required him to rely on his imagination (plate 4).

Eighteenth-century Quebec consisted of an upper town, on a headland between the confluence of the St. Charles and St. Lawrence rivers; and beneath it, a lower town, at water level. Benjamin West's painting of the death of General Wolfe is set on the Plains of Abraham, a plateau west of the upper town, where British attackers and French defenders fought a set-piece battle in the open field in September morning light.

Trumbull had to show a different battle, unfolding in a different hour and season. In the fall of 1775 two American armies invaded Canada, one led by Richard Montgomery, the other by Benedict Arnold. Arnold, a New Haven merchant, had already shown tactical verve in early fighting in New York. Montgomery, from a family of Irish Protestant gentry, was a veteran of the French and Indian War, and a friend of Charles James Fox and Edmund Burke; he bought a farm in the Hudson valley and took up the patriot cause. In December 1775 the two American commanders converged on Quebec, Montgomery coming down the St. Lawrence from Montreal, Arnold bushwhacking across the wilderness of Maine. In the face of this invasion, the British fell back to their defenses in the upper town. Montgomery planned to enter the lower town by sweeping along the shore of the St. Lawrence to the south, while Arnold followed the path of the St. Charles to the north; after they met, they would scale the walls of the upper town.

The Americans attacked in a blizzard on New Year's Eve. Trumbull's painting is therefore a night piece. This suited him, since he had never seen Quebec (he would not visit it until 1807, two decades after his painting was finished). His imaginary vantage point is closer than it was in *Bunker's Hill,* maybe five yards from the nearest of the action, but much of what he and we see is darkness and confusion. As in *Bunker's Hill,* an army advances toward us, American this time, but it seems to be looming up from a cavern, or the grave. Snow on the ground and smoke in the air provide almost the only brightness in the setting. The flags of the American vanguard melt into the branches of a twisted, barren tree.

Three figures in the center, at the head of the march, pick up a beam of light from somewhere; their golden breeches and waistcoats, and the golden linings of their topcoats, reflect it back. Their lower and inner garments have been exposed to us by death. A blast of grape shot from an enemy cannon, out of the picture to the left, has killed them all: Major General Montgomery, and two aides, Captain Jacob Cheeseman and Captain John MacPherson. Montgomery falls to his knees, head thrown back, supported by a comrade; Cheeseman and MacPherson lie entangled on the snow. Their poses are both religious and sensuous. The dead officers are patriot saints, in the moment of giving their lives for their country, and supple forms, as if foreshadowing *The Rokeby Venus* Trumbull would copy decades later. Spirit and eros, personified by Marys and Magdalenes, Sebastians and Davids, had commingled in European art for centuries. Now they appear on the battlefield. The reactions of the dead men's comrades yank us away from such meditations. One officer, in a red cap and collar, struggles to hold Montgomery up; another, supporting Montgomery's outstretched arm, leans forward, as if to help Cheeseman and MacPherson too (too late). Two blue-coated officers, just behind these men, look stunned: *My God, what has happened?* A third officer, down and to the right, stops in midstride, as if his body, lagging behind his mind, is still intent on their interrupted advance.

The most dramatic reactions are on the left. Three Americans, in red, blue, and brown uniforms, respectively, look back at their slaughtered comrades, waving their arms in shock. Their muskets and bayonets seem to share their distress. In David's *Oath of the Horatii,* which Trumbull would see shortly after finishing *Quebec,* the arms and legs of the men making their vow move in harmony, like spokes of the wheels of will (see figure 5). These firearms jab and cross, like pieces of a busted wheel. A broken cannon at the soldiers' feet repeats the effect of collapse.

A fourth gesturing officer stands to the left of the central group, facing the direction of the deadly cannon. White men knew him as Joseph Louis Cook, or informally as Colonel Louis (his rank would be conferred officially by the Continental Congress four years later). His Mohawk name is Akiatonharonkwen. He was of mixed race, which was not uncommon on the colonial frontier; his father was black, his mother an Abenaki Indian. Mohawks captured him in a raid in the 1740s and raised him as one of their own. He had no love for Britain; he fought for France in the French and Indian War, for America in the Revolution.

He had come to the walls of Quebec in Arnold's army, but Trumbull places him at Montgomery's death, where he serves, like the Indian in West's *Death of General Wolfe,* as a patch of local color; his beaded accoutrements and feathered headdress are carefully rendered. More important, Trumbull shows the man's fighting spirit (he would serve through the Revolution and even, as an old man, in the War of 1812). West's Indian sits contemplating the white hero's death. Colonel Louis brandishes his tomahawk in defiance.

Quebec is a surreal composition. The details we can see are quite precise: the uniforms of the three gesturing officers on the lower left are copied from the clothing that Charles Willson Peale had sent West from America when West thought of painting the history of the Revolution himself. Yet they float in a nightmarish void. We clearly see only twelve men, two of whose faces are hidden. There are no visible enemies (*Bunker's Hill* was crowded with them). Death falls like fate. Where is the light that shines on the dead coming from? Heaven? History?

Montgomery's sudden death threw the remaining officers into despair; his force was ordered to retreat. Arnold's, on the other side of town, was beaten back, much of it captured. Come spring the British would reinforce Quebec by water, and proceed to undo all of America's Canadian conquests.

Trumbull, in his catalogue, described the scene thus: "The earth covered with snow,—trees stripped of their foliage,—the desolation of winter, and the gloom of night, heighten the melancholy character of the scene."⁹ Once again, the enemy wins.

The Declaration of Independence

Not outside, but in a room. Not armies, but a meeting of delegates. Not gunfire, but quiet, with perhaps the sound of a few voices. The scene of Trumbull's third painting is the Assembly Room of the Pennsylvania State House in Philadelphia, where the Second Continental Congress had been meeting since May 1775 (plate 5).

The Continental Congress was different from today's. Each colony's delegation cast one vote, however populous the colony was, or however many delegates it sent. Day-to-day business was conducted by committees; there was a president, but he was a presiding officer of Congress's sessions, not an executive. In the year before the moment depicted here, Congress had picked a commander in chief, organized an army, and secretly courted possible foreign allies.

On June 7, 1776, Richard Henry Lee of Virginia presented another item of business, moving "that these United Colonies are, and of right ought to be, free and independent States." America and Britain had been fighting pitched battles for fourteen months; Lee wanted to cut the cord. His motion was debated for the remainder of the month; meanwhile Congress named a five-man committee to prepare a declaration of independence.

On July 2 Lee's motion was approved, nine states to four. The following day three of the holdout states joined the majority (New York abstained for a while longer, lacking instructions from its provincial Congress). Meanwhile the delegates revised a draft declaration that had been prepared by Thomas Jefferson, and lightly edited by Benjamin Franklin and John Adams. The final version was done by July 4.

Trumbull gives us a straight-ahead view of the Assembly Room's west wall, with the south and north walls reaching toward us diagonally, left and right. We, the viewers, seem to be standing at the east wall, behind the dais visible in the foreground. For the floor plan, Trumbull relied on the sketch given him in Paris by Jefferson (his own first idea for a possible painting is drawn on the back of the sheet). Jefferson had misremembered the room, however, putting two doors on the west wall, when there was only one, in its center. Trumbull made a few changes of his own, covering the windows in drapes rather than Venetian blinds, and furnishing the room with French-style oval-backed chairs, rather than the spindle-backed Windsor chairs that were actually there.

The president of Congress, Trumbull's old nemesis, John Hancock, sits at his desk, angled so that we are not looking at the back of his head. In front of him the drafting committee—Adams; Roger Sherman of Connecticut; Robert Livingston, a young New York grandee; Jefferson; and Franklin—have come forward to offer their handiwork. Jefferson, the draftsman, holds the document itself. Behind and beside them fortytwo other men spread out, standing and seated, witnessing the moment.

What moment is it? July 4, as the date on both the document and the painting suggest? The day when Jefferson and the committee first presented their draft to Congress, which had been June 28? Or is it the day on which the delegates began signing, which would not be until August 2?

Trumbull has painted what looks like a moment, but he is actually making a comprehensive statement about the Declaration, telescoping events and juggling characters. He knew, as the notes in his catalogue show, that "the usual practice" of committees reporting an act was for one member, typically the chairman, to rise from his chair in the body of the room and offer it for consideration. Instead, Trumbull brings all five members of the drafting committee forward.[10] He also knew that not every man who signed in August had been present on July 4 (among the latecomers was William Williams of Connecticut, who was married to Trumbull's sister Mary). Finally, he knew that important patriots who had been intimately involved in debating and creating the Declaration had not signed it. Robert Livingston of the drafting committee was called back to New York before August 2. John Dickinson of Pennsylvania, who, thanks to a decade of patriotic polemics, was a more famous advocate in 1776 than young Jefferson, had refused to sign, not because he had turned Loyalist, but because he questioned the timing (the people of his colony, he thought, "were not yet ripe for bidding adieu to British connection," though "they were fast ripening").[11] Trumbull is presenting a deed, both context and fruition; a piece of paper, and the men whose discussion had brought it into being.

Trumbull labored to collect as many accurate likenesses as he could, capturing faces in Europe and America; ten had to be copied from portraits by other artists.[12] In Trumbull's lifetime keys identifying the characters appeared, one when the life-size version in the Rotunda was offered as an engraving, another when all four Rotunda images were installed. The keys made a few mistakes: Dickinson is supposed to be the middle man in the cluster of three to the left of Hancock's chair, though he is more likely the man in the hat standing by the west wall.[13] (Dickinson had Quaker parents and a Quaker wife; Quakers rejected doffing hats as a worldly honorific.)

How was Trumbull to make a roomful of men, most of them immobile, visually interesting? In 1828 Representative John Randolph, an eccentric, sharp-spoken cousin of Jefferson's, judged the result in a phrase that was characteristic of his rhetoric: amusing, malicious, mem-

orable, and wrong. The painting, Randolph said, ought "to be called the
Shin-piece, for, surely, never was there, before, such a collection of legs
submitted to the eyes of man."[14] Trumbull in fact so varied the poses of
his subjects—eighteen are standing, most of them behind other members, while most of the thirty who are seated are behind desks or each
other—that only four pairs of legs stand out. Trumbull arranged other
small contrasts of position and attitude. A few congressmen are not paying complete attention: there are three small conversations going on,
two on the left, one on the right. A couple of additional delegates glance
away from the main event. So it is at any particular moment in a large
gathering, even on the most solemn occasions. These visual eddies offer
a pictorial relief; if Trumbull's blocking has a flaw, it is in the long, straight
line made by the heads of the seated members, running from George
Wythe on the left edge to Samuel Huntington on the right.

Too much variety among the onlookers might, however, detract
from the central action, which is happening at Hancock's table. Benjamin Franklin, oldest member of the drafting committee, and of Congress, looks almost straight at us, the only man in the room doing so. At
age seventy, he has seen a lot; he has a lot more to see (diplomacy in
France, a constitutional convention eleven years later in the same room).
Robert Livingston and his wavy black hair, at the back of the group, adds
a devil-may-care note. But Adams, Sherman, and Jefferson are determined, focused on the business at hand. Adams and Jefferson, the two
members Trumbull consulted with, are given time-honored poses. Adams's hand on hip recalls Washington's in Trumbull's 1790 portrait, and
Charles I's in the Van Dyck that Trumbull imitated. Jefferson handing
the Declaration to Hancock—it could be two pages, or a large one folded,
it is not clear which—modifies a pose from Roman sculpture, *adlocutio,*
in which an emperor, arm extended, addresses his troops. Here the gesture of the general and the king is given to a lawyer in a brown suit; of
the emperor, to a tall planter with a red waistcoat and reddish hair. The
body languages of the military, royalty, and despotism are transferred to
representative government.

Jefferson, with author's pride, had wanted to make sure that Trumbull's revolutionary series included him and his document. With author's
touchiness, he had resented every cut and alteration that Congress made

to his draft (they were roughest on his bill of indictment against George III and the British people). With a great thinker's honesty, he declared that the ideas expressed in his introductory paragraphs on human nature and just government were common to everyone in the room, Dickinson included (and indeed Congress hardly touched them). They were common to everyone of the patriot party in America. They were, as he put it the year before he died, "the common sense of the subject.... the harmonizing sentiments of the day, whether expressed in conversation, in letters, printed essays, or in the elementary books of public right, as Aristotle, Cicero, Locke, Sidney, etc."[15] Jefferson had put the common sense of the subject on paper. Standing at Hancock's desk, the tallest man in the room and the reddest, he is for this moment the star of Trumbull's image, the star of the show. But the cast is as important as he is.

Although this is a scene of politics, there is a war going on, as Trumbull reminds us with the captured British flags hanging on the west wall. He imagined that they were trophies won from early victories in Canada, on Montgomery's march north from New York and down the St. Lawrence, before the defeat at Quebec. In his catalogue Trumbull admitted they may not have been hanging there—"the artist ... took the liberty of embellishing the background" by displaying them. But he added, almost immediately, that they "probably were actually placed in the hall."[16] They appear, faintly, in his very first sketch, on the reverse of Jefferson's floor plan. Perhaps Jefferson told him such trophies were there; or maybe Trumbull's own memories of the war in the north prompted him to include them.

Flags or no flags, Congress was well aware of the war. The enemy had begun landing an expeditionary force on Staten Island on July 2, as a build-up to the battles that would conquer all of New York City and its environs by November, and all of central New Jersey by the following month.

The war would continue. But Congress had said for what (independence) and why (to secure "certain unalienable rights").

The Capture of the Hessians at Trenton

The Capture of the Hessians at Trenton is the last military scene in Trumbull's series to which he had any personal connection, and it was very slight: he was posted briefly in December 1776 to Washington's army, where it lay on the Pennsylvania side of the Delaware River, opposite Trenton, New Jersey (plate 6).

Five months earlier Washington had had the Declaration of Independence read to his men in New York. The noble document may have come to seem vain as they were driven successively from Long Island, Manhattan, White Plains, and the state of New Jersey, in what Trumbull, in his catalogue, called "one continued series of disasters." At last, he wrote of the spot where he joined them, "the exhausted troops enjoyed a few days of repose."[17] Trumbull left them there when he was dispatched to Rhode Island.

Trenton commemorates the reversal that occurred only days later. On the morning of December 26 Washington surprised an advance post of the enemy at Trenton, routing three regiments and taking almost nine hundred prisoners and their weapons, with minimal American losses.

Accounts of the Battle of Trenton, whether verbal or painted, have highlighted the nighttime crossing of the Delaware that preceded the attack. Washington's first biographer, Mason Locke (Parson) Weems, set the tone. "Washington and his little forlorn hope, pressed on through the darksome night, pelted by an incessant storm of hail and snow. On approaching the river . . . they heard the unwelcome roar of ice, loud crashing along the angry flood."[18]

Trumbull focuses instead on the moment of victory. We are seeing, from ten yards away, an after-action report. The remains of battle—a fallen banner, an abandoned musket and drum—litter the ground. So do the dead and wounded, both Hessian—in reddish breeches and waistcoats—and American. The after-motions of combat still ripple through the scene: suddenly reined-in horses bow or twist their necks; in the background a mounted American still gallops, while another swings his sword. As in *Bunker's Hill,* the sky takes part in the action, with black clouds to the left, and dark smoke to the right. (The weather that morning had actually been much worse, pelting snow turning to rain.) In the center of Trumbull's sky the weather breaks in a patch of white, which outlines the head of the mounted American commander in chief, George Washington.

He and two of his staff are riding toward a party of senior officers to the right, among them Major General Nathanael Greene, a bland-faced military tyro and genius; Brigadier General Henry Knox, chief of artillery, who had spent the previous night muscling cannon onto the boats that took them across the Delaware; and Colonel John Glover, whose regiment of Massachusetts sailors had steered the armada. But Washington, on his splendid chestnut horse, turns suddenly aside to acknowledge another senior officer. It is Colonel Johann Rall, his defeated opponent.

Rall was a subject of Hesse Cassel, a central German state whose sovereign hired out his army to foreign princes. The Hessians' current assignment was to assist Britain in suppressing the Revolution in America. Rall, fifty, had followed his father into the service when he was a teenager and risen through the ranks. He was a fighter, popular with his men, though his junior officers would criticize his skills as a commander.

Trumbull's account of the battle in his catalogue perpetuated an American myth. Since "German troops," he wrote, "were accustomed to keep Christmas with great festivity . . . the revelry of the night [left] them off their guard."[19] Hungover Hessians have gone down in history, but there were none in Trenton. Rall had been warned of a possible attack, but assumed that a minor feint by patriot militia earlier in the night had been the real thing. The fog of war, not indiscipline, accounted for his guard being down on December 26.

When the Americans appeared at dawn on the northern edge of town, Rall quickly dressed and mounted, leading his men in a maneuver (foiled) to outflank the attackers, then plunging them into a melee to recover two cannon the enemy had seized. In this fight he was shot in the flank, and carried, first to a nearby church, then back to his headquarters.

Here he stands, supported by an American officer, but he is dying. By day's end his outflung right arm would be as limp as Joseph Warren's or Richard Montgomery's. Washington's right arm is extended too, in a mounted *adlocutio*. But his is a gesture not of imperial address, but of humane compassion. He appears almost to want to touch Rall. Trumbull explained in his catalogue that he "chose this subject and composed this picture for the express purpose of giving a lesson to all living and future soldiers in the service of his country, to show mercy and kindness to a fallen enemy—their enemy no longer when wounded and in their power."[20]

Here, unlike in *Bunker's Hill,* the gesture of mercy does register. There is no clash of arms overhead to compete with it. Washington's position, on horseback, but turning aside to something more important than a staff meeting, is visually more interesting than Major Small's striding. Most important, Washington is the American commander in chief, not an enemy mid-rank officer. The best man is doing the best thing.

Trumbull assured Silliman that the scene was true to life. "Washington's face," he said, "varied extremely ... in different circumstances." In the circumstances Trumbull records here, it showed "deep sympathy and concern." He accordingly asked Washington, when he was painting him during his presidency, "to place himself as nearly as possible in the position which he occupied at that moment."[21]

In the welter of after-battle events—reviewing what had just happened, deciding what to do next (find more enemy to fight, or retire back across the Delaware?)—Washington seems to have encountered both Rall and another mortally wounded Hessian senior officer; he directed that Rall be allowed to remain in the house that had been his headquarters, rather than be moved, as a prisoner of war, a third time. (Rall died there that night.) In an early sketch, Trumbull separated Washington and the wounded Hessian. In his painting, he brings them side by side, to emphasize Washington's magnanimity.[22]

There is another seriously wounded man identifiable in *Trenton,* who will fare better than Rall. Almost directly behind Rall's right hand is a prone American's face, even paler than Rall's. This is the face of Lieutenant James Monroe, eighteen years old, shot during the struggle for the cannons in which Rall was mortally wounded. A musket ball severed an artery in Monroe's chest; his bleeding was stopped, and his life saved, by the quick thinking of a local doctor who had volunteered to join the American attack only the night before.[23] Silliman recalled Trumbull saying, rather cattily, that "that ball made [Monroe] president of the United States."[24] That, and the friendship of Thomas Jefferson, and years of hard political work.

Considered as a work of art, *Trenton* loses energy as it moves from left to right. Like so many painters before him, historical and otherwise, Trumbull has arranged three foreground groups: officers, Washington and Rall, officers. The officers on the left wave and twist, grab reins, and grip a flag. Those on the right recall the sedate British officers on the right of *The Sortie Made by the Garrison of Gibraltar,* or even the seated delegates in *The Declaration of Independence.* Although they are out-doors, on the field of a just-concluded battle, six heads make a straight line. The only variety comes from the standing officer, Captain William Washington, a cousin of the commander in chief; his hands are bandaged from wounds sustained in Monroe's and Rall's melee.

Although *Trenton* was well along by the early 1790s, Trumbull still tinkered with it decades later. One of his last additions is the Hessian who lies face down between Washington's and Greene's curveting hors-es. Trumbull told Silliman he put the dead man there to give the horses "something to snort at"; otherwise, "some critic might say [they] were making bows at each other."[25] The Hessian's right shoulder looks mis-shapen, almost deformed, the color of his uniform is blocky and dull. As for the horses, either you know you can paint them at moments of high tension, or you don't. The hypothetical jibes of critics should not matter. Washington's gesture, posture, and mount; the activity on the left and in the atmosphere; and the painterly pizzazz that still infuses most of the canvas, keep *Trenton* in Trumbull's first rank.

It is also noteworthy as an American victory.

THIRTEEN

The next painting in Trumbull's series is, like *Bunker's Hill* and *Quebec*, a battle piece; like *Bunker's Hill*, it is a synopsis, bringing different episodes at the turning point of the struggle into one image.

The Death of General Mercer at the Battle of Princeton

After their victory at Trenton, Washington and his senior officers decided to take their captives and their spoils across the Delaware River to Pennsylvania. But Washington did not want to give the enemy a free hand in New Jersey that winter, so he brought his army back over the river, posting a small holding force in Trenton, with the main body of his troops on the south bank of Assunpink Creek, just below town.

The British meanwhile sent General Charles Cornwallis and eight thousand men to dispatch the rebels. The British arrived in Trenton at dusk on January 2, 1777, pushing the holding force before them and trading artillery fire with the Americans on the far side of the creek. Although Cornwallis tried and failed to force the lone bridge that spanned the Assunpink, he expected to overwhelm the Americans in the morning.

"Gen. Washington," wrote Trumbull in his catalogue, "saw his danger [and] resolved to extricate himself by falling into the rear of the enemy." Leaving his campfires burning, "he withdrew his troops in the dead of night, with the most profound silence," and marched over frozen backroads toward Princeton, twelve miles away.[1]

Trumbull's painting shows what happened next (plate 7). "Trumbull 'thought' with drawings," as a twentieth-century catalogue put it, and an unusually large number of studies for this particular painting survive.[2] He made line drawings using pen, ink, and pencil; to later drawings, he added patches of shade with washes of diluted ink. In the next-to-last version, he put a layer of light oil paint over a sketch in black chalk. In each iteration he moved men, horses, and objects back and forth across the field of his inner eye, seeking the arrangement that would best edit the story, and present it most effectively.

At dawn on January 3, after marching all night, the Americans were two miles from Princeton. At the same time a smaller British force was moving in the opposite direction along a parallel road, intending to join Cornwallis in Trenton. Outliers from each side encountered each other in an apple orchard.

The Americans were led by General Hugh Mercer, a Scottish doctor who had settled in Virginia and was a friend of Washington. His men and the enemy exchanged volleys, then the British charged with bayonets. A man with a bayonet can cover a short distance faster than a man with a musket can reload. So it now happened.

In the center foreground of Trumbull's painting, about five yards from us, Mercer lies on the ground, alongside his dead gray horse. He flourishes his sword, but two British infantrymen come in for the kill. No gallant Major Small is there to impede these bayonet thrusts. Mercer tries, grasping the blade of his nearest enemy, but he will not succeed.

To the left, another American, an artillerist, is being bayoneted at his gun. Contemporary keys identified him as Lieutenant Charles Turnbull, of the Pennsylvania artillery. But Turnbull moved to New York after the war, married, owned a farm in what is now Brooklyn, and died in 1795.[3] This artillerist is dying before our eyes. He has been correctly identified as Lieutenant Daniel Neil of the New Jersey artillery. The enemy pays too. At the right Captain William Leslie, second son of a Scottish earl, has taken a mortal shot, though he is still standing. Across the foreground lie five dead or dying men, two British, three American. No key identifies them. The pair of dead combatants on the right almost lie in each other's arms. So many bodies make a harem of the expiring.

In the battle, Mercer's surviving troops fell back before the British bayonet charge and mingled in confusion with a party of Philadelphia militia coming up to support them. If the confusion had spread, the British might have won the day. But Washington, who had been ahead of the fighting, rode back to lead a charge of reinforcements against the enemy.

Trumbull shows this moment in the upper center of his painting, as if it were happening a few yards behind Mercer and at the moment of his death. Washington rides toward us on a chestnut horse, looking to the left, where most of the Americans in the painting are, but pointing with his sword to the right, where most of the British are. On the battlefield, he reportedly shouted, "Parade with us, my brave fellows! There is but a handful of the enemy, and we will have them directly."[4] In the painting, he says it with a gesture. To the left, and behind his head, swords are swinging and stabbing; the blasted wintry tree of *Quebec* has transplanted itself to New Jersey and looms over him. But he is composed, as if out for a ride (a serious ride). Washington's horse, though his right eye is wide with excitement, shares his rider's composure, as well-ridden horses will. The horse might have panicked, the Americans might have panicked, but Washington sees them through. The cloud of smoke behind his head is white. The town of Princeton, his goal, appears in the distance as a pair of toy buildings.

Trumbull valued this painting above all the others in his series; he told Silliman that if he could save only one from some disaster, this was the one he would pick. He has shown Washington post-combat at Trenton, and he would show him in two others settings, even more sedate. This is his only painting of Washington in battle; hence its value to him. He worked hard to get the details right. When a British artist told him that Captain Leslie secured his sword by a leather thong attached to his right wrist, he adjusted the painted weapon accordingly. Leslie himself was included as a tribute to Dr. Benjamin Rush, the Philadelphia physician and signer of the Declaration, shown riding into the battle behind Washington. Trumbull featured Rush so prominently because he had helped rally the local militia before the fight and tended the wounded afterward. Rush knew Leslie from his youth, when he was studying medicine at Edinburgh. He only learned of Leslie's wounds at Princeton when it was too late to be of any help. After Washington learned that Rush and Leslie were friends, he had Leslie buried with military honors in a local churchyard.

Trumbull painted Hugh Mercer's son, also named Hugh, in Fredericksburg, Virginia, in 1791, as a stand-in for the dead hero. As the painting progressed Trumbull altered the position of the head of Mercer's horse. In earlier versions it reared up in a death agony. In the end Trumbull lowered it, so as not to distract from Washington's chestnut horse behind it.[5]

Trumbull included, in the gallery of his paintings at Yale, the last study he had made of Princeton, in oil over black chalk. He wrote in the catalogue that he hung it as a lesson, "to explain to future artists" how a painting was made: "the ground was white on which the work was first merely sketched,—then faintly stained with positive colors,—and finally," as in the completed picture, "each head and figure [was] carefully finished from nature."[6]

Hanging the two pictures in the same room has had the unfortunate effect of upstaging the final version. The unfinished study, like *Bunker's Hill*, shows a sweeping action, although now the American resistance, instead of falling away, surges back, led by Washington. The colors blaze; Goethe would have noticed that the American artillerist wears a red waistcoat, matching the British uniforms (in the final version his waistcoat becomes white). The unfinished quality of the painting seems to make the scene pulse before our eyes.

In the final version drawing and colors have both become more definite. The overall effect is darker, drabber. The rush of action crystallizes, like a chemical solution, into a collection of separate scenes. The synopsis breaks up into its constituent parts: Neil, Mercer, Leslie, Washington; three casualties, one victor.

Modern art historians attribute the change in Trumbull's style and emphasis to a loss of talent. Although he began *Princeton* in the 1780s, when all the preliminary studies, including the one he hung at Yale, were done, he was still working on the final version forty years later. The catalogue of a 1982 Trumbull show at Yale cites "the two versions of the Battle of Princeton" as "ready evidence of his retrogression as a painter," his work "suffer[ing] an almost catastrophic decline in quality."[7] The Yale critic attributed Trumbull's falloff to moving home; in America he lost touch with the Old Master models that had inspired him in England and France. If that were the case, why had he not regained his touch when he moved

back to England, in 1794–1804, or 1808–15? A better reason for his decline might be age: the 1820s were forty years and a Constitution later
than the 1780s. The world had changed; so had Trumbull's eye and hands.

If there is an aesthetic justification for the look and feel of the final
version of *Princeton,* it must be found in its highlighting of the dead. The
battle was fought in broad morning; there could be no unexplained
nighttime spotlight on a military pietà, as in *Quebec.* If these fallen warriors are to get their pictorial due, their limbs, torsos, and faces, even
Mercer's dead horse, have to be lightened and blocked against darker
backgrounds. The signers of the Declaration pledged their lives; these
men have given theirs, the British for empire, the Americans for liberty.
Washington, gesturing behind and above them with his sword, is not
performing a classic *adlocutio;* his arm is stretched across his chest,
while his head turns back; he is rallying troops, leading a charge. It is not
the commander but the artist who is telling us, with his blunt colors and
bleak lighting, *Look at these fallen men.*

After Washington's successful charge, the Americans moved on to
take the town of Princeton. Washington had thought of pushing on to
Brunswick, where the British had a supply depot. But his men, after an
all-night march and a battle, were too fatigued for further combat. They
went instead to Morristown, on higher ground north of the state's central plain, where they spent the winter. The British for their part retired
to strongholds opposite New York City and Staten Island; the prospect
of a triumphal progress through the mid-Atlantic states after the capture
of New York City was over. If the Americans were to lose the war, it
would be after a long slog, not a quick sweep.

Princeton, like *Bunker's Hill* and *Quebec,* shows the death of an
American general; but this time, the painting shows an American victory. The Trenton/Princeton campaign had been, in a later phrase, not
the beginning of the end, but the end of the beginning.

The Surrender of General Burgoyne at Saratoga

Trenton showed the enemy at the moment of defeat, *Princeton* at
the moment just before, when the tide of battle has turned. In *The Surrender of General Burgoyne at Saratoga,* the enemy surrenders (plate 8).

Although the subjects are all military men and the setting is outdoors, it is as formal an occasion as *The Declaration of Independence.*

Trumbull took no part in the ceremony of surrender, or the battles that preceded it—he had angrily left the army months before—but this painting brought him back to a landscape—upstate New York—and a commander—Horatio Gates—he had known in his earlier service. After clearing the Americans out of Canada, the British decided to invade New York in 1777, according to an ambitious and complicated plan drawn up by General John Burgoyne, a playwright, a veteran, and an anti-American member of Parliament. While General Howe was to move up the Hudson from occupied New York, two British armies would attack from Canada, one swinging in from the western end of Lake Ontario, while the principal force, under Burgoyne himself, would proceed directly south, via Lake Champlain. All three would converge on Albany, knocking New York out of the war and splitting the rebellious colonies apart.

Everything went wrong. Howe, whose orders were unclear, chose to take Philadelphia instead. The attack from the west was stopped at a ferocious frontier battle at Oriskany (American casualties ran as high as fifty percent). Burgoyne's progress was slowed by felled trees and dammed streams, obstacles put in his path by the defenders. Patriot militias, smelling victory, swelled the ranks of the regular American army. Burgoyne lost two battles in succession, only fifteen miles north of Albany, and surrendered on October 17, 1777.

The surrender of an entire British army at Saratoga was a decisive event, encouraging France to ally openly with the rebels it had been supporting on the sly. Trumbull had planned from the earliest days of his project to paint it. But he did not do so until he made the life-size version for the Capitol Rotunda. The small painting in the Trumbull Gallery was a follow-on.

The central figure is his old commander, Horatio Gates. Gates, who died in 1806, needed pictorial rehabilitation. His reputation and his head swollen by his triumph at Saratoga, he spent the rest of 1777 scheming to replace George Washington as commander in chief (the scheme collapsed when one of Gates's aides talked about it in a tavern, and word got back to Washington). In 1780 Gates was sent to repel a

British invasion of South Carolina, only to suffer a crushing defeat. At war's end, he became the willing tool of disaffected officers and politicians who hoped to use the army to threaten Congress into fiscal responsibility; only Washington's appeal to his comrades quashed the plot. Gates's great victory at Saratoga, however, could not be denied him. In Trumbull's composition, he refuses, with a slightly turned away left hand, the sword of General Burgoyne. With his extended right hand, he invites his defeated enemy to his tent for a meal. Through such civilities the mutual esteem of the officer corps was maintained across national lines. Behind Burgoyne is William Phillips, a British major general; in the background, peeking over Burgoyne's sword hand, is Friedrich Riedesel, commander of his German allies.

American officers spread out on either side, respectful spectators. The most visually interesting are Colonel Daniel Morgan, the Virginia rifleman, in his white leggings and hunting shirt, and to the left Captain Thomas Seymour, wearing a dragoon's crested metal helmet, then a newish cavalry fashion, imported from France.

Missing is Gates's second in command, General Benedict Arnold. Gates was an organizer and an overseer; he led from his tent. Arnold had been in the thick of the fray, as he had been at Quebec almost two years earlier. "Arnold was our fighting general, and a bloody fellow he was," one veteran of Saratoga remembered. "He didn't care for nothing; he'd right ride in. It was 'Come on, boys'" 'twasn't 'Go, boys.' He was as brave a man as ever lived."[8] Among the things Arnold did not care for was any cause greater than his own sense of honor. Annoyed by slowness of promotion and accusations of corruption, in 1780 he planned to betray West Point to the British, fleeing to their lines when his plot was discovered. The greatest painting ever done could not rehabilitate him.

Saratoga, like the *Declaration,* is in great part a collection of portrait heads, the arrangement here somewhat improved by Trumbull's having abandoned the straight lineup he made of the delegates to the Continental Congress. The portraits themselves, however, are a sad disappointment. The faces are crude, almost cartoonish. In Trumbull's how-to description of the last study of *Princeton,* he wrote that "each head and figure" was added, at the last moment, onto a preexisting sketch. But here the head of Lieutenant Colonel John Brooks, whose hand rests on the barrel of the foremost cannon, does not sit correctly atop his body; it is too far to the left. The heads behind Brooks to the right, belonging to a chaplain and one of Gates's aides, were no doubt painted smaller because the men they belong to are standing farther back, but the perspective is so casually established that they seem child-sized. The main actors center stage are equally bad, dully arranged and poorly painted. Burgoyne's and Phillips's identical strides make them look like cutouts decorating a cake. Gates wears an unpleasant frown; is he sorry to have won? The contrast between his doughy visage, and the pinpoint faces of Trumbull's Adams, Jefferson, Franklin, or almost any of his Washingtons, is painful. The cast of characters in *Saratoga* justify the critic's judgment of catastrophic decline.

There is one interesting character in this painting, and it is, surprisingly, nature. Trumbull had once proposed doing a panorama of Niagara Falls, and he had painted a few picturesque views of Connecticut as well. But he was not, by inclination, an artist of the outdoors. The turn in American painting, early in the nineteenth century, from history to nature left him artistically marooned. Here, however, nature softens and soothes the scene. The blasted tree that traveled from Quebec to Princeton reappears in New York, though now it is cut off and prostrate in the foreground. Around its roots are several almost alarmingly leafy groundcover plants. Huge, healthy trees in autumnal foliage—beeches, perhaps, by their bark and the shape of their leaves—fill the upper air and the countryside. In the distance sits a blue mountain, which Trumbull had sketched on a trip to Saratoga in 1791, and which he seemingly liked so much he doubled its peak in the painting.

Trumbull's verdure and views reflect a truth about the campaign of 1777. Although northern New York had been the setting of forts, marches, and battles going back to the French and Indian War, it was wild and difficult terrain. James Fenimore Cooper's historical romance, *The Last of the Mohicans,* published in 1826, described the scene for later generations of Americans: "Armies larger than those that had often disposed of the scepters of the mother countries were seen to bury themselves in these forests, whence they rarely returned but in skeleton bands that were haggard with care or dejected by defeat."[9] The British, and General Burgoyne, their main planner, had miscalculated the difficulties they would face in their three-pronged invasion, and suffered the consequences.

Burgoyne surrenders to Gates, but he surrenders even more to the landscape.

The Surrender of Lord Cornwallis at Yorktown

The Surrender of Lord Cornwallis at Yorktown, the seventh painting in Trumbull's series, depicts the last surrender, the moment that persuaded George III and his ministers that the war was lost (plate 9).

The siege of Yorktown was fruit of the Franco-American alliance that the battles of Saratoga had first made real. After several frustrating joint campaigns, including one in which Trumbull served (the failed attempt to take Newport), in the fall of 1781 the two allies settled on a plan, far more complicated than Burgoyne's invasion of New York, and miraculously pulled it off.

Their target was Charles Cornwallis, whom both of Trumbull's commanders had tangled with: Washington had outfoxed him at Princeton, Gates had been demolished by him at Camden. Gates's replacement in the South, Nathanael Greene, had maneuvered so craftily that Cornwallis had left the Carolinas for Virginia. There the allies resolved to trap him.

Cornwallis positioned himself at Yorktown, on the mouth of one of the wide rivers that empty into Chesapeake Bay, awaiting reinforcements from occupied New York. What came instead was an Anglo-French expeditionary force consisting of a French army, under the comte de Rochambeau, which marched south from Rhode Island; an American army, under Washington, which joined the French in upstate New York and continued south with them; a small French fleet from Rhode Island, commanded by the comte de Barras; and a large French fleet, which had sailed north from the West Indies, led by the comte de Grasse. When the combined French naval forces defeated a last-minute English rescue fleet off the mouth of Chesapeake Bay in September, Cornwallis's escape by water was sealed. Rochambeau and Washington, joining the American forces on the spot, which were commanded by the marquis de Lafayette, laid siege to Yorktown on land. After three weeks of pummeling, Cornwallis submitted.

The ceremony of surrender took place on October 19. The protocol was shaped by losers' resentment, and victors' revenge. Cornwallis refused to surrender in person, claiming illness, sending his deputy, Brigadier General Charles O'Hara, in his place. O'Hara, snubbing Washington, offered his sword to Rochambeau, who, even though the French had outnumbered the Americans at Yorktown, refused it, directing him to Washington instead. Washington would not accept the surrender of a number two, and pointed O'Hara to General Benjamin Lincoln. Lincoln had a backstory: in May 1780 he had been on the losing side, surrendering Charleston, South Carolina, to Cornwallis after a month-long siege. Cornwallis then had denied the defeated the honors of war—a last march into captivity with flags flying and bayonets fixed. Washington stipulated that the British troops receive the same treatment now, and that Lincoln (who had returned to combat after a prisoner exchange) receive the symbol of victory.

Trumbull fussed with the arrangement of the scene. In every study he arrayed the French on the left and the Americans on the right, with the act of surrender in the center, but his first effort showed Lincoln, mounted, from behind. Horses' hindquarters—horses' asses—appeared in military and other paintings without any obvious intent to insult or raise a laugh, but the view was not appealing. Lincoln himself, viewed from the rear, showed a male-pattern bald spot. Trumbull's solution was to reverse Lincoln, showing him face forward, with his hat on. Lincoln is performing a ritual for his comrades, French and American, but Trumbull's blocking makes him also perform it for us.

We are at Trumbull's favorite vantage point, between five and ten yards distant. The allied officers stretch toward us in two lines that diverge, so that we may not miss anyone present. The scene is as choreographed as a ballet, and so it should be, for the end of an empire is an important occasion.

Yorktown is a visual lecture on the geopolitics of the Revolution. France and Britain had been at war off and on since the late seventeenth century, and France had been aching to avenge its defeats in their last round of fighting, the Seven Years' War. As early as 1768, she had sent Johann de Kalb, a German officer in the French service, to North America to assess the colonists' willingness to revolt. (Kalb reported that they were unhappy, but not yet rebellious; when the Revolution did come, he joined the American army out of conviction, and was killed at Camden.) The money, men, and ships that France poured into the American cause were an elaborate, and expensive, payback. Loans and payments do not make riveting pictures, but Trumbull's collection of French officers in Yorktown pays tribute to their military exertions.

He collected French faces when he stayed with Jefferson in Paris in 1787; while there he also made a careful sketch of a French uniform. He painted in Americans in New York in 1790. Hence the portraiture in Yorktown is early, the skill level is high. Most interesting to us is Lieutenant Colonel Alexander Hamilton, to the right of the white horse in the American lineup. He is flush with military glory. Siege warfare was a step-by-step process, regular as a mathematical proof, of digging trenches, moving mortars into them, then pushing the trenches closer. To complete the trenchwork at Yorktown, however, two British redoubts, forward posts, had to be captured. The marquis de Lafayette led one nighttime charge, Hamilton led the other. He stands in Trumbull's painting, young, fresh, with the world ahead of him. Next to him stands his dear friend, Lieutenant Colonel John Laurens (the letters of the two men, charged with the language of sensibility, express their love for each other). Trumbull did not get Laurens's image in New York; he had been killed in one of the skirmishes that occurred, here and there, in the interval between Yorktown and the final signing of the Treaty of Paris, a year and a half later. Among the mounted American officers are Lafayette, second in from the end of the line on the left, and to his right, Baron von Steuben. Lafayette is even younger than Hamilton, and looks it; Steuben, the Prussian professional who taught Americans how to maneuver in the field, is stout, solid. Like Kalb, both men had taken the American cause as their own. For them the struggle for liberty knew no boundaries. Lafayette would return to France, though he made sure that he was buried in soil brought from America; Steuben would retire to Utica, New York.

The American officers are also a Trumbull family affair. His older brother, Jonathan, Jr., is there, two men to the right of Steuben, serving, as John briefly had, as an aide to Washington. Also present, as an aide to Lincoln, is Ebenezer Huntington, brother-in-law of Trumbull's unfortunate sister Faith. Although Trumbull himself was in Europe, recently sprung from prison, when the surrender happened, he could be present by proxy.

Washington is set slightly apart from the American line, highlighted both by a white cloud and by the contrast of his white leggings with his chestnut mount. His closed mouth almost shows a smile.

Trumbull's loathing of the French Revolution no doubt had something to do with the fates it visited on the men who had helped win America's liberty. The comte de Rochambeau, the French general in chief, on the dark horse at the far end of the French line, would be arrested in the Reign of Terror, and spared only by the fall of Robespierre. The comte de Custine, third from the left standing, and the duc de Lauzun, above him in the tall plumed hat, were not so lucky: they would be arrested and guillotined. Four other officers—the marquis des Deux-Ponts, the marquis de Saint-Simon, the comte de Damas, and the baron de Vioménil—would fight the Revolution in the armies of royalist émigrés or of France's enemies. A Swede attached to the French court, the comte de Fersen, fourth to the right of Lauzun, helped Louis XVI in a vain attempt to escape France in 1791; Fersen later became the lover of Marie Antoinette. The marquis de Choisy would serve in the army of the new regime without complaint.

Two of Trumbull's Frenchmen would die before the storm struck. The marquis de Chastellux would publish *Voyages . . . dans L'Amérique septentrionale* (Travels in North America), an insightful account of his experiences there, including character sketches of Washington, and of Trumbull's father, the punctilious governor. The comte de Grasse would enjoy no victories after Yorktown. The British would beat him soundly in the Battle of the Saintes off Dominica the following year, a defeat that ended his career. He and Chastellux both died in 1788.

For the rest, the poses of the horses are varied and engaging (Trumbull felt no need to paint dead Britons to explain them). The flags of the victors—Trumbull has given the American flag three extra stripes—flap with carefree curls. A sedate background shows a rank of British prisoners, a bit of the York River, and the brick house that had been Cornwallis's headquarters until the allied bombardment forced him to retire to an underground grotto in the garden where, one assumes, he is still sulking. There is smoke in the sky, but also patches of blue.

If the Revolution had been only military, *Yorktown* would be a fitting end to Trumbull's series.

The Resignation of General Washington

Trumbull's series does not end, however, until he shows an event that happened two years and two months after *Yorktown*. What filled the interval?

Although George III, his ministers, and Parliament realized that the war in North America was lost, skirmishes, such as the one in which John Laurens lost his life, continued to occur. European powers meanwhile engaged in major battles. France, and Spain (which had joined the war as an ally of France, though not of the United States), made a plan to sweep Britain from the Caribbean. De Grasse's defeat at the Battle of the Saintes in April 1782 scotched that, and weakened France's hand in postwar negotiations.

The diplomats assembled in Paris disputed the shape of the postwar world. Spain coveted large tracts of what would become Alabama, Mississippi, and Kentucky. France also preferred an independent America that would be small; a runt country would need to rely on French friendship. On the other hand, Benjamin Franklin, America's senior negotiator, told the British that if they simply gave the Americans Canada, there could be no future occasions for Anglo-American conflict. A treaty awarding the new nation everything south of Canada, east of the Mississippi, and north of Florida and Spain's Gulf Coast, was finally signed in September 1783.

The American army's last encampment, at Newburgh, New York, was broken up, the quarters of the soldiers and officers sold to local farmers (a few buildings survived, as sheds and chicken coops, into the twentieth century). The British evacuated New York City at the end of November. Early the following month Washington bade farewell to a small group of officers at a tavern near the waterfront. He asked Congress what he was then to do, and was told to deliver to it the commission under which he served.

Congress had been on the move since June when an unruly crowd of junior officers surrounded the State House in Philadelphia, demanding to be paid. The lawmakers had decamped to Princeton, New Jersey, for four months, then settled in Annapolis in the Maryland State House, a handsome building on a small hill. Washington appeared there in the Senate Chamber on December 23, 1783.

The most affecting account of what happened was written by James McHenry, a thirty-year-old surgeon and veteran, then serving in the Maryland state senate. "To day my love," he wrote to his wife, "the General at a public audience made a deposit of his commission and in a very pathetic manner took leave of Congress. . . . The spectators all wept, and there was hardly a member of Congress who did not drop tears. The General's hand which held [his] address shook as he read it. . . . But when he commended the interests of his dearest country to almighty God, and those who had the superintendence of them to his holy keeping, his voice faltered and sunk, and the whole house felt his agitations. After the pause which was necessary for him to recover himself, he proceeded to say in the most penetrating manner, 'Having now finished the work assigned me I retire from the great theater of action.'"[10]

Trumbull had sketched the interior of the Senate Chamber in 1822. We are looking at the northwest wall. He has, however, simplified the room, banishing a window, a mantel, and a hanging portrait that might distract us from the main event, which is George Washington, center stage, delivering his commission. Behind and above Washington, to the right, is the visitors' gallery; ahead of him, on the left, is a shallow niche, in front of which the members of Congress sit or stand.[11]

Trumbull had trouble, so many years after the event, collecting likenesses of those who were present. A few—Thomas Jefferson, Elbridge Gerry—had served in the Congress that had signed the Declaration. A number of "ideal"—that is, made-up—heads had to be included, however, to populate the room.[12] One head—James Madison's, to the right of the left-most door—had been added even though he had been at home in Virginia at the time, because Trumbull wanted all the founding presidents depicted in his series, and all the Virginian presidents in this painting.

The painting is far from ideal (plate 10). The flaws that marred other pictures in his revolutionary series seem gathered in one spot. There is a line of ten heads running across the left background. Proportion and perspective are out of whack. The president of Congress, Thomas Mifflin, standing at the left edge, seems larger and therefore closer to us than the seated delegate who is in fact in front of him. Heads in the second rank of the group standing behind Washington seem smaller, and therefore farther from us, than the space of the room would allow. The colors are blunt and dull, the portraits undistinguished. The most disappointing likeness is Washington's. His eye sockets are dark, his chin jowly, his skin tone bland. He has been serving, it is true, for eight and a half years; he deserves to look tired. But Trumbull seems to have been more tired painting him than Washington was postwar.

The Resignation of General Washington is notable for two things. One is the presence of women. This is the first time that half of America appears in Trumbull's series.

There were women in the visitors' gallery that day; we have a letter from one of them, Mary Ridout, daughter of a former governor, whose description of the scene tracks McHenry's: the general "addressed Congress in a short speech but very affecting many tears were shed."[13]

Women's absence in Trumbull's earlier paintings is not altogether surprising. "There are certain appropriate duties assigned to each sex," wrote Mercy Otis Warren, a contemporary historian of the Revolution. "It is the more peculiar province of masculine strength ... to repel the bold invader of the rights of his country and of mankind."[14] At a time when armies were so composed, military paintings would naturally exclude women. Political paintings would exclude them too, for although intelligent, public-spirited women—like Mercy Otis Warren—commented on current events, they did not hold office. Yet here, in the visitors' gallery on the upper right, and on the floor of the chamber, are nine women, plus two girls. The girls are daughters of the congressman in the gray suit, Charles Carroll of Carrollton, who protectively clasps one of them. Carroll was a Maryland lawmaker and grandee. The girls are present as members of his family. Martha Washington, looming in the center of the visitors' gallery, is also obviously there as a family member, though her regular attendance on her husband at winter encampments of the army (including Valley Forge) entitle her to credit as an auxiliary in the struggle.

Who are the others? Left of Martha is her granddaughter Eleanor Custis, the child of her son by her first marriage (she and George had no offspring of their own). Left of Eleanor is Harriet Wadsworth, Trumbull's almost-fiancée.

These women were not at Annapolis. Martha and her family were awaiting George at Mount Vernon, Harriet lived with her family in Hartford. Trumbull introduces them to represent the everyday life of peace: what Washington is going back to (he would arrive home on Christmas Day); what Trumbull would not achieve for years after the war, and not with Harriet.

The other noteworthy feature of the picture is Washington's gesture of returning his commission, the reason for the painting. It is the one thing Trumbull has to get right, and he does.

A triangle of light, issuing from an unexplained source, points down toward Washington's outstretched right hand, which holds the commission. The white of the paper is picked up in his neckcloth, in the dresses of many of the women, and on the foreheads of a few congressmen, especially that of Jefferson, highlighted against the left jamb of the leftmost door in the wall.

John Holmes, a senator from Maine, complained in 1825 about the amount of money Congress had spent on Trumbull's Rotunda paintings, especially the life-size version of the *Resignation,* which he called "the most solemn daubing [I] ever saw. . . . What do you see in the picture? Why, a man looking like a little ensign, with a roll of paper in his hand, like an old newspaper, appearing as if he were saying, 'Here, take it—I don't want to give it up.' "

Holmes prefaced his remarks by saying that he "did not pretend to be a critic in painting."[15] He wasn't. Washington is saying, visually, *Here, take it,* because the commission is not his. It belongs to Congress, which assigned it to him for the performance of a task. The task performed, it returns to them. He has fought and won a war—all that he was asked to do, and only what he was asked.

There were those who wanted him to do more. Some months after Cornwallis's surrender at Yorktown, Lewis Nicola, an army colonel, had written Washington a private note recommending that he became a peacetime king. "This war must have shown to all, but to military men in particular, the weakness of republics. . . . the same abilities which have led us . . . to victory and glory . . . would be most likely to conduct and direct us in the smoother paths of peace."[16] Washington rejected Nicola's proposal with indignation. But he had received from parties more serious—his former aide, Alexander Hamilton, now a congressman—suggestions both more plausible and (because more subtle) more mischievous. The army, about to be disbanded with the arrival of peace, had yet to be paid; Congress needed to be reformed and strengthened. Might not Washington "guide the torrent, and bring order, perhaps even good, out of confusion"?[17]

In the *Resignation,* Trumbull placed on the chair behind Washington a reddish-purple cloak. It is wintertime, he will need to wrap up when he leaves. But it is important to the painting that he turns his back to it. Cloaks, and robes, were acknowledged artistic symbols, the trappings of emperors, and emperors-to-be; purple and red were the colors of majesty. Early in the nineteenth century, Trumbull's friend Jacques-Louis David created a stirring image of Napoleon, then First Consul of France, leading his army across the Alps to victories in Italy. David put him astride a rearing steed, pointing onward, a red cloak billowing round him. A few years later, David painted him, in a grander cloak yet, placing an imperial crown on his own head.

Not this general, not here, not ever. His job done, he will go home to his wife and his step-granddaughter.

The marquis de Chastellux, one of the French officers in *Yorktown,* understood politics, and greatness, better than his more famous countryman. In his memoirs of his time in North America, Chastellux wrote of Washington, "He has commanded the army, and ... he has obeyed Congress; more need not be said."[18]

And more need not be painted. The hero serves, the people's representatives rule. This is the end of Trumbull's series.

FOURTEEN

Each of Trumbull's eight revolutionary paintings tells a story. What story do they tell all together? How do they tell it?

The most obvious theme of the entire series is that revolution is hard. It is the parent and offspring of war. The state begins in violence.

Three of the paintings show battles, and one the immediate aftermath of another. These four condition our response to the two calmer images of military surrender that follow: we have seen these uniformed men, their mounts and their weapons, before, in action. They are not trying to kill each other now, at Saratoga and at Yorktown, but that is what they are equipped and drilled to do, and what they have been doing.

War is hard because defeats are inevitable. In *Bunker's Hill,* the very first picture, the enemy sweeps all before him; in *Quebec,* the second, we the heroes are about to retire in shock. Viewers in Trumbull's lifetime, and viewers who are history buffs today, know that the enemy's first depicted victory was Pyrrhic—the losses the British suffered in their first attempts to take Bunker's Hill would prey on the mind of their commander, Lord Howe, as long as he remained in America; while the American campaign against Quebec, two armies converging from hundreds of miles apart, was gallant—in Trumbull's catalogue for the Yale gallery, he compared Benedict Arnold's march across Maine "for brilliancy of conception and hardihood of attempt ... with the passage of the Alps by either the ancient or the modern Hannibal" (the modern Hannibal being Napoleon).[1] The paintings, however, don't show any of that. The British swarm up Bunker's Hill; the Americans at Quebec stand, at the edge of Stygian darkness, frozen as if by some destroying divine hand. What we see before our eyes is overthrow and loss.

Even victories are bought with injury and death. After Trenton, Lieutenant Monroe lies in a comrade's arms, helpless; Captain William Washington can stand, but shows his bandages. At Princeton, General Mercer, Lieutenant Neil, and other dying or dead Americans litter the field.

A secondary, subtler theme of the battle pictures is that, for all the carnage, the enemy cannot simply be hated. The British are relentless: grenadiers with the battle fury on them wield their bayonets when their side is winning (*Bunker's Hill*) and when it is losing (*Princeton*). But the British are not demonic. Trumbull may have miscalculated the degree of prominence he gave Major Small's gracious gesture to the dying General Warren at Bunker's Hill. But there are other enemy officers who obviously merit our sympathetic attention: the Hessian Colonel Rall after Trenton, Captain Leslie at Princeton.

Missing from Trumbull's battle paintings is the enemy as monster, or buffoon. He is not giving us propagandistic garbage of the sort churned out by cartoonists and designers of posters and placards, then and since. Trumbull's mentor Benjamin West tucked an image of that kind into one edge of his painting *The Battle of La Hogue*. On the right a British officer grips the coat of a bug-eyed Frenchman who has lost his hat and wig. *Ho ho, look at Frenchie run.* Trumbull eschews schoolyard emotions. His story is too serious for them.

Trumbull's series is not all military, however. Twice, a third of the way in and at the climax, we get images of politics. Congress in Philadelphia receives the Declaration of Independence, and Congress in Annapolis receives General George Washington's resignation. Thomas Jefferson, the star of the first painting, suggested the subject to Trumbull; Trumbull himself conceived of the second.

The *Declaration* is a painting of a theory. We cannot see any text, much less read it, but the kind of theory Congress has adopted is implied by Trumbull's composition. These men are representatives, chosen in the states that sent them by elected representatives. They are civilians, or, if any of them have had military experience, they are there in a civilian capacity. (George Washington, delegate from Virginia, had attended the Continental Congress wearing his old uniform from the French and Indian War, but he has already been sent, as commander in chief, to the front.) The men present have presumably talked and argued but now, apart from a few stray conversations, they are quiet and paying attention; they have made up their minds. They have deliberated.

They seem to be peers. The members of the drafting committee and the president of Congress are front and center, but they are of the same scale as their colleagues around and behind them. Their coats and shirtfronts, breeches and stockings, show no distinctions of rank: no jewels or ermines, such as decorate the necks and shoulders, painted and real, of royalty and nobility. (Jefferson has the best sense of color; John Dickinson, Quaker-adjacent, wears a hat.) Jefferson presents the paper he is holding alongside four apparent coauthors; they have evidently taken some time to produce it. ("Prudence, indeed, will dictate that Governments long established should not be changed for light and transient causes.") But now almost everyone in the room—Dickinson will hold out—is going to endorse what the paper says. ("For the support of this Declaration, with a firm reliance on the guidance of Providence, we mutually pledge to each other our Lives, our Fortunes and our sacred Honor.") The drums and flags hanging on the wall remind us of the men in the field, who have been risking, and losing, their lives. What the men in this room are doing is stating what the fight is for.

That is fine, and thanks to Jefferson's way with words, memorable. But how will it work out? The war had been going on for fifteen months when the Declaration was adopted; it would continue for more than five years until Yorktown, for more than seven until the last belligerents would go home. In that stress and strain, those defeats and victories and longueurs, what characters would emerge, what grudges or ambitions be nourished?

The Resignation of General Washington, at the end of the series, gives the answer. For all Washington's faltering as he made his remarks, and all the spectators' tears as they heard him, his words have not survived as Jefferson's have. His action does (or it deserves to). He comes before Congress as the man in uniform, attended by uniformed comrades. They bear the weight of battles and surrenders; they carry the memory of brothers who have not lived to see this day. (General Hugh

Mercer lived in Fredericksburg, Virginia, across the Rappahannock River from Washington's childhood home.) Politicians to the left, military men to the right: with just a little pictorial and historical tweaking, this could be an all-too-common scene, Cromwell and his men dismissing Parliament, Napoleon and his abolishing the Directory. *We have been bleeding while you were talking. We are force, we will now be law.*

But here the leader of the warriors gives to the men in civilian clothes what belongs to them, not to him: the authority to command and kill. He held it for a time, but it has always been theirs. Now it returns to them, until they should choose to assign it again. Senator Holmes compared Trumbull's Washington to "a little ensign." Once he turns to leave, he will not be even that; he will be a civilian once more.

The *Declaration* is theory; the *Resignation* is practice. The *Declaration* expresses the ideal. The *Resignation* shows it being made real.

Hence the prominence of the women and girls at the series' end. They are more than the heroes' reward. They represent the goal of the new nation as a whole, of any society worth defending. Revolutions deal in death, but if they do not bring peace and life, they amount to robbery and murder.

When the Capitol was to be built on its ashes after the War of 1812, Trumbull envisioned large versions of his series encircling the Rotunda like a patriotic panorama. That did not happen. So for Yale College he completed the series at his favorite, two-by-three-foot size, and hung the paintings on a single wall.

Painters had been experimenting with large-scale arrangements of images for centuries—arguably since primitive men covered cave walls with hunting scenes and hand prints. When Trumbull made his first trip to Paris, he saw at the Luxembourg Palace an entire gallery of enormous Rubenses depicting, one by one, episodes in the life of Marie de Medici, queen of France: birth, wedding to Henri IV, motherhood, political travails, ultimate apotheosis. One could read the story of her life, moving from painting to painting, as if turning pages in a book. Trumbull, amazed as he always was by Rubens, called the series "the empire of color, allegory, and composition."[2]

Trumbull's series is more modest in size, but more ambitious in scope: Rubens shows a queen adopting, and helping to rule, a great kingdom; Trumbull shows the birth of a new order of politics.

Trumbull weaves a composition with two melodies, military and congressional. The rhythm of it is 2 + 1 + 2 + 2 + 1. The military paintings appear in pairs: two defeats; two victories; two surrenders. They move from the chaos of collapse to the choreography of triumph. In the first pair of paintings, the rebels are smashed; in the second, they find their feet; in the third, the empire gives way. Meanwhile, on a parallel path, the singleton congressional paintings echo each other across the military scenes between them, forming a mirror image. This double take shows the form the liberated colonies will assume. In each scene, one individual adopts the *adlocutio* pose. Jefferson hands the Declaration of Independence to the right, Washington hands his commission to the left. Jefferson's gesture says, *This is ours.* Washington's, *This is yours.*

Trumbull eschews allegory; his idol Rubens surrounded Marie de Medici with crowds of gods, goddesses, graces, fates, and cupids; the most Trumbull ventures is a possibly divine ray of light. Trumbull's command of color weakens as the series proceeds (though it can shine as far along as Yorktown). His sense of composition carries him through, within each painting, and across them. The details of scale and portraiture waver, the broad outlines never.

Techniques of representation would change in ways Trumbull could not have imagined in the years after he finished his series—photography and motion pictures, obviously, but also different forms of printing. Trumbull's series anticipates the trailer of a movie, except that it includes a full conclusion, not just a teaser. It is also like the picture section of a book, whether history or biography, travel or natural history, in which the main points are illustrated. What it most resembles is the graphic novel. At Yale, Trumbull displayed a graphic epic.

What did Trumbull leave out?

In 1790 he projected six scenes that he never got around to painting: the treaty with France that brought her formally into the war; the Battle of Eutaw Springs in South Carolina, just before Yorktown; the Treaty of Paris, ending the war; the British evacuation of New York City in November 1783; Washington's reception at Trenton in 1789 as he rode to his first inauguration; and the inauguration itself.

Trumbull may have felt that the points to be made by these pictures were adequately covered by the paintings he completed. France's

role, which would be featured in the treaty scenes, was handsomely recognized in Yorktown, as was Britain's departure from our shores. The
images of war giving way to the peace of Washington's presidency had
been symbolized in the decisive moment of his resignation.

Eutaw Springs may have fallen by the wayside for a personal reason. Memorializing that battle would have implicitly rebuked Horatio
Gates, one of the two commanders Trumbull had served as aide. The
reason Nathanael Greene was commanding at Eutaw Springs was that
Gates had suffered ignominious defeat at Camden the year before.
Trumbull, so careful to praise Gates at Saratoga, may have been unwilling to criticize him, even indirectly. For whatever reason, Trumbull's war
stops at Virginia. The bitter campaign in the South drops out of his story,
as it has out of American popular memory.

Trumbull's story is overwhelmingly a story of leaders: officers, and
political officeholders. He tells a top-down tale, reflecting his own experience as a colonel, an aide-de-camp, and a governor's son. There are
more foreign officers in his paintings, both allies and enemies, than
American enlisted men. Trumbull cared, even obsessively, about recording actual faces. These tended to be the faces of the prominent; ordinary
folk get noticed only on the occasion of some unusual action by or in-
volving them. The women and girls at Annapolis mark a late turn away
from elite men, but only as far as elite women.

Blacks and Indians make token appearances—Asaba and a
faint Peter Samuel in *Bunker's Hill*, Joseph Louis Cook in *Quebec*.
Blacks, free and enslaved, and Indian nations played roles in the Revolution. The British tried, with some success, to lure the slaves of patriots
to defect and take up arms against their former masters. Patriots, to
a lesser extent, profited from enlisting free blacks, and from slaves serving in their masters' places. Indian alliances were a factor in several
theaters: the Iroquois Confederacy of western New York fought for
the British, except for the Oneidas, who took the American side. (Colonel Louis, the Abenaki-turned-Mohawk, was a freelance.) Trumbull
includes men of color, but minimally. He had painted a fanciful William
Lee, Washington's slave and personal servant throughout the war, in
his first portrait of the commander in chief, but never depicted him
again.

Loyalists are entirely missing from Trumbull's story. You would not guess, from his paintings, that, as John Adams said, a third of the American people supported the Revolution, a third opposed it, and a third were neutral. Adams's breakdown is endlessly quoted because it is pithy, and because no one has better numbers (Adams was just guessing). Trumbull may have ignored the Loyalists because there were so few of them in Connecticut (although they could be ferocious: his father had been threatened with assassination). Patriotism and Puritanism held his home state in their grip.

The thing most strikingly missing from his series, because it was so ubiquitous and so obvious in so many of the events he portrays, is blood. The first American casualty at Bunker's Hill was a militiaman decapitated by a cannonball, "so near me," Colonel William Prescott recalled, "that my clothes were besmeared with his blood and brains which I wiped off, in some degree, with a handful of fresh earth."[3] At wintry Princeton, said an anonymous sergeant, "the ground was frozen and all the blood which was shed remained on the surface."[4] Trumbull shows bodies in every attitude of death, kneeling, falling, twisted, prone, stepped on. Yet the only blood he shows us is a trickle from the neck of General Mercer's mount in *Princeton,* and a trace on Captain William Washington's bandaged hand in *Trenton.* General Montgomery, killed in *Quebec* by a blast of grape shot, wears a uniform that looks as if it had been freshly laundered. Trumbull's tidiness is an aesthetic, and beyond that a psychological choice. Even in religious art, where the blood of Christ and of martyrs has theological significance, painters traditionally titrated their doses. Goethe praised Trumbull's skill in handling red uniforms. Red blood would be too shocking. Art, even realistic art, can bear only so much reality.

In 1827, irked by criticisms of his paintings in the Rotunda, Trumbull drafted a letter defending his project to freshman congressman Edward Everett of Massachusetts. "It seems to be supposed that historical painters abound in this country," Trumbull began testily. "Talent does indeed abound. . . . Portrait painters are many, but the difference between portrait and historical painting is almost the same as that between a cabinet-maker and an architect."[5] The first may do exquisite details, but only the second—that is, Trumbull himself—can manage the grand design.

He then ran through his peers—his old friend from West's studio, Gilbert Stuart; other students of West, including William Dunlap; Thomas Sully, whom Trumbull had instructed; Charles Willson Peale and his son Rembrandt. Some of these were portraitists; "in that branch of the profession," Trumbull wrote handsomely, "the name of Stuart stands almost without a rival, in this or any country, or in any age." Some of them had done individual historical paintings of revolutionary events. The elder Peale had filled a museum in Philadelphia with images of America's founders (as well as stuffed animals, and a mastodon skeleton).[6] But, Trumbull concluded, "from among all these you find not one instance of any attempt to record the glory of our country."[7] *My fellow painters have given us faces, even an event or two. Only I have told the story.*

Among his revolutionary paintings in his gallery, Trumbull hung another work, not belonging to the series, but related to it, and commenting on it. This is the life-size standing portrait of George Washington that Trumbull painted in Philadelphia in 1792 (plate 11).

This was the image, commissioned by the city of Charleston, that was declined on completion on the grounds that it was too eventful. Trumbull gave the Charlestonians a simpler portrait—"calm, tranquil, peaceful"—and kept the first one, giving it to the Connecticut branch of the Society of the Cincinnati.[8] Yale bought it from them for Trumbull's gallery.

Its title is *General George Washington at Trenton,* though what it depicts is a night scene a week after the Battle of Trenton, when the British under Lord Cornwallis have retaken the town and cornered Washington and his army, as they think, on the far side of Assunpink Creek, which runs into the Delaware River to the south. There had been a sharp skirmish at dusk for possession of the one bridge across. American muskets and artillery had held the British off, but the enemy was confident they could outflank the Americans by fording the Assunpink upstream in the morning. Conferring with his officers, Washington decided to foil them by a night march, via back roads, toward Princeton to the north.

Trumbull explained in his catalogue that he wanted to paint Washington in this situation in order to represent "his military character in the most sublime moment of its exertion. ... I told the president my object [Washington was in his first term when he posed]; he entered into it warmly, and, as the work advanced, we talked of the scene, its dangers, its almost desperation." Desperate indeed. Only a drop in temperature that night had allowed New Jersey's muddy roads to freeze, making a march of any speed possible. Meanwhile the enemy would have to be deceived by lit campfires, suggesting that the Americans had stayed put. As painter and subject talked, Washington "*looked* the scene again, and I happily transferred to the canvas, the lofty expression of his animated countenance, the high resolve to conquer or to perish."⁹ Those were the options. After four months of disasters, Washington had won a surprise victory at Trenton. He was now about to extend his streak to two, or throw it all away.

He stands, all six feet plus of him. Behind him is the iconography of catastrophe. All the elements are there. Darkness and smoke, tinged with red. (Sunset? The sun had already gone down.) In the far distance, points of light. (Enemy campfires, or enemy musket flashes?) An American gun crew is working their cannon. Closer to us, a barrel, dismounted from its carriage, lies on the ground, useless. The blasted tree of *Quebec* has come south and looms behind Washington's head, like a witch. To his left, a dragoon struggles with a horse. This animal is rearing, frightened. *Where is my rider? What is happening to me?*

Washington stands in front of all this, close enough to us that by stretching we could shake his hand, if he were in a hand-shaking mood. He wears a uniform fit for a formal dinner, an expression fit for his predicament. He is determined, concentrating; has decided to act, is about to act. The seals dangling on a ribbon below his waistcoat gesture discreetly toward the neighborhood of his crotch: he is the Father of His Country. Let the art historians decode that; there won't be a country if he doesn't get the job done now. Time to move.

The risk of sandwiching this large painting, eight-and-a-half by five feet, into a series of paintings less than half that size is to tilt the whole group in Washington's direction. Along with *Trenton, Princeton, Yorktown,* and the *Resignation,* he now appears in more than half the canvases. As an old man John Adams feared that the executive summary of Revolution would be that Benjamin Franklin struck the ground with his electric rod, and out sprang George Washington, leaving everyone else (especially John Adams) in the shade. Here, minus Franklin's rod, it almost comes to pass.

The activity and the number of other characters in the smaller paintings that include Washington tug the viewer away from that mistake. So does his gesture in this life-size image. It is what is by now our old friend, the *adlocutio.* Here Washington's right arm holds out a spyglass. There is every reason for him to have one, even though it is now night. Come the morning, if he ever gets to Princeton, he may need it, perhaps to see what is happening with General Mercer in his rear.

The gesture points to the moment he is in, and is addressed to the viewer in the future. See where we were; see what we had to do.

When the painting is hung, as Trumbull hung it, with its eight cousins, Washington is saying much more. See the entire story. *We had to lose and die, kill and succor. We had to be bold and generous, thoughtful and consistent. When we wrote new rules, we had to follow them ourselves. When we were done, we went home, to normal life—the life we wanted, the life we wanted for you. We did this; some day, you may have to.*

After forty-five years, Trumbull found his wall and made it tell a story.

FIFTEEN

In Trumbull's letter to Representative Everett, defending the Rotunda versions of his series, he had identified himself as "President of one of the principal academies of the fine arts in this country," as if he could not make an argument without calling the roll of his achievements.[1] He had been president of the American Academy of the Fine Arts for a decade and a half when his gallery at Yale opened. His tenure had been an honor, recognizing his preeminence among American artists. But as the years passed, it had increasingly become a source of discord.

The Academy, since its inception, was run by its stockholders, all civic leaders, either actual officeholders or public-spirited rich men; Trumbull's predecessor as president had been the archetypal Gotham statesman and wire-puller DeWitt Clinton. With Trumbull the Academy acquired the sheen of an actual artist at the helm. It also gained Trumbull's energy and commitment; Clinton had been more interested in running for governor and promoting the Erie Canal. Trumbull, for his part, gained an annuity of $900, in return for giving the Academy a cache of paintings, his own and a few of his European acquisitions (including the supposed Raphael).

One function of the Academy, as with the Royal Academy in London, was to educate artists and the public. Sir Joshua Reynolds, the Royal Academy's first president, had done this with annual lectures, or discourses, which he then published. Trumbull did not follow suit. He and the painters who most inspired him—West and Copley—had in fact violated Reynolds's rules for history painting, with their details of uniforms and weapons, geography and local color. So, tacitly, had Reynolds himself when he praised the results they had achieved. Trumbull taught not by theorizing, but by doing, and by showing what he had done.

Trumbull could be helpful to beginners whom he met one-on-one—more helpful, certainly, than Reynolds had been to him. In the early 1820s Thomas Cole, an untrained immigrant from England, showed three paintings he had done of upstate New York scenery in the window of a bookstore on Broadway. Trumbull, happening to see them, bought one for twenty-five dollars, and brought Asher Durand, the engraver of his Rotunda paintings, and William Dunlap to admire the young talent; they bought the other two canvases.[2] Cole showed regularly at the American Academy after that. Trumbull's appreciation of him was the more generous because Cole was working in a genre, landscape, that Trumbull himself had tried and dropped, except as a background for *Saratoga*.

But if younger artists at the Academy pushed or pressed Trumbull beyond the bounds of what he considered proper, he could be as stiff as in his letter to Edward Everett.

Beginning artists were allowed to come to the Academy between six and nine in the morning to draw its casts of ancient statuary. The curator, however, opened up when he felt like it. One morning in the mid-1820s two young artists, finding the door shut, turned away. A director of the Academy and Trumbull himself then appeared on the scene. (Trumbull was arriving to work in the room allotted to him; the director was walking by. New York City was still small enough for such encounters to happen spontaneously.) The curator opened the door to the president, whereupon the director remarked that the young artists who had just left had not been so lucky. Trumbull replied that when he was starting out there were no casts in the country at all: "I was obliged to do as well as I could." Casts cost money, which had been provided by the Academy's patrons. "*The gentlemen,*" as Trumbull put it, "have gone to a great expense" to acquire them. As for the young learners, "they must remember that beggars are not to be choosers."[3]

Trumbull may have had the Academy's finances on his mind because his deal for an annuity had recently fallen through; the Academy lacked sufficient funds to pay him, so the collection of paintings he had donated reverted to him. Whatever his reasons, Trumbull would come to regret the scene at the door.

In 1826, nine years into his tenure, disgruntled New York artists formed a rival group, called the National Academy of Design. Its declared intent was to provide an academy for artists, run by artists themselves. They would be their own choosers, beggars no more.

An equally powerful impetus for the National Academy was ambition. Trumbull had turned seventy in 1826. How long did he intend to hang on? The first president of the new group, Samuel Finley Breese Morse, was thirty-five years Trumbull's junior. In his later years Morse would pursue two careers: inventing the telegraph, and churning out anti-Catholic polemics. On a trip to Naples, he wrote the first description by an American of pizza which, along with those who ate it and the religion they professed, he loathed: "a species of most nauseating looking cake . . . like a piece of bread that had been taken reeking out of the sewer."[4] But before he took up those vocations, Morse was a painter, whose portraits have a quirky interest.

Morse originally aspired to become president of the American Academy himself. "Colonel T—— is growing old," he wrote his wife in 1823. "I may possibly be promoted to his place."[5] That had not happened, so Morse and his peers simply created a new place for themselves.

The two academies existed side by side, attempts to rejoin them foundering on the issue of who should rule, stockholders or artists. The American Academy, shrugging off the defection, built an exhibit space all its own on Barclay Street, around the corner from its previous home at the Institution of Learned and Scientific Societies. Trumbull designed this building, a functional three-story structure with skylights on the top floor.

By the 1830s Trumbull could expect to enjoy a golden old age, and a golden reputation. Yale ensured him the annuity the American Academy had failed to provide. His life's project had been teased in the Capitol Rotunda, and fully realized at his gallery in New Haven. In 1834, however, he found himself attacked, not by ignorant congressmen, but by a fellow artist and longtime acquaintance, William Dunlap.

Trumbull and Dunlap had known each other since the 1780s, when they met in London studying under Benjamin West. They shared, in addition to their interest in painting, a disability: Dunlap had lost his sight in his right eye in a childhood accident.

Dunlap was younger than Trumbull by a decade, born and raised in Perth Amboy, New Jersey. His family were Loyalists; his father had fought in the ranks under Wolfe at the Battle of Quebec. Perhaps in reaction, the son became a full-throated American patriot, painting when he was only seventeen a portrait of George Washington. When the adult Dunlap found that painting could not support him, he turned to the theater, managing companies in New York.

American theater at that turn of the century was a rough-and-ready world. Drunks demanding popular songs disrupted performances; the holders of cheap tickets in the galleries bombarded the prosperous patrons in the orchestra with fruit, vegetables, and other missiles. "They are only amusing themselves a little at our expense," an experienced playgoer told a young Washington Irving. "Sit down quietly and bend your back to it."[6] A traveling star from England—or so the yokels would consider him—might hold the audience enthralled for an evening, but after a binge the next day would forget all his lines on his second night.

To expand the repertoires of his troupes beyond the staples of the day—Shakespeare and Addison, *The School for Scandal* and *The Beaux' Stratagem*—Dunlap became a playwright, churning out farces, melodramas, history pieces, tragedies. After a success with a version of a play by August von Kotzebue, a then-popular German dramatist, he decided he had better study the language in earnest and work the lode. A rush of German translations followed. Whenever the theater turned temporarily fallow, he returned to his brush, painting portrait miniatures or scenes from the life of Christ. Trumbull's survey of American history painters, written for Everett, mentions him. "William Dunlap, N.Y. Studied a short time under Mr. West, in early life, left the pursuit of the arts for many years and engaged in . . . literature, the theater, etc.; a few years ago resumed the pencil and has painted several historical pictures, generally ancient and sacred subjects, which have been generally seen, but has made no attempt at modern history so far as I know."[7] In addition to all this activity Dunlap kept a diary, copious even though many of its volumes have been lost. He had great energy and some ability. In an age when American society had more money to spend on culture, he would have found some sinecure, academic or journalistic.

In 1834 Dunlap produced a three-volume work entitled *A History of the Rise and Progress of the Arts of Design in the United States.* Judged by his resume, Dunlap was the perfect man for the job. He had been in and out of the art world for most of his life, knew most of the major players personally, and lived in New York City, one of the country's art hubs, such as they then were. What he did not know firsthand, he picked up from investigation, or from gossip.

Dunlap could tell a story, and his account of Trumbull is decorated with a number of them, from different phases of the artist's life. He told of Trumbull's first meeting with Copley when the youngster was on his way to Harvard: Copley's "high repute as an artist" and the "elegance displayed ... in his style of living" made a "permanent impression in favor of the life of a painter."[8] He described Trumbull and Stuart in London, playing their flutes together, and Stuart's humorous explanation of how their master, West, painted hair.[9] He gave an account of Trumbull's efforts to display a panorama of Niagara Falls in London, and of Trumbull discovering Thomas Cole in a New York bookshop; Dunlap indeed was the first person Trumbull told of the new talent.[10] Another event at which Dunlap was present, unfortunately, was the scene at the door of the American Academy when the young artists were turned away, and Trumbull said "beggars are not to be choosers." "We may consider this," Dunlap concluded sternly, "as the condemnatory sentence of the American Academy of the Fine Arts."[11] (Dunlap was a charter member of the National Academy of Design.)

When it came to aesthetic judgment, Dunlap varied condemnation with bright bits of praise. *Bunker's Hill* and *Quebec* were "beautiful pictures," the "composition, coloring and touch" of the first "admirable," and the chiaroscuro in the second "perfect."[12] He called the small portraits in the *Declaration* and *Yorktown* "among the most admirable miniatures in oil that ever were painted," and even professed to like *The Woman Taken in Adultery.*[13]

On the whole, however, Dunlap judged Trumbull to be both disappointing and misguided. He burned out young, and his theory of history painting was wrong. Dunlap flayed the technique of paintings that was in fact weak. In the Rotunda canvases, "the touch and the coloring were not there." *Saratoga* showed "a lamentable falling off," the *Resignation* was "still worse."[14] He attacked a painting that was splendid: the standing portrait of Washington after Trenton "has not a feature like the hero."[15] Not a feature, except for the face, the form, the expression, and the character.

Even the paintings Dunlap reckoned beautiful failed because of Trumbull's mistaken intentions. Dunlap offered two sorts of criticism of these. One deserves serious consideration, and that is that Trumbull, although claiming to record actual events, got details wrong. The site of General Montgomery's death in Quebec hangs in space, whereas in fact the Americans were stopped by the cannon's blast on a cliff-side street of the lower town. If the painterly historian, wrote Dunlap, "cannot tell the whole truth, he must at least not violate the known truth."[16]

This assumed that history paintings should aspire to the condition of photography (as of 1834, barely invented yet). To present an event, they must show accurate details. But to convey the context and the meaning, they will introduce elements that no eye could have seen at any one time. That might include, as in *Quebec,* stripping scenery away to highlight the actors; it might mean, as in the *Declaration,* assembling all the signers in a complete, though imagined tableau.

Dunlap's second criticism was simply stupid—patriotic fustian. Trumbull claimed to be the bard of the American Revolution, yet, Dunlap chided, he had painted British victories. *Bunker's Hill* depicted "the moment of the overthrow of [Trumbull's] countrymen, and the triumph of their enemies." *Quebec* showed "another triumph of Britain over America." West had shown Wolfe at Quebec, expiring at the moment of victory; Trumbull's dying men, by contrast, were "nothing more than—dying men."[17]

To which, one can only say: good men die in wars; defeats are the price of victory. The critic needs to grow up.

Dunlap had obviously been offended by Trumbull's toploftiness in running the American Academy. The governor's son took his presidential prerogatives too seriously. The man who had resigned his colonel's commission because Congress misdated a promotion would not take guff from art students.

But there was a deeper source of Dunlap's dislike—envy. Trumbull was a legacy child: "emphatically well-born ... reap[ing] as is generally the case, through life, the advantages resulting from the accident."[18] Money had been showered on him. "No American painter has ever received from government such patronage as Mr. Trumbull."[19] His end would be as easy as his beginning: the Yale annuity, plus his army pension, will "afford those comforts and enjoyments which old age so much requires to smooth the passage to the tomb."[20] What Dunlap said was true, which only made it harder for him to bear. Trumbull was a gentleman who never lived below his station, though often beyond his means, and the federal government had honored and rewarded him above all other American painters. The freelancer, hustling from opening night to opening night and canvas to canvas, could not forgive him for his good fortune.

If anyone ever taxed Dunlap about his portrayal of Trumbull, he might have answered that the half was not told, for his diary contained a trove of gossip about Trumbull's wife: King's surprise at the rush job of the wedding ceremony, the rumors that Sarah was Lord Thurlow's love child.[21] These tidbits went decorously unmentioned in the *History.* Dunlap did not wish to injure the dead, only to defame the living.

Trumbull's friends rallied round him. Philip Hone, a wealthy art patron, and former mayor of New York, wrote to Trumbull that, although he had found "some entertainment" in Dunlap's book, he was "vexed and annoyed" by the "bad temper which characterizes every page of it. . . . I was willing to make some allowance for the irascibility of an old man, who has not always been on the sunny side of the hill; but the ill-natured remarks in which he has indulged [and] his bad feelings towards you, have excited my indignation."[22]

Benjamin Silliman, Trumbull's attentive nephew by marriage, offered more concrete solace. He had been suggesting for years that Trumbull write his memoirs. In a letter of 1828 he had laid out the reasons. Trumbull's memoirs would benefit posterity. "Few of the accomplished gentlemen of talent and experience of the old school are left . . . and when they are gone the treasure of knowledge which they possess, unless previously secured, will be irrecoverably lost." Memoirs would also benefit Trumbull's reputation. "Such a work, in connection with and in illustration of the productions of your pencil, would associate your memory with the most interesting period of American history." Memoirs were another form of dissemination and brand-building, like prints. Trumbull could tell readers and future readers what he had seen, and his words would increase the fame of his paintings, and his standing as a participant and witness.

Silliman proposed to ease the process of writing by offering his home in New Haven as a one-man writer's colony. "This house would be at your service . . . while engaged in your literary labor, and all the assistance from books which we, or the college, or the town could furnish would be accessible to you."[23]

So long as Trumbull was angling to fill the Rotunda, or striking his paintings-for-annuity deal with Yale, he put off embarking on such a project. Dunlap's attack gave him the necessary prod.

In previous quarrels, from wrangling with Congress over his promotion to wrangling with congressmen who disliked his Rotunda paintings, he had sent, or sometimes only drafted, combative, self-justifying letters. One of them had been addressed to John Randolph, who, Trumbull imagined, might top his shin-piece insult by challenging him to a duel (the eccentric Virginian had provoked a duel with Henry Clay). Trumbull readied a grand brush-off: "I beg leave to say . . . that I have done with fighting. The last of my fields was on Quaker Hill . . . the day after the siege of Newport was raised." *Don't trifle with me, young civilian.* Trumbull never had occasion to deliver it; even Randolph was not eccentric enough to duel a septuagenarian.[24]

Dunlap's pages of rancor required a real answer, at book length. Trumbull would not reply directly to his tormentor, or even mention him at all, but simply and with dignity remind the world who he was and what he had done.

Silliman readied his home for his uncle. He and his wife lived in a two-story clapboard house a fifteen-minute walk north of the Yale campus. To accommodate Trumbull he added a gallery, fifty feet long and thirteen-and-a-half feet wide, atop the wood shed at the back of the main house. This extension was divided into two rooms by a chimney and closets. Trumbull could paint in the longer of the two, and read and write in the smaller.[25]

Trumbull left New York City for New Haven in July 1837. He had resigned as president of the American Academy the year before, leaving it in the capable hands of Rembrandt Peale, second son of Charles Will-son Peale. (Peale's brothers also included a Raphaelle, a Titian, and a Rubens—an entire gallery at home.)

New Haven, at over ten thousand souls, was the largest city in Con-necticut, attracting factories and Irish immigrants. Trumbull would be spending his time not on shop floors or in the newly built Catholic church, but with the city's elite, formerly defined by religion and politics—which, in New Haven, had meant Congregationalism and Federalism—now also marked by its cultural engagement, centered on Yale College, though not restricted to it: Silliman's public chemistry lec-tures were only one among several forms of adult education that civic-minded New Havenites enjoyed. Trumbull was entering a small, earnest, attentive world.

He debarked from the steamboat at the city wharf in style, accom-panied by seven truckloads of boxes, many of them filled with books; his clothes and his bed were still to come. "Your Papa," Silliman's wife wrote to their daughters, "went down to the boat to meet [Uncle Trumbull] and bring him up and we waited dinner for him. . . . He now seems to be in earnest about making this his home."[26]

Silliman, while offering his uncle every convenience, put him to work, for Yale and for himself. Trumbull gave lectures to the students about his pictures, laughing at what he called his new "trade." He also gave readings from his autobiography, as he wrote it, to Silliman's inti-mates. The Hillhouses and the Whitneys, whose names decorate New Haven's history and streets, would come by Saturday evenings to listen to Trumbull's latest pages until nine o'clock, when the author would serve his audience grapes and champagne; the Sillimans supplied cake. "Very pleasant little meetings," one of the Silliman daughters called them.[27]

Trumbull relished these performances. Like many authors, he found that reading aloud what he had written helped him write. He also enjoyed being the center of attention, the grand old man. The shy boy who had never been a public speaker had become a good conversation-alist. Well-connected, well-traveled, widely read, he had met everyone and had opinions on everything. He could say it all now to these inter-ested, intelligent, and respectable folk without fear of contradiction from blustering Virginians, or of embarrassment from a beloved but difficult wife. "He was particularly acceptable," Silliman noted, "to ladies of refinement and cultivation, whom he, in turn, greatly admired."[28]

During his New Haven years Trumbull continued to paint, and think about painting. When Daniel Wadsworth had proposed a second Trumbull gallery in Hartford, in addition to the one at Yale, Trumbull had made two large copies of *Trenton* and *Princeton* for permanent installation there. These were half life-size (half the scale of the Rotunda images). Once Wadsworth suggested rotating the original small versions between the two galleries, Trumbull put his foot down, and the Hartford scheme collapsed. But he continued to paint half life-size replicas of the *Declaration, Bunker's Hill,* and *Quebec.* Trumbull thought they were better than his small originals. They are not: they are dark and dull, as if seen through colored glass (or faded talent). They did allow him to fix a mistake: the wall of the Assembly Room directly facing us in his third version of the *Declaration* is rendered with one door, not two. So the floor plan Jefferson had sketched for him in Paris almost half a century earlier was finally corrected. Although he painted no more revolutionary replicas after 1834, he continued to hope that some public building might buy them for display, and allow him to paint the remaining three.

Two paintings he did do in New Haven were sacred, not secular. Like the replicas, they were based on some very old work of his.

Timothy Dwight, educator and clergyman, although born in Massachusetts, had a family connection to Yale: his maternal grandfather was the theologian Jonathan Edwards, Yale class of 1722. Dwight became president of the college in 1795—he was the man who hired Silliman to teach chemistry—serving until his death in 1817, when Trumbull painted a memorial portrait of him (unfortunately he did an inert, brownish job).

Among Dwight's talents was versifying. Several of his hymns found popular favor, and one short poem, "The Smooth Divine," is an effective satire of oleaginous clergymen who never offend their flocks (unlike Dwight himself, whose theology was rough, rigid orthodoxy).

Early in his career, in 1785, Dwight wrote an epic poem in eleven books, *The Conquest of Canäan,* recounting the battles of the Book of Joshua, in which Israel subdued its promised land. Dwight compared this struggle to the Revolutionary War, and included a flash-forward vignette of the Battle of Bunker's Hill, and a prophecy of America's future greatness.

It is a dreadful poem, imitating the dullest battle scenes in *Paradise Lost,* which themselves imitate the dullest battle scenes in the *Aeneid,* all squeezed through an eighteenth-century sieve of heroic couplets.

From this mess Trumbull lit upon two lines, describing Joshua at the siege and destruction of the Canaanite city of Ai.

> From glowing eyeballs flashed his wrath severe
> Grim death before him hurl'd his murdering spear.[29]

Trumbull sketched a scene suggested by these lines in 1786. Fifty years later, he wrote to Silliman to say that he had "found courage to commence a picture of it," *Joshua at the Battle of Ai—Attended by Death,* which he managed to finish while he was in New Haven.[30]

Joshua and the Israelites roll in from the left, their Canaanite victims reel back on the right. Behind Joshua, stride for stride, comes Death, a bright-white skeleton. Skulls were a popular memento mori in religious art and secular still lifes. Skeletons may seem odd as action figures in realistic art, even realistic allegory, because, in most people's experience, they do not actually move under their own power. But Trumbull's skeleton brims with energy—his right hand balances a substantial spear, five feet long by the look of it—and even wit: one foot treads on the body of a Canaanite, as if to say, *Stay down, dead guy!* A black cloak billowing behind him highlights his bright bone-tone. The out-there literalism with which he was drawn anticipates horror comics before the congressional hearings of the 1950s reined them in.

A second late picture of Trumbull's, realizing an equally early sketch, was inspired by the Flood in Genesis. *The Last Family Who Perished in the Deluge* shows a tiny, box-like Noah's ark, floating to safety in the left background. We hardly notice it, because the entire foreground is filled with the titular family, gathered on the last dry rock left on earth: a mother, exhausted and in shock, cradling a dead infant in her lap; a husband toppling, at her feet, headfirst into the rising waters; behind her, a white-haired patriarch, gesturing at the lightning-charged sky. Trumbull's notes to the Yale gallery explain that he is praying for immediate destruction.[31] Trumbull made the sketch in 1786 and the painting in New Haven.

He had seen an image of the Deluge by Nicolas Poussin at the Louvre the year he did his sketch, though his praise of it was tepid ("generally considered a very fine work"), and his own composition does not resemble it.[32] A more likely model for one detail—the long neck of the grieving mother—can be found in a Virgin by the Italian Renaissance painter Parmigianino, although when one looks at the neck Trumbull painted one cannot help recalling Sarah's lovely neck in her portrait with the spaniel.[33] Trumbull had still to meet Sarah when he did his sketch; evidently women's necks and throats, the longer the better, were features that he liked, in the flesh and on canvas.

Both New Haven paintings reflect Trumbull's time of life when he did them. When Silliman met him at the New Haven wharf he had just turned eighty-one. *The Last Family* shows the ages of man—infancy, prime, and old age, Trumbull's own. Only the man in the last phase is still—for the moment—viable. And of *Joshua at the Battle of Ai,* Trumbull could say, when Death finally came for him, *I have painted your portrait.*

His main task in New Haven, however, was writing. He had begun his memoirs in New York City. He would not need to borrow many books, from the college or the town: his own library held over five hundred volumes. He had also brought with him a mass of correspondence and an old journal, which he drew on liberally.

He worked away in New Haven for three years, and finished his manuscript after moving back to New York City in 1840. The Sillimans had done for him all that he could have asked, but at age eighty-four he wanted to live near his New York doctor. "He walks out when the weather will admit," wrote Silliman, still solicitous. He no longer painted, for "he does not allow himself to use [his eyes] much as all their strength is required to correct the proofs of his book which is now printing. . . . The interest and excitement caused by its progress will help keep up his spirits and energy."[34]

The Autobiography, Reminiscences and Letters of John Trumbull, from 1756 to 1841, was published by Wiley and Putnam, a New York publishing house that had a branch in London—the first ever for an

American publisher. The *Autobiography* ran to 294 pages of text, plus a 140-page appendix of letters and documents, beginning with William Kneeland reporting to the governor about young John at Harvard, and ending with the old artist cataloguing his works at the Trumbull Gallery at Yale. There were also twenty-three illustrations. The price was steep, as befitted an art book—three dollars a copy.

Trumbull was a raconteur, and his book was studded with anecdotes that had, after long thought and no doubt many verbal iterations, become set pieces. Most detail his life as an artist: copying his sister's productions on the parlor floor; his first meeting with Copley; his father informing him that Connecticut was not Athens; Joshua Reynolds unwittingly admiring his coloring; his visual education in the palaces and galleries of Paris; painting President Washington. Some anecdotes are of wider historical interest: Trumbull gives us the most dramatic account we have of Alexander Hamilton and Aaron Burr on the eve of their final interview.

His descriptions of Bunker's Hill and the aftermath of Quebec are nowhere near as vivid as the paintings he made of those battles; they are remote views only, necessarily so, given how far he had been from the action. But they are tiles, small but real, in the collective memory mosaic of those events.

His account of his arrest in London is a case study in miniature of the operation of arbitrary power. His experience cannot compare with the arrest, imprisonment, and escape of Casanova as described in his own memoirs, an account from Trumbull's era; still less with the survivors' stories of the camps and killing fields of our era. Trumbull, given his own connections and the decency of most of his captors, was never in real danger. But features of his ordeal—the shock, the disorientation, the depression, the boredom; the combination of fruitless appeals and arbitrary bursts of good luck—ring true to the experience of countless others who suffered far worse. They offer a primer of life gone wrong under the modern state.

He included twenty pages of description, taken from a journal, of a trip he took down the Rhine and through the Low Countries in 1786, after leaving Jefferson and the Cosways in Paris—a long holiday detour on his way back to London. It is eighteenth-century wallpaper, as charming as it is thin: a young man in new places, the weather, the women, the palaces, the inns; tiny mishaps, little adventures.

One thread that runs through the volume is Trumbull's interest in Indians, from his childhood temptation of Zachary, through his sketching of the Creek negotiators, to his suggestion that Washington help place an Aztec and an Inca on the thrones of Mexico and Peru. His language is stagy, invoking the stock character of the noble savage, sometimes weighted toward nobility, as in Zachary's reproof, sometimes toward savagery, as when the Creeks marvel at two-dimensional representation. His pencil sketches of the Creeks, reproduced in the volume and bristling with personality, improve and correct his choice of words.

Unfortunately, Trumbull's book is full of gaps. Their absence is felt as a presence, unbalancing the entire narrative, as in a building whose architect forgot to add enough walls. After the death of his father, his family disappears. There is not one word about John Ray— understandable, given the conventions of the day. But his brother the governor, his nieces, the loyal Silliman are almost never mentioned either. He only describes his wife—"beautiful beyond the usual beauty of women!"—when she dies.[35]

Long years and many acquaintances slide by uncharacterized. The Trumbull who recorded his Rhine journey could have evoked teeming London, deadly Bath, brash New York. Dear friends, like Christopher Gore and Rufus King, and famous ones, like Lafayette, are mere wraiths. But Trumbull had kept no notes of these places and people, and he had, by his early eighties, lost the power to bring them back to life.

In their places he quoted dull documents at dull length: long details of his work on the Anglo-American claims commission, an excerpt from the French historian Adolphe Thiers to establish how awful the French Revolution was. Instead of solid structure, he patched up tar paper.

He had no editor. He talked the work over with Silliman, and let him read the proofs. But the nephew admired the grand old man too much to make serious suggestions—"I found little to correct, and rarely ventured to expunge."[36] The work was published as Trumbull wrote it.

A twentieth-century editor managed to make the *Autobiography* digestible only by adding an armature of footnotes and appendices almost as long as the text itself. It fails, therefore, at its intended purpose, as a draw for Trumbull's paintings. Readers seek it out only if they are already interested in the artist. They find a disorganized warehouse, containing a number of interesting items.

Trumbull's last days in New York City were spent in the boarding-house he had occupied before moving to New Haven, near the home of his doctor, James Washington. Dr. Washington was a very distant cousin of George, and had met Lafayette while studying medicine in Paris. So the old colonel enjoyed pleasing associations as well as medical advice.

One of his late visitors, before he left New Haven, was Sylvester Genin, a young Ohioan with an interest in the arts. Genin studied the paintings in the Trumbull Gallery, and called on the artist to ask for advice on how to become a painter. Trumbull gave him precise practical tips: in flesh tints use no red brighter than Indian red, no yellow brighter than Roman ocher (this applied, of course, to the flesh of white subjects). He also warned against trusting to painting alone as a source of income. "I would have been a beggar had I wholly relied on painting for my support." Better that Genin become a lawyer, which would free him to paint in his spare time.

The mixture of world-weariness, skill, and old-fashioned courtesy in this advice reflected the man who gave it. Trumbull was ever vexed by the need to hustle for work, yet he was willing to impart, if asked politely, what his lifetime's work had taught him.[37]

If the young man had asked him how to become a painter like Trumbull, what could he have said? *Take part in the most important event of your time and paint what you have seen and learned, so that others may see it long after the event and all its witnesses are gone.*

Trumbull died on November 10, 1843, age eighty-seven. After his paintings had been hung in his gallery at Yale, he had told Silliman that they were his children and he wished to be buried beneath them. "Those whom they represent have all gone before me. Let me be buried with my family—I have long lived among the dead."[38]

His body was brought by steamboat to New Haven on November 11 and taken to Silliman's house. His wife was already in New Haven, having been disinterred from her New York City grave in 1834 and re-buried against the day when she and her husband would be reunited. On

the twelfth there was a funeral service for Trumbull in the college chapel. The sermon, preached by Eleazar Fitch, professor of divinity, took as
its text Genesis 25:8–10. "Then Abraham gave up the ghost, and died in
a good old age, an old man, and full of years .... there was Abraham
buried, and Sarah his wife." On the thirteenth John and Sarah were laid
to rest together, beneath his gallery.

Over the spot, at Silliman's direction, was placed a black marble
tablet, inscribed with the dates of their deaths, and this tribute:

Colonel John Trumbull

Patriot and Artist

Friend and Aid

Of

Washington

. . .

To his country he gave

His sword and his pencil[39]

SIXTEEN

Trumbull's paintings, and the ever-growing number of those by other artists in Yale's collection, would be moved from the gallery he designed to successor galleries in styles more whimsical than his— Venetian gothic after the Civil War, a Florentine palazzo in the 1920s. Trumbull's neoclassical building was converted to administrative offices, with windows punched in the walls, then ultimately torn down. At each move of his paintings, however, he and his wife followed them, respectfully reburied. The Trumbull Gallery is now on the second story of the palazzo (known as the Old Yale University Art Gallery after it was joined by a brutalist extension in the 1950s). A memorial tablet is sunk into the floor of the story below Trumbull's gallery. His and Sarah's remains lie in the basement below that.

What of his reputation? In 1853 William Makepeace Thackeray, the English novelist who had studied art in Paris as a young man and who illustrated his literary works with lively little sketches, was taken on a tour of the Capitol with Senator Charles Sumner. "Trumbull is your painter," he told his host after scanning the Rotunda. "Never neglect Trumbull."[1]

No one in the art world would now say that Trumbull was America's painter. Thomas Cole, the young artist he had discovered in a Manhattan bookshop window, marked the dramatic and, as it turned out, final turn away from the kind of public art Trumbull did. Cole is unfortunately best known for his over-the-top allegories, *The Course of Empire* and the *Voyage of Life,* in which dramatic landscapes form a background for solemn lessons about the human condition. But his love of nature, his real skill in depicting it, and the country's seemingly endless supply of it turned painters out of doors. When they came back to humanity, as they inevitably did, it was for scenes of ordinary life, high or low—heiresses, or heavyweight fighters, surgeons lecturing, or lonely souls in late-night diners. Modernisms in their infinite variety took up shapes, lines, and colors; postmodernisms, ads and graffiti. Figurative art is so old that it has become new again, but it has not turned its attention to battles or sessions of Congress.

Serious American artists after Trumbull occasionally depicted public events, but they did so obliquely—Winslow Homer's Union veteran reaping wheat, Childe Hassam's Fifth Avenue flags celebrating the end of World War I—or ironically—Grant Wood's storybook Paul Revere, Andy Warhol's multicolored Maos. There was civic art for the walls of high schools and post offices, and scholars study it now because everything gets studied, but it is a niche field and a special taste.

Beginning in the mid-nineteenth century, people expected catastrophes and celebrations, slaughter and progress, faces famous, notorious, or merely ordinary, to be photographed rather than painted. When Abraham Lincoln, aspiring presidential candidate, came to New York City in 1860 to make his East Coast debut with an address at Cooper Union, he did not go to a painter to have his portrait done; he went to Mathew Brady's studio on Broadway instead. As posed stills were succeeded by live-action shots, then joined by motion pictures, from newsreels to smartphone clips, traditional artists were relegated to sketching courtrooms, where cameras are forbidden, and editorial cartooning. They still had worlds to occupy them, but history in the making slid out of their portfolio. Trumbull and his work belonged to an aesthetic dead end.

Trumbull thought of himself as an artist, bound to the world of art—worshipper of Rubens, follower and supplanter of West and Copley. The thought of being excluded from, or demoted in, that company by an otherwise-minded future would have grieved him. But he thought of himself even more as a recorder and interpreter of events. The art world might abandon history; he was true to it. He was, as he called himself in the catalogue for the Yale gallery, "the graphic historiographer of . . . the great events of his time," preserving them and teaching them to later generations.[2] Did he succeed in that task?

His contemporaries—West, Copley, Peale, Stuart—left a number of portraits of the Revolution's great men, though only a few of these made an impression on the public mind. West's painting of the signers of the Treaty of Paris was abandoned, unfinished. In 1772 Copley painted a splendid image of Samuel Adams (paid for by John Hancock), which is simultaneously learned and menacing—Adams points to the Charter of Massachusetts, asserting the province's violated rights, and he crowds the visual field as if about to burst off the canvas. But Loyalist Copley left America and its revolutionaries for Britain two years later. Peale and his children were prolific portraitists, and filled his Philadelphia museum—America's first—with images of famous contemporaries, a great service to the viewing public in one of the new country's largest cities, however bland most of the images were. Stuart's Athenaeum portrait of George Washington (so-called because the Boston Athenaeum bought it from Stuart's daughter after his death) certainly became famous: Stuart never delivered it to its subject, keeping it unfinished so he could churn out copies. It was engraved many times, and supplied the model for the current one-dollar bill. Unfortunately it is a stiff and forbidding likeness; Stuart and Washington never hit it off in their sittings, and it shows.[3] Stuart's old age portrait of John Adams, done when the painter was seventy-eight and the subject eighty-seven, is by contrast masterly, a fiery spirit burning in a ruined frame, fully justifying Trumbull's high opinion of the abilities of his old friend.

Foreign artists also contributed portraits of America's founders. After his arrival in France 1776, Benjamin Franklin was portrayed as that intellectuals' fashion-of-the-moment, the noble savage. A print, based on a sketch by Charles Cochin, and a terra-cotta medallion, by Jean-Baptiste Nini, depicted him wearing a souvenir of a diplomatic mission to Canada, a cap made of marten fur, which happened to resemble a fur hat sported by Rousseau in a famous 1766 painting: the forests of America and the philosopher of nature together supplied Franklin's headgear. Two years later a canvas by royal painter Joseph-Siffred Duplessis promoted Franklin to a symbol of humanity itself, calm, wise, wry, a septuagenarian who had seen it all and understood it all. The inscription on Duplessis's frame simply said "VIR," Latin for "man." Franklin, ever mindful of the power of images, knew this was his perfect portrait, and declined to sit for any other.[4]

Foreign sculptors lent a hand. Jean-Antoine Houdon, Trumbull's acquaintance, did a modern dress statue of Washington, commissioned by the state of Virginia, and displayed in its State House. Antonio Canova, making a different aesthetic choice, showed "Giorgio Washington" in a toga, destined for the North Carolina State House; building and statue were both destroyed in a fire in 1831.

But as Trumbull himself said when surveying his fellow painters, these likenesses were faces, bodies, and, at best, character studies only. It was vital to preserve the images and personalities of great men, but even more important to show what they had done. Portraitists give us their subjects' appearances and personalities; history painters tell us why we should care about them.

Trumbull's only competitor in that regard was posthumous: Emanuel Leutze, a nineteenth-century German who came to America as a child, then divided his adult life as a painter between his native and his adopted countries. In the wake of the failed European revolutions of 1848, he sought to encourage German liberals with an image of the American Revolution. The result was *Washington Crossing the Delaware*, exhibited in New York City in 1851. It is an enormous canvas—twelve by twenty-one feet—in a hyperrealistic style, every detail of the lead boat in the foreground popping as if spotlit. Like Trumbull's *Trenton*, Leutze's image includes both Washington and young James Monroe, the latter here as yet un-wounded, clasping an American flag. Like Trumbull's *Bunker's Hill*, *Washington Crossing the Delaware* shows a black man, this one manning an oar (the Fourteenth Massachusetts, which managed the boats that night, was composed of Marblehead sailors, including blacks and Indians). Trumbull painted the two important battles that followed the crossing, but the crossing itself has captured the popular imagination, Leutze's image inspiring innumerable reproductions and many homages and spinoffs. Larry Rivers (*Washington Crossing the Delaware*) deconstructed it; Robert Colescott (*George Washington Carver Crossing the Delaware: Page from an American History Textbook*) turned it into a minstrel show. A&E (*The Crossing*) filmed it, Tony Millionaire (*Maakies*) reviewed it.

Trumbull's images lodged as deeply in the American mind, two of them as iconic as Leutze's. Trumbull's complete narrative, his wall telling the story, is visible only at Yale, and not always even there. Although his revolutionary series and his standing portrait of Washington after Trenton are hung in the art gallery, according to his bequest, their arrangement on its walls varies according to the ideas of the curators. When I was an undergraduate, in the late seventies, they were placed as Trumbull had placed them. Now they are arranged differently: Trumbull the artist rather than Trumbull the historian is featured. Standing Washington introduces the visitor into the rooms dedicated to him, the small portraits hanging in a small space by themselves, and the revolutionary series intermixed with other paintings, including Stuart's 1818 portrait of his fellow artist. Trumbull's copies of five of his revolutionary paintings, at half life-size, were bought after his death by his old friend Daniel Wadsworth, who installed them in a new museum he had founded in Hartford, the Wadsworth Atheneum. (So a collection of Trumbulls would hang in Hartford after all.) The Capitol Rotunda holds his four life-size copies.

The life-size Rotunda images have been disdained since they were hung, Thackeray notwithstanding. "It is tragic," wrote Trumbull's twentieth-century editor, "that much of his fame rests on these pictorial failures."[5] They were painted, writes another twentieth-century critic, at a time when "the deterioration in Trumbull's abilities becomes evident."[6] His palette has dulled, his flair has departed. But artwork hung at a distance in active public spaces may satisfy different criteria than easel paintings, meant to be seen on the walls of galleries or private residences. Broad strokes can survive even when the zest-giving details are invisible, or absent.

Trumbull's paintings in the Rotunda, where the greatest number of people by far see them, reduce his Revolution to four scenes—the *Declaration, Saratoga, Yorktown,* and the *Resignation.* Two are military, two are political. That is not a bad selection. The military scenes are by definition staid, since they depict ceremonial surrenders. The uniforms, the mounts, the flags, and the weapons suggest, however, what was happening before the parties agreed to meet. The military paraphernalia is not on parade merely; these men have recently been using it, in the hope of killing or at least subduing each other.

To what end? The political paintings suggest an answer. In the *Declaration* the statement of a goal, self-rule by representative government, is being offered to the political class; in the *Resignation,* the military respectfully and wholeheartedly accepts it. This is a war animated, and justified (if that is possible) by an idea.

The Capitol loses Trumbull's images of struggle and death, forged from his own experience of smoke and corpses, his memories of the sound of artillery and the smell of gunpowder. That is a pity. But we know that struggle has occurred, and we are shown why. That is a fair executive summary of his project, and of the Revolution.

The most tenacious of his images is the one he had not planned until Jefferson suggested it. The *Declaration* decorates textbooks and, since 1976, the reverse of the two-dollar bill. The original Broadway production of *1776* ended with a tableau of the actors arranged to mimic it. Every nation has an origin myth. The writing and approving of the Declaration has become ours. The death of Jefferson and John Adams, draftsman and first reader, on the fiftieth anniversary of the Fourth of July, enhanced the Declaration's status enormously; the use made of it by later politicians as diverse as Abraham Lincoln, Calvin Coolidge, and Martin Luther King, Jr., has burnished it still further. Jefferson's own way with words is of course the fundamental reason that the Declaration is remembered. Trumbull's image, flashed like an ad on the nation's retina, has also imprinted, and continues to imprint the message.

But nations are more than documents. The ideas that animate them have to be upheld, sometimes defended, in the world. It is appropriate that the second iconic image from Trumbull's revolutionary series is a battle scene. *Bunker's Hill* did not make it to the Capitol. It marches on from sheer pictorial force. Horace Walpole said, absurdly, that Trumbull's *Sortie Made by the Garrison of Gibraltar* was the best painting ever done north of the Alps. *Bunker's Hill,* truly, is one of the best battle paintings of the last two hundred and fifty years. As Abigail Adams testified, it makes the frame contract, and the blood shiver. It satisfies the same passions, base but indelible, as horror movies: you are there, where you don't want to be. It would be violence porn, if it were not real: *we did this, we survived this.*

Copies of varying quality of *Bunker's Hill* flooded the print market for decades. One interesting detail in this plethora of reproduction is the changing image of Asaba, the armed black slave in the lower-right corner. Although it can be difficult to attribute intent to works as crude as Currier & Ives prints, some of them show him, correctly, as black, while others appear either to lighten his skin tone or to hide him almost entirely behind his then-master, Lieutenant Grosvenor. A black man supporting the cause of independence might be problematic, a black man slinging a gun even more so. Abolitionists, by contrast, highlighted him in their reproductions. An 1855 tract, *Colored Patriots of the American Revolution,* eliminated Lieutenant Grosvenor, so that Asaba stands, and fights, alone.[7]

So as far as the averagely intelligent, moderately visual American is concerned, Trumbull's lifework boils down to two images: a document and a battle. This is what we have left of what he left us of the Revolution—the epitome of the summary. Even a man as proud as Trumbull might console himself for the loss of art-world standing with such a real-world result.

Is the result worthy? Trumbull told Jefferson, when his project was fresh in his soul, that he meant to give men "glorious lessons of their rights, and of the spirit with which they should assert and support them."[8] Are his lessons worth learning? Are they glorious?

The bicentennial of independence in 1776 inaugurated a founders' revival, which has been carried on by academics with a gift for writing, and by popular historians. The climax of it may have been Lin-Manuel Miranda's *Hamilton: An American Musical,* based on Ron Chernow's best-selling biography of one of Trumbull's many subjects.

The 250th anniversary of independence is unlikely to be greeted with similar enthusiasm. The protests and riots that followed the murder of George Floyd in 2020 were accompanied by a wave of iconoclasm as public statues of historical figures were removed, defaced, or destroyed. First to go were monuments to Confederate leaders, reasonably enough— these were not memorials of the dead in cemeteries, but civic expressions, fossilized in stone, of Lost Cause revanchism. The rebels were followed in disgrace by images of founding fathers and even heroes of the Union. (A statue of Hans Christian Heg, Wisconsin abolitionist and U.S. Army colonel killed at the Battle of Chickamauga, was toppled, decapitated, and thrown in a lake.) To the vandals, the murder of Floyd, and all the travails of black men and women since the first slaves were brought to Jamestown in 1619, express the essence of the country. All its symbols deserve to fall.

Trumbull cannot be untangled from this indictment by arguing that his racial attitudes were proto-enlightened. They weren't. His interest, as a man and an artist, in the status of black Americans was all but nonexistent. He had more thoughts about American Indians, and drew them more often, but even these concerns were relatively slight.

His career as a revolutionary, and a revolutionary artist, was concerned with a greater issue: the issue of self-rule. Those who enjoy self-rule as a matter of course forget how novel and fragile the concept was and is. In the summer of 1619, before the first African slaves were off-loaded in Jamestown, the colony, the oldest British settlement in what would become the United States, convened its first General Assembly, a meeting of the governor, his council, and elected burgesses or representatives. Over the four days that they met, they approved regulations of tobacco prices, morals, and Indian relations, and asserted a desire to adjust any orders from London "which did presse or binde too harde."[9] This was the seed of American self-rule, planted subsequently in all the colonies, including the two—Connecticut and Massachusetts—in which Trumbull was born and raised. For a century and a half, colonial self-rule flourished by increments until, after the French and Indian War, London resolved to trim it back. Then Trumbull and his peers and his elders went to war to secure it. Every subsequent revolution, whether in the first, second, or third world, has addressed the issue, directly or willy-nilly.

Self-rule is the first and fundamental right. Others are vital: property, worship, speech. Self-rule may threaten them all, but without it, no lasting defense of any of them is possible. In America self-rule maintained slavery; but self-rule abolished it. Self-rule imposed legal racism; but self-rule overthrew it. Trumbull is the bard, in pictures not words, of American self-rule.

As such, he rebukes false friends, who can be as dangerous as open enemies. One of the most striking images of the Capitol riot on January 6, 2021, is of the smiling trespasser, toting the lectern of the Speaker of the House across the Rotunda as he waves at the photographer. Behind him hangs Trumbull's *Saratoga*. At his trial the man pleaded guilty to entering and remaining in a restricted building, and expressed remorse for what he had done; he was fined, and sentenced to seventy-five days in prison. At the time of his pose, however, he or his fellow rioters might have said that they were applying Trumbull's glorious lessons: an election had been stolen, they had stormed the Capitol to see justice done (figures 9 and 10).

Figure 9. A trespasser totes the Speaker of the House's lectern through the Capitol Rotunda.

Figure 10. National Guard members stand in the Rotunda with the U.S. Capitol tour.

They needed to study the *Declaration* and the *Resignation*. Direct action is a serious matter. The warrant to employ it depends on more than the assertions of an aggrieved loser. Trumbull's revolution was declared by "the Representatives of the united States of America, in General Congress, Assembled . . . by Authority of the good People" who chose them. Its shock troops were not brawlers and rioters but armies who, when summoned to do so, surrendered to Congress "the trust committed" to them. That sets the bar of legitimate revolution high. But "all experience hath shewn, that mankind are more disposed to suffer, while evils are sufferable, than to right themselves by abolishing the forms to which they are accustomed."

Only when the conditions outlined by Jefferson and obeyed by Washington are met can deadly combat be justified, and the lasting peace forecast in the right side of Trumbull's image of the Annapolis State House be expected: women and children; wives; a father holding his arm behind his daughters' shoulders.

A boy on the floor, copying his sister's embroidery.

Appendix: Thirteen Trumbulls Online

1. *George Washington and William Lee*, 1780
   Oil on canvas, 36 x 28 in. (91.4 x 71.1 cm)
   Metropolitan Museum of Art, Bequest of Charles Allen Munn, 1924
   https://www.metmuseum.org/art/collection/search/12822

2. *The Death of General Mercer at the Battle of Princeton* (unfinished version)
   c. 1786–88
   Oil on canvas, 26 x 37 in. (66 x 94 cm)
   Yale University Art Gallery, Trumbull Collection
   https://artgallery.yale.edu/collections/objects/102

3. *Thomas Jefferson*, 1788
   Oil on panel, 4¾ x 3 in. (12.1 x 7.6 cm)
   White House Collection/White House Historical Association
   https://www.whitehousehistory.org/photos/thomas-jefferson-by-john-
   trumbull

4. *The Sortie Made by the Garrison of Gibraltar*, 1789
   Oil on canvas, 71 x 107 in. (180.3 x 271.8 cm)
   Metropolitan Museum of Art, Purchase, Pauline V. Fullerton Bequest; Mr. and
   Mrs. James Walter Carter and Mr. and Mrs. Raymond J. Horowitz Gifts; Erving
   Wolf Foundation and Vain and Harry Fish Foundation Inc. Gifts; Gift of Han-
   son K. Corning, by exchange; and Maria DeWitt Jesup and Morris K. Jesup
   Funds, 1976
   https://www.metmuseum.org/art/collection/search/12828

5. *Washington at Verplanck's Point*, 1790
   Oil on canvas, 30¹⁄₁₆ x 20¹⁄₁₆ in. (76.5 x 51.1 cm)
   Winterthur Museum, Garden, and Library, Gift of Henry Francis DuPont
   http://museumcollection.winterthur.org/single-record.php?view=gallery&re
   cid=1964.2201%20A

6. *Alexander Hamilton,* 1792
   Oil on canvas, 86¼ x 57½ in. (219.1 x 146.1 cm)
   Jointly owned by Crystal Bridges Museum of American Art and the Metropolitan
   Museum of Art, Gift of Credit Suisse, 2013
   https://www.metmuseum.org/art/collection/search/20893

7. *John Adams,* 1793
   Oil on canvas, 25⅝ × 21⅝ in. (65.1 × 54.9 cm)
   National Portrait Gallery, Smithsonian Institution
   https://npg.si.edu/object/npg_NPG.75.52

8. *Lemuel Hopkins,* 1793
   Oil on wood, 3⅞ x 3¼ in. (9.8 x 8.3 cm)
   Yale University Art Gallery, Trumbull Collection
   https://artgallery.yale.edu/collections/objects/111

9. *Harriet Wadsworth,* c. 1793
   Oil on wood, 3⅞ x 2⅞ in. (9.8 x 7.3 cm)
   Yale University Art Gallery, Trumbull Collection
   https://artgallery.yale.edu/collections/objects/7410

10. *Mrs. Thomas Sully,* 1806
    Oil on canvas, 30⅛ x 24¹⁄₁₆ in. (76.5 x 61.1 cm)
    Five Colleges and Historic Deerfield Museum Consortium, Bequest of
    Herbert L. Pratt (Amherst Class of 1895)
    https://museums.fivecolleges.edu/detail.php?t=objects&type=ext&id_
    number=AC+1945.83

11. *Mrs. John Murray,* c. 1806
    Oil on canvas, 30 x 24 in. (76.2 x 61 cm)
    Metropolitan Museum of Art, Morris K. Jesup Fund, 1922
    https://www.metmuseum.org/art/collection/search/12827

12. *The Woman Taken in Adultery,* 1811
    Oil on canvas, 94³⁄₁₆ x 67⅛ in. (239.2 x 170.5 cm)
    Yale University Art Gallery, Trumbull Collection
    https://artgallery.yale.edu/collections/objects/126

13. *Joshua at the Battle of Ai—Attended by Death,* 1839–40
    Oil on canvas, 40¼ x 50⅜ in. (102.2 x 128 cm)
    Yale University Art Gallery, Trumbull Collection
    https://artgallery.yale.edu/collections/objects/176

Notes

Abbreviations of Persons

AA   Abigail Adams
GW   George Washington
JA   John Adams
JT   John Trumbull
TJ   Thomas Jefferson

Abbreviations of Institutions

CHS   Connecticut Historical Society, Hartford
CSL   Connecticut State Library, Hartford
FO   Founders Online, https://founders.archives.gov
N-YHS   New-York Historical Society, New York
NYPL   New York Public Library, New York
YUL   Yale University Library, New Haven

Introduction

1. Irma B. Jaffe, *John Trumbull* (Boston: New York Graphic Society, 1975), 277.
2. JT to TJ, June 11, 1789, FO.
3. John Trumbull, *Autobiography, Reminiscences and Letters of John Trumbull, from 1756 to 1841* (New York: Wiley & Putnam, 1841), 89.
4. Jaffe, *Trumbull*, 225.

Chapter One

1. Trumbull, *Autobiography*, 5.
2. Alice Morse Earle, *The Sabbath in Puritan New England* (New York: Charles Scribner's Sons, 1891), 6.
3. Trumbull, *Autobiography*, 6.

4. Hartford and New Haven served as the colony's twin capitals.

5. Kevin Phillips, *1775: A Good Year for Revolution* (New York: Penguin, 2012), 54; Jonathan Trumbull, *Jonathan Trumbull: Governor of Connecticut* (Boston: Little, Brown, 1919), 68.

6. Trumbull, *Autobiography,* 7–8.

7. Ibid., 11.

8. Ibid., 13.

9. Ibid., 11.

10. Ibid.

11. For Copley, see Jane Kamensky, *A Revolution in Color: The World of John Singleton Copley* (New York: W.W. Norton, 2016).

12. C.A. du Fresnoy, *The Art of Painting,* trans. John Dryden (London: J. Hepinstall, 1695), 4.

13. Trumbull, *Autobiography,* 13.

14. Copley wrote of the status of painting in Boston in 1767, "The people generally regard it no more than any other useful trade ... like that of a carpenter, tailor, or shoe maker." Susan Rather, *The American School: Artists and Status in the Late-Colonial and Early National Era* (New Haven: Yale University Press, 2016), 17.

15. Trumbull, *Autobiography,* 297–98.

Chapter Two

1. Jaffe, *John Trumbull,* 24.

2. Trumbull, *Jonathan Trumbull,* 115.

3. Trumbull, *Autobiography,* 15.

4. Trumbull, *Jonathan Trumbull,* 146.

5. Ibid., 268.

6. Ibid., 258.

7. Trumbull, *Autobiography,* 48.

8. Ibid., 20.

9. Benson Bobrick, *Angel in the Whirlwind: The Triumph of the American Revolution* (New York: Simon & Schuster, 1997), 143.

10. Trumbull, *Autobiography,* 22.

11. Ibid.

12. TJ to Walter Jones, January 2, 1814, FO.

13. AA to JA, July 16, 1775, FO. "Those lines of Dryden" Abigail Adams recalled, from Dryden's tragedy *Don Sebastian, King of Portugal* (1689), originally described a heroine: "Mark her majestic fabric," etc. Adams performed a sex change on them to make them apply to Washington—and, more subtly, to project herself as a woman into the revolutionary struggle.

14. Trumbull, *Autobiography,* 23.

15. Ann Brandwein, "An Eighteenth-Century Depression: The Sad Conclusion of Faith Trumbull Huntington," *Connecticut History Review* 26 (November 1985): 25; JT to Faith Huntington, October 5, 1775, CHS; JT to David Trumbull, October 12, 1775, CHS.

16. Brandwein, "Eighteenth-Century Depression," 26.

17. Trumbull, *Autobiography*, 22.

18. Ibid., 24.

19. Ibid., 302.

20. Ibid., 28.

21. JT to Joseph Trumbull, September 25, 1776, CSL.

22. *The Historical Magazine* 1 (October 1857): 289.

23. Ibid., 290.

24. Ibid.

25. Ibid., 291.

26. JA to AA, May 22, 1777, FO.

27. Trumbull, *Autobiography*, 305-6.

28. Ibid., 53.

Chapter Three

1. For Smibert, see Rather, *American School*, 13, 72.

2. Lewis Einstein, *Divided Loyalties: Americans in England* (Boston: Houghton Mifflin, 1933), 94.

3. Almost certainly they hadn't. See Rather, *American School*, 209, 287.

4. Trumbull, *Autobiography*, 58.

5. Ibid., 58-59.

6. JT to David Trumbull, August 6, 1779, YUL.

7. William Sawitzky, *Matthew Pratt, 1734-1805* (New York: New-York Historical Society, 1942), 19.

8. Trumbull, *Autobiography*, 67.

9. James Thomas Flexner, *Gilbert Stuart* (New York: Alfred Knopf, 1955), 49.

10. William Dunlap, *A History of the Rise and Progress of the Arts of Design in the United States* (Boston: C.E. Goodspeed, 1918), 1:214.

11. Colonel C.P. Stacey, "Benjamin West and 'The Death of Wolfe,'" *National Gallery of Canada Bulletin* 4, no. 1 (1966).

12. John Galt, *The Life, Studies and Works of Benjamin West, Esq.* (London: T. Cadell & W. Davies, 1820), 47-49.

13. Helen Zimmern, ed., *Sir Joshua Reynolds' Discourses* (London: Walter Scott, 1887), Third Discourse (December 14, 1770), 34.

14. Even after independence, Americans still sometimes thought and calculated in British currency, in which twelve pence made a shilling, twenty shillings made a pound, and twenty-one shillings made a guinea. Apart from periods of inflation—extreme in America during the Revolution, bad in Britain during the late Napoleonic Wars—the pound was worth about four and a half dollars.

15. See West's portraits of Frederick William Ernest, count of Schaumburg Lippe, and John Manners, marquess of Granby.

16. John Caldwell et al., *American Paintings in the Metropolitan Museum of Art* (New York: Metropolitan Museum of Art, 1994), 1:201.

17. Trumbull, *Autobiography*, 72.

18. William Bell Clark, "In Defense of Thomas Digges," *Pennsylvania Magazine of History and Biography* 77, no. 4 (October 1953): 421–24.

19. Francis Steuart, ed. *The Last Journals of Horace Walpole from the Reign of George III* (New York: John Lane, 1910), 2:337–38.

20. *The Political Magazine and Parliamentary, Naval, Military and Literary Journal* 1 (November 1780): 739–40.

21. Steuart, *Walpole*, 364.

Chapter Four

1. Trumbull, *Autobiography*, 88.

2. Ibid.

3. Ibid., 89.

4. Ibid., 90.

5. James Boswell, *The Life of Samuel Johnson*, selected by Edmund Fuller (New York: Dell Publishing, 1960), 68 aetat. 43 1752.

6. JT to Jonathan Trumbull, Jr., March 10, 1784, YUL; JT to David Trumbull, June 17, 1784, CHS.

7. Trumbull, *Autobiography*, 92.

8. GW Address to Congress on Resigning His Commission, Annapolis, Md., December 23, 1783, Founders' Online (GW to United States Congress December 23 1783).

9. JT to Jonathan Trumbull, Jr., March 10, 1784, YUL.

10. Helen A. Cooper et al., *John Trumbull: The Hand and Spirit of a Painter* (New Haven: Yale University Art Gallery, 1982), 29.

11. JT to Jonathan Trumbull, Jr., March 10, 1784, YUL.

12. JT to Jonathan Trumbull, Jr., November 15, 1784, YUL.

13. JT to Jonathan Trumbull, Jr., September 13, 1785, YUL.

14. Jonathan Trumbull, Jr., to JT, October 27, 1786, YUL.

15. Ron Chernow, *Alexander Hamilton* (New York: Penguin Press, 2004), 134.

16. Theodore Sizer, ed., *The Autobiography of Colonel John Trumbull: Patriot-Artist, 1756–1843* (New Haven: Yale University Press, 1953), 90.

17. Trumbull, *Jonathan Trumbull*, 220–21.

18. See David Menschel, "Abolition without Deliverance: The Law of Connecticut Slavery 1784–1848," *Yale Law Journal* 111, no. 1 (October 2001): 183.

19. Trumbull, *Jonathan Trumbull*, 306.

20. Jonathan Trumbull, Jr., to JT, December 10, 1784, YUL.

21. Jonathan Trumbull, Sr., to JT, April 29, 1785, CHS.

22. JT to David Trumbull, January 31, 1786, CHS.

23. Charles Francis Adams, ed., *Letters of Mrs. Adams, the Wife of John Adams* (Boston: Wilkins, Carter, 1848), 277 (AA to Mrs. Shaw, March 4, 1786).

24. William Dunlap, *Diary of William Dunlap (1766–1839)* (New York: New-York Historical Society, 1943), 1:196.

25. Jaffe, *John Trumbull*, 317.
26. Trumbull, *Autobiography*, 93.
27. Ibid., 95.

Chapter Five

1. Kenneth R. Bowling and Helen E. Veit, eds., *The Diary of William Maclay and Other Notes on Senate Debate* (Baltimore: Johns Hopkins University Press, 1988), 275.
2. Trumbull, *Autobiography*, 104.
3. Ibid., 109.
4. Ibid., 107.
5. Ibid.
6. Ibid., 112.
7. Ibid., 105–6.
8. Ibid., 108.
9. Ibid., 113.
10. Ibid., 112–15.
11. TJ to Maria Cosway, October 12, 1786, FO.
12. TJ to JT, October 30, 1786, FO.
13. JT to TJ, March 16, 1788, FO.
14. Maria Cosway to TJ, March 6, 1788, FO.
15. Maria Cosway to TJ, April 19, 1788, FO.
16. Maria Cosway to TJ, August 19, 1788, FO.
17. TJ to JT, August 24, 1788, FO.
18. Maria Cosway to TJ, April 6, 1790, FO.
19. Trumbull, *Autobiography*, 145.
20. Trumbull, *Jonathan Trumbull*, 190–91.
21. Trumbull, *Autobiography*, 147.
22. TJ to JT, February 23, 1797, FO.
23. Trumbull, *Autobiography*, 150.
24. JT to Jonathan Trumbull, Jr., December 27, 1786, YUL.
25. JT to Jonathan Trumbull, Jr., February 6, 1788, YUL.
26. JT to Jonathan Trumbull, Jr., February 26, 1788, YUL.
27. JT to Jonathan Trumbull, Jr., September 7, 1789, YUL.
28. JT to Benjamin West, October 8, 1789, YUL.
29. Sizer, *Autobiography*, 150.
30. TJ to JT, May 21, 1789, FO.
31. JT to TJ, June 11, 1789, FO.

Chapter Six

1. Jaffe, *John Trumbull*, 154.
2. Joel Barlow, *The Vision of Columbus* (Hartford: Hudson and Goodwin, 1787), 209–10.

3. GW to Henry Knox, January 1, 1789, FO.

4. George Washington Diary, January 23, 1790, and February 10, 1790, FO.

5. GW to Frances Hopkinson, May 16, 1785, FO.

6. GW Diary, March 1, 1790.

7. Trumbull, *Autobiography*, 164–65.

8. Virginia Pounds Brown and Linda McNair Cohen, *Drawing by Stealth: John Trumbull and the Creek Indians* (Montgomery, Ala: NewSouth Books, 2016), 12. See also John Quincy Adams's comments on Chickasaws smoking a peace pipe with Washington in Philadelphia in 1794 "as if they were submitting . . . in compliance with *our* custom." David Waldstreicher, ed., *John Quincy Adams Diaries* (New York: Library of America, 2017), 1:45.

9. JT to Harriet Wadsworth, May 17, 1788, YUL.

10. JT to Harriet Wadsworth, February 27, 1790, YUL.

11. Jeremiah Wadsworth to Harriet Wadsworth, February 14, 1790, YUL.

12. JT to Harriet Wadsworth, December 15, 1790, YUL.

13. Jeremiah Wadsworth to Harriet Wadsworth, January 30, 1792, YUL.

14. JT to Harriet Wadsworth, January 28, 1791, YUL.

15. Sizer, *Autobiography*, 333–34.

16. Ibid., 336.

17. Edward Warren Capen, *The History and Development of the Poor Law of Connecticut* (New York: Columbia University Press, 1905), 38–40, 126–32.

18. Sizer, *Autobiography*, 333.

19. Trumbull, *Autobiography*, 166.

20. Ibid., 116–17.

21. GW to William Moultrie, May 5, 1792, FO.

22. Trumbull, *Autobiography*, 339–40.

23. GW to Lafayette, November 21, 1791, FO.

24. Bowling and Veit, *Diary of William Maclay*, 365.

25. Trumbull, *Autobiography*, 170–72.

Chapter Seven

1. Trumbull, *Autobiography*, 177.

2. Ibid., 180–81.

3. James Monroe, *A View of the Conduct of the Executive in the Foreign Affairs of the United States* (Philadelphia: Benjamin Franklin Bache, 1797), 155–56.

4. James Grieg, ed., *The Farington Diary* (New York: George H. Doran, 1923), 1:192.

5. The elaborate process by which Trumbull became the fifth commissioner is explained in Richard B. Lillich, "The Jay Treaty Commission," *St. John's Law Review* 37, no. 25 (1963).

6. Trumbull, *Autobiography*, 191–92.

7. JT to Rufus King, September 2, 1797, N-YHS.

8. JT to Rufus King, September 18, 1797, N-YHS.

9. Trumbull, *Autobiography*, 222.

10. Ibid., 224–25.

11. Ibid., 227–28.

12. William Spence Robertson, *The Life of Miranda* (Chapel Hill: University of North Carolina Press, 1929), 53.

13. JT to GW, March 24, 1799, FO.

14. Trumbull, *Autobiography,* 395–97; JT to Jonathan Trumbull, Jr., April 5, 1799, FO.

15. GW to JT, June 25, 1799, FO. See also Marshall Smelser, "George Washington Declines the Part of El Libertador," *William and Mary Quarterly* 11, no. 1 (January 1954): 51.

16. See Lillich, "Jay Treaty Commission," 279–80.

17. Trumbull, *Autobiography,* 227–28.

18. GW to JT, June 25, 1799, FO.

19. Trumbull, *Autobiography,* 399–400.

20. Ibid., 400–402.

Chapter Eight

1. JT to William Williams, July 16, 1803, N-YHS.

2. JT to Jonathan Trumbull, Jr., May 1, 1801, YUL.

3. Dunlap, *Diary,* 3:738–39.

4. Ibid., 738.

5. Fox's joke appears in slightly different forms in a number of places. See, for example, "Lord Holland's Memoirs of the Whig Party," *London Quarterly Review* (American edition) 94 (1854): 205.

6. Mark Argent, ed., *Recollections of R.J.S. Stevens: An Organist in Georgian London* (London: Macmillan, 1992), 159–60.

7. Dunlap, *Diary,* 3:800–801.

8. Sizer, *Autobiography,* 347.

9. JT to Jeremiah Wadsworth, July 26, 1799, YUL.

10. Jeremiah Wadsworth to JT, February 1, 1801, YUL.

11. JT to Jonathan Trumbull, Jr., August 16, 1800, YUL.

12. JT to Jonathan Trumbull, Jr., January 18, 1785, YUL.

13. "I am your spaniel, and, Demetrius, / The more you beat me, I will fawn on you." Shakespeare, *A Midsummer Night's Dream,* II.i.

14. Sizer, *Autobiography,* 352 (John M. Trumbull to Solomon Williams, May 1, 1801).

15. Milton Lomask, *Aaron Burr: The Years from Princeton to Vice President, 1756–1805* (New York: Farrar, Strauss, Giroux, 1979), 87.

16. Trumbull, *Autobiography,* 244.

17. Sizer, *Autobiography,* 237.

18. Gouverneur Morris quoted in John W. Francis Papers, NYPL.

19. David Humphreys to JT, December 22, 1802, CSL.

20. Thanks to Dr. Will Sencabaugh of the First Congregational Church of Lebanon, Conn., who discovered the dimensions while measuring the sanctuary for Covid compliance.

21. Sizer, *Autobiography,* 338.

22. Sizer, *Autobiography,* 352.

23. JT to Faith Wadsworth, December 13, 1806, YUL.

24. Jonathan Trumbull, Jr., to JT, January 25, 1808, CSL.

25. John Lambert, *Travels through Canada and the United States* (London: Baldwin, Craddock & Joy, 1816), 2:64–65.

Chapter Nine

1. Boswell, *Life of Samuel Johnson,* 99 aetat. 54 1763.

2. TJ to Charles McPherson, February 25, 1773, FO.

3. Benjamin Silliman Notebook (hereafter BSNB) II, 124, YUL.

4. JT to Benjamin Silliman, May 19, 1822, YUL.

5. Sizer, *Autobiography,* 339.

6. John Ray to JT, June 22, 1811, YUL.

7. JT to John Ray, July 10, 1811, YUL.

8. John Ray to JT, September 24, 1811, YUL.

9. JT to John Ray, October 26, 1811, YUL.

10. John Ray to Sarah Trumbull, September 23, 1812, YUL.

11. JT to Rufus King, August 19, 1812, YUL.

12. JT to Samuel Williams, May 5, 1814, YUL.

13. Emily Robertson, ed., *Letters and Papers of Andrew Robertson, A.M.* (London: Eyre and Spottiswoode, n.d.), 61.

14. JT to John Ray, August [?], 1814, YUL.

15. Diana Strazdes, "John Trumbull's Nude Venus," *Master Drawings* 51, no. 1 (Spring 2013): 49–62.

16. Cooper, *Hand and Spirit,* 225.

17. Dunlap, *History,* 1:272–73.

Chapter Ten

1. Edwin G. Burrows and Mike Wallace, *Gotham: A History of New York City to 1898* (New York: Oxford University Press, 1999), 467.

2. Henry Adams, *History of the United States in the Administrations of James Madison* (New York: Library of America, 1986), 1013.

3. JT to TJ, December 26, 1816, FO.

4. Ibid.

5. JA to JT, January 1, 1817, FO.

6. TJ to JT, January 10, 1817, FO.

7. TJ to James Monroe January 10, 1817, FO.

8. TJ to James Barbour, January 19, 1817, FO.

9. Trumbull, *Autobiography,* 262–63, 267–72.

10. Benjamin Henry Latrobe, *The Journal of Latrobe* (New York: D. Appleton, 1905), 51.

11. Trumbull, *Autobiography,* 267–72.

12. See Egon Verheyen, "John Trumbull and the U.S. Capitol," in Cooper, *Hand and Spirit,* 260–71.

13. JT to John Ray, July 26, 1815, YUL.

14. JT to John Ray, October 20, 1817, YUL (emphasis in the original).

15. JT to John Ray, September 6, 1818, YUL (emphasis in the original).

16. Sizer gives a selection: Sizer, *Autobiography,* 362–63.

17. Charles Rufus King, ed., *Life and Correspondence of Rufus King* (New York: G.P. Putnam's Sons, 1900), 6:57–59.

18. William Howe Downes, "Boston Painters and Paintings," *Atlantic,* July 1888, 96.

19. JT to James Madison, October 1, 1823, FO.

20. Trumbull, *Autobiography,* 358.

21. Ibid., 359.

22. Ibid., 402.

23. *Annals of Congress,* 15th Congress, 2nd sess., 1142.

24. Sizer, *Autobiography,* 363.

25. Jaffe, *John Trumbull,* 248. Thanks to Sarah Ruden for analyzing the badness of the Latin.

26. Charles Francis Adams, ed., *Memoirs of John Quincy Adams* (Philadelphia: J.B. Lippincott, 1875), 4:128 (September 1, 1818).

27. Waldstreicher, *John Quincy Adams Diaries,* 2:144 (November 28, 1826).

28. Ibid.

Chapter Eleven

1. Paul Staiti, *Of Arms and Artists: The American Revolution through Painters' Eyes* (New York: Bloomsbury Press, 2016), 237.

2. Sizer, *Autobiography,* 349; John Ray to JT, January 7, 1823, YUL.

3. Sizer, *Autobiography,* 349; JT to John Ray, May 20, 1827, YUL.

4. Sizer, *Autobiography,* 349; John Ray to JT, March 16, 1829, YUL.

5. George P. Fisher, *Life of Benjamin Silliman* (Philadelphia: Porter & Coates, 1866), 242.

6. Helen M. Morgan, ed., *A Season in New York, 1801: Letters of Harriet and Maria Trumbull* (Pittsburgh: University of Pittsburgh Press, 1969), 152–53.

7. BSNB, 4, YUL.

8. Cooper, *Hand and Spirit,* 170.

9. BSNB, 38.

10. Ibid., 40.

11. Sizer, *Autobiography,* 284.

12. Ibid., 170.

13. BSNB, 48.

14. Ibid., 49.

15. Trumbull, *Autobiography,* 285.

16. JT to Benjamin Silliman, November 30, 1831, YUL.

17. Sizer, *Autobiography,* 284. Yale has the draft of JT's letter, Harvard the copy that Quincy received. I believed the story that Harvard would get the paintings if Yale ever backslid, and recounted it several times as a laugh line in history talks. This is my apology.

18. Ibid., 374.

19. Ibid., 376, discusses architectural fashion.

20. Trumbull, *Autobiography,* 290.

21. BSNB, 56.

22. Ibid., 27.

Chapter Twelve

1. Trumbull, *Autobiography,* 410.

2. BSNB, 65, YUL.

3. Adams, *Letters of Mrs. Adams,* 277.

4. Benjamin Hichborn to JA, December 10, 1775, FO.

5. Trumbull, *Autobiography,* 411.

6. BSNB, 67. For Asaba's bondage and subsequent freedom, see George Quintal, Jr., *Patriots of Color: "A Peculiar Beauty and Merit": African Americans and Native Americans at Battle Road and Bunker Hill* (Boston: National Historical Park, 2004), 115.

7. Kamensky, *Revolution in Color,* 320–23, discusses the polemical role of Copley's black marksman.

8. Adams, *Letters of Mrs. Adams,* 277.

9. Trumbull, *Autobiography,* 416.

10. Ibid., 417.

11. See TJ, "Autobiography" (June, 7, 1776), in Jefferson Looney et al., eds., *The Papers of Thomas Jefferson,* Retirement Series, vol. 16, *1 June 1820 to 28 February 1821* (Princeton: Princeton University Press).

12. JT to TJ, December 28, 1817, FO.

13. Jaffe, *John Trumbull,* 114–17.

14. *Register of Debates in Congress,* January 9, 1828, vol. 4, pt. 1, 94.

15. TJ to Henry Lee, May 8, 1825, FO.

16. Trumbull, *Autobiography,* 418.

17. Ibid.

18. Mason Locke Weems, *A History of the Life and Death, Virtues and Exploits of General George Washington* (Cleveland: World Publishing, 1965), 139.

19. Trumbull, *Autobiography,* 418–19.

20. Ibid., 420.

21. BSNB, 74.

22. David Hackett Fischer, *Washington's Crossing* (New York: Oxford University Press, 2004), 253–54, 521.

23. Ibid., 247; Tim McGrath, *James Monroe: A Life* (New York: Dutton, 2020), 33.

24. BSNB, 75.

25. Ibid.

Chapter Thirteen

1. Trumbull, *Autobiography,* 422.

2. Cooper, *Hand and Spirit,* 65.

3. "Turnbull," interestingly, was the original, Scottish form of Trumbull's surname.

4. Fischer, *Washington's Crossing,* 334.

5. Cooper, *Hand and Spirit,* 67–72.

6. Trumbull, *Autobiography,* 416.

7. Cooper, *Hand and Spirit,* 70.

8. Isaac N. Arnold, *The Life of Benedict Arnold: His Patriotism and His Treason* (Chicago: A.C. McClurg, 1905), 29.

9. James Fenimore Cooper, *The Last of the Mohicans* (1826; repr., New York: Signet Classics, 1962), 13.

10. James McHenry to Margaret Caldwell, in John Rhodehamel, ed., *The American Revolution: Writings from the War of Independence* (New York: Library of America, 2001), 796.

11. Note that JT has shifted the axis of the room. Congress should be sitting to the viewers' right, the visitors' gallery should be on the viewers' left

12. Cooper, *Hand and Spirit,* 89.

13. Mary Ridout to Anne Tasker Ogle, January 16, 1784, Maryland State Archives, Annapolis.

14. Mercy Otis Warren, *History of the Rise, Progress, and Termination of the American Revolution* (Boston: Manning and Loring, 1805), iv.

15. *Register of Debates in Congress,* 18th Congress, 2nd sess., February 18, 1825, 625.

16. Lewis Nicola to GW, May 22, 1782, FO.

17. Alexander Hamilton to GW, February 13, 1783, FO.

18. Marquis de Chastellux, *Travels in North America,* trans. "An English Gentleman" (New York: n.p., 1828), 72.

Chapter Fourteen

1. Trumbull, *Autobiography,* 414.

2. Ibid., 108.

3. John Warner Barber, *Interesting Events in the History of the United States* (New Haven: J.W. Barber, 1831), 108.

4. Fischer, *Washington's Crossing,* 332.

5. Sizer, *Autobiography,* 369–71.

6. See Linda Crocker Simmons, "Politics, Portraits and Charles Peale Polk," in *The Peale Family,* ed. Lillian B. Miller (New York: Abbeville Press, 1996).

7. Sizer, *Autobiography,* 369–71.

8. Trumbull, *Autobiography,* 167.

9. Ibid., 166–67.

Chapter Fifteen

1. JT to Edward Everett, January 12, 1827, FO.

2. Dunlap, *History,* 1:351, 3:149.

3. Ibid., 3:51–53.

4. Kenneth Silverman, *Lightning Man: The Accursed Life of Samuel F.B. Morse* (New York: Alfred Knopf, 2003), 102.

5. Edward Lind Morse, ed., *Samuel F.B. Morse: His Letters and Journals* (Boston: Houghton Mifflin, 1914), 1:249.

6. Washington Irving, *Letters of Jonathan Oldstyle* (New York: Columbia University Press, 1941), 19.

7. JT to Edward Everett, January 12, 1827, YUL.

8. Dunlap, *History,* 1:120.

9. Ibid., 1:202, 214

10. Ibid., 1:214, 2:52

11. Ibid. 3:149, 3:52–53.

12. Ibid. 1:305, 2:35.

13. Ibid. 2:39, 2:54.

14. Ibid., 2:57–59.

15. Ibid., 3:75.

16. Ibid., 2:35.

17. Ibid., 2:33, 55.

18. Ibid., 2:13.

19. Ibid., 2:76.

20. Ibid.

21. Dunlap, *Diary,* 3:738–39.

22. Sizer, *Autobiography,* 324.

23. BSNB, 8, YUL.

24. JT to John Randolph, January 13, 1828 (not sent), YUL.

25. Sizer, *Autobiography,* 298.

26. Ibid.

27. Ibid., 299.

28. BSNB, 12.

29. Timothy Dwight, *The Conquest of Canäan* (Hartford: Elisha Babcock, 1785), VI, l.645–46.

30. JT to Benjamin Silliman, June 21, 1836, YUL.

31. See JT note in Trumbull, *Autobiography,* 429.

32. Ibid., 116.

33. Cooper, *Hand and Spirit,* 202–4; Patricia Mullan Burnham "Trumbull's Religious Paintings: Themes and Variations," in Cooper, *Hand and Spirit,* 180–93.

34. Benjamin Silliman to Faith W. Silliman, May 18, 1841, YUL.

35. Trumbull, *Autobiography,* 276.

36. BSNB, 9.

37. Sylvester Genin, *Selections from the Works of the Late Sylvester Genin, Esq.* (New York: Maigne & Hall, 1855), 37–39.

38. BSNB, 27.

39. BSNB, 33–34.

Chapter Sixteen

1. Richard Henry Stoddard, *Anecdote Biographies of Thackery and Dickens* (New York: Scribner, 1874), iv.

2. Trumbull, *Autobiography,* 407.

3. James Thomas Flexner, *George Washington* (Boston: Little, Brown, 1969), 4:308.

4. See Bernard Bailyn, *To Begin the World Anew: The Genius and Ambiguities of the American Founders* (New York: Alfred Knopf, 2003), 68–92.

5. Sizer, *Autobiography,* 257.

6. Cooper, *Hand and Spirit,* 86.

7. Staiti, *Of Arms and Artists,* 294.

8. JT to TJ, June 11, 1789, FO.

9. William J. Van Schreeven and George H. Reese, eds. *Proceedings of the General Assembly of Virginia . . .* (Jamestown, Va.: Jamestown Foundation, 1969), 255.

Bibliography

Trumbull's papers are hither and yon, with important deposits at Yale, the Connecticut Historical Society, the Connecticut State Library, the Massachusetts Historical Society, the New-York Historical Society, and Fordham University. Trumbull published a number of letters by, to, and about him in his *Autobiography*. Theodore Sizer, Irma Jaffe, and Helen Cooper and her coauthors published much else. I am in their debt. My notes give the correspondents, the dates, and the locations of the originals.

All correspondence of George Washington, John Adams, and Thomas Jefferson is available at Founders Online, https://founders.archives.gov.

Books and Pamphlets

Adams, Charles Francis, ed. *Letters of Mrs. Adams, the Wife of John Adams*. Boston: Wilkins, Carter, 1848.

———. *Memoirs of John Quincy Adams*. Philadelphia: J.B. Lippincott, 1875.

Adams, Henry. *History of the United States in the Administrations of James Madison*. New York: Library of America, 1986.

Annals of Congress.

Argent, Mark ed. *Recollections of R.J.S. Stevens: An Organist in Georgian London*. London: Macmillan, 1992.

Arnold, Isaac N. *The Life of Benedict Arnold: His Patriotism and His Treason*. Chicago: A.C. McClurg, 1905.

Bailyn, Bernard. *To Begin the World Anew: The Genius and Ambiguities of the American Founders*. New York: Alfred Knopf, 2003.

Barber, John Warner. *Interesting Events in the History of the United States*. New Haven: J.W. Barber, 1831.

Barlow, Joel. *The Vision of Columbus*. Hartford: Hudson & Goodwin, 1787.

Bobrick, Benson. *Angel in the Whirlwind: The Triumph of the American Revolution*. New York: Simon & Schuster, 1997.

Boswell, James. *The Life of Samuel Johnson*. Selected by Edmund Fuller. New York: Dell Publishing, 1960.

Bowling, Kenneth R., and Helen E. Veit, eds. *The Diary of William Maclay and Other Notes on Senate Debate.* Baltimore: Johns Hopkins University Press, 1988.

Brown, Virginia Pounds, and Linda McNair Cohen. *Drawing by Stealth: John Trumbull and the Creek Indians.* Montgomery, Ala.: NewSouth Books, 2016.

Burrows, Edwin G., and Mike Wallace. *Gotham: A History of New York City to 1898.* New York: Oxford University Press, 1999.

Caldwell, John et al. *American Paintings in the Metropolitan Museum of Art.* Vol. 1. New York: Metropolitan Museum of Art, 1994.

Capen, Edward Warren. *The History and Development of the Poor Law of Connecticut.* New York: Columbia University Press, 1905.

Chastellux, marquis de. *Travels in North America.* Translated by "An English Gentleman." New York: n.p., 1828.

Chernow, Ron. *Alexander Hamilton.* New York: Penguin Press, 2004.

Cooper, Helen, et al. *John Trumbull: The Hand and Spirit of a Painter.* New Haven: Yale University Art Gallery, 1983.

Cooper, James Fenimore. *The Last of the Mohicans.* 1826. Repr., New York: Signet Classics, 1962.

Du Fresnoy, C.A. *The Art of Painting.* Translated by John Dryden. London: J. Hepinstall, 1695.

Dunlap, William. *Diary of William Dunlap (1766–1839).* New York: New-York Historical Society, 1943.

———. *A History of the Rise and Progress of the Arts of Design in the United States.* Boston: C.E. Goodspeed, 1918.

Dwight, Timothy. *The Conquest of Canäan.* Hartford: Elisha Babcock, 1785.

Earle, Alice Morse. *The Sabbath in Puritan New England.* New York: Charles Scribner's Sons, 1891.

Einstein, Lewis. *Divided Loyalties: Americans in England.* Boston: Houghton Mifflin, 1933.

Fischer, David Hackett. *Washington's Crossing.* New York: Oxford University Press, 2004.

Fisher, George P. *Life of Benjamin Silliman.* Philadelphia: Porter & Coates, 1866.

Flexner, James Thomas. *George Washington.* Boston: Little, Brown, 1969.

———. *Gilbert Stuart.* New York: Alfred Knopf, 1955.

Galt, John. *The Life, Studies and Works of Benjamin West, Esq.* London: T. Cadell & W. Davies, 1820.

Genin, Sylvester. *Selections from the Works of the Late Sylvester Genin, Esq.* New York: Maigne & Hall, 1855.

Grieg, James, ed. *The Farington Diary.* New York: George H. Doran, 1923.

Irving, Washington. *Letters of Jonathan Oldstyle.* New York: Columbia University Press, 1941.

Jaffe, Irma B. *John Trumbull.* Boston: New York Graphic Society, 1975.

Kamensky, Jane. *A Revolution in Color: The World of John Singleton Copley.* New York: W.W. Norton, 2016.

King, Charles Rufus, ed. *Life and Correspondence of Rufus King.* New York: G.P. Putnam's Sons, 1900.

Lambert, John. *Travels through Canada and the United States.* London: Baldwin, Craddock & Joy, 1816.

Latrobe, Benjamin Henry. *The Journal of Latrobe*. New York: D. Appleton, 1905.

Lomask, Milton. *Aaron Burr: The Years from Princeton to Vice President, 1756–1805*. New York: Farrar, Strauss, Giroux, 1979.

Looney, Jefferson, et al., eds. *The Papers of Thomas Jefferson*, Retirement Series, vol. 16, *1 June 1820 to 28 February 1821* (Princeton: Princeton University Press).

McGrath, Tim. *James Monroe: A Life*. New York: Dutton, 2020.

Miller, Lillian B., ed. *The Peale Family*. New York: Abbeville Press, 1996.

Monroe, James. *A View of the Conduct of the Executive in the Foreign Affairs of the United States*. Philadelphia: Benjamin Franklin Bache, 1797.

Morgan, Helen M., ed. *A Season in New York, 1801: Letters of Harriet and Maria Trumbull*. Pittsburgh: University of Pittsburgh Press, 1969.

Morse, Edward Lind, ed. *Samuel F.B. Morse His Letters and Journals*. Boston: Houghton Mifflin, 1914.

Phillips, Kevin. *1775: A Good Year for Revolution*. New York: Penguin, 2012.

Quintal, Jr., George. *Patriots of Color: "A Peculiar Beauty and Merit": African Americans and Native Americans at Battle Road and Bunker Hill*. Boston: National Historical Park, 2004.

Rather, Susan. *The American School: Artists and Status in the Late-Colonial and Early National Era*. New Haven: Yale University Press, 2016.

Register of Debates in Congress.

Rhodehamel, John, ed. *The American Revolution: Writings from the War of Independence*. New York: Library of America, 2001.

Robertson, Emily, ed. *Letters and Papers of Andrew Robertson, A.M.* London: Eyre & Spottiswoode, n.d.

Robertson, William Spence. *The Life of Miranda*. Chapel Hill: University of North Carolina Press, 1929.

Sawitzky, William. *Matthew Pratt, 1734–1805*. New York: New-York Historical Society, 1942.

Silverman, Kenneth. *Lightning Man: The Accursed Life of Samuel F.B. Morse*. New York: Alfred Knopf, 2003.

Sizer, Theodore, ed. *The Autobiography of Colonel John Trumbull: Patriot-Artist, 1756–1843*. New Haven: Yale University Press, 1953.

Staiti, Paul. *Of Arms and Artists: The American Revolution through Painters' Eyes*. New York: Bloomsbury Press, 2016.

Steuart, Francis ed. *The Last Journals of Horace Walpole from the Reign of George III*. New York: John Lane, 1910.

Stoddard, Richard Henry. *Anecdote Biographies of Thackery and Dickens*. New York: Scribner, 1874.

Trumbull, John. *Autobiography, Reminiscences and Letters of John Trumbull, from 1756 to 1841*. New York: Wiley & Putnam, 1841.

Trumbull, Jonathan. *Jonathan Trumbull: Governor of Connecticut*. Boston: Little, Brown, 1919.

Van Schreeven, William J., and George H. Reese, eds. *Proceedings of the General Assembly of Virginia . . .* Jamestown, Va.: Jamestown Foundation, 1969.

Waldstreicher, David, ed. *John Quincy Adams Diaries*. New York: Library of America, 2017.

Warren, Mercy Otis. *History of the Rise, Progress, and Termination of the American Revolution*. Boston: Manning & Loring, 1805.

Weems, Mason Locke. *A History of the Life and Death, Virtues and Exploits of General George Washington*. Cleveland: World Publishing, 1965.

Zimmern, Helen, ed. *Sir Joshua Reynolds' Discourses*. London: Walter Scott, 1887.

Articles and Papers

Benjamin Silliman Notebook, Yale University Library.

Brandwein, Ann. "An Eighteenth Century Depression: The Sad Conclusion of Faith Trumbull Huntington." *Connecticut History Review* 26 (November 1985): 19–32.

Clark, William Bell. "In Defense of Thomas Digges." *Pennsylvania Magazine of History and Biography* 77, no. 4 (October 1953): 381–438.

Downes, William Howe. "Boston Painters and Paintings." *Atlantic*, July 1888.

The Historical Magazine 1 (October 1857): 289–92.

John W. Francis Papers, New York Public Library.

Lillich, Richard B. "The Jay Treaty Commission." *St. John's Law Review* 37, no. 25 (1963).

"Lord Holland's Memoirs of the Whig Party." *London Quarterly Review* (American edition) 94 (1854): 388.

Maryland State Archives, Annapolis.

Menschel, David. "Abolition without Deliverance: The Law of Connecticut Slavery 1784–1848." *Yale Law Journal* 111, no. 1 (October 2001): 183–222.

The Political Magazine and Parliamentary, Naval, Military and Literary Journal 1 (November 1780): 739–40.

Smelser, Marshall. "George Washington Declines the Part of El Libertador." *William and Mary Quarterly* 11, no. 1 (January 1954): 42–51.

Stacey, Colonel C.P. "Benjamin West and 'The Death of Wolfe.'" *National Gallery of Canada Bulletin* 4, no. 1 (1966).

Strazdes, Diana. "John Trumbull's Nude Venus." *Master Drawings* 51, no. 1 (Spring 2013): 49–62.

Acknowledgments

The researching of this book was made more than usually complicated thanks to Covid. I am as ever grateful to all who helped me.

Mark Mitchell of the Yale University Art Gallery, besides his many other responsibilities, is a devoted custodian and student of John Trumbull's art. He opened the gallery for me and helped clear up a number of points.

In Lebanon, Connecticut, Blysse Scoby showed me the Governor Jonathan Trumbull House and the War Office. Dr. Will Sencabaugh showed me the First Congregational Church.

Alexander Rose gave me the benefit of his knowledge of eighteenth-century spies and spy craft. Sarah Ruden translated shaky Latin. Douglas Bradburn and Jessie MacLeod at George Washington's Mount Vernon described what William Lee actually wore, not what Trumbull fancifully painted. Hassaan Qadir helped with research at Yale. Shawn McKinney shared his thoughts on painting, and listened to mine. Matthew Malec and Frank Filocomo at the National Review Institute wrangled permissions. Nicole Seary gave me invaluable assistance.

In 1977 Ronald Poulson let me write the college paper that was the seed of my first biography, and of this one.

I must thank my editor and photographer, William Frucht, and my agent for thirty years, Michael Carlisle.

When I was trying to think of an idea for a third book, I made a list of ten subjects. My wife, Jeanne Safer, told me to add George Washington to the list. She was right. She has heard every word of my books, and improved many.

Illustration Credits

Plates

Plate 1
Faith Trumbull
Milking Scene Needlework, 1754
Embroidery; silk and metallic threads, ink, and paint on a satin-woven silk ground; linen string, wood strainer, iron nails, 15⅝ x 18⅜ in. (39.7 x 46.7 cm)
The Connecticut Historical Society, gift of Jonathan Trumbull Rogers, in memory of Eleanor Root Silliman Rogers; The Newman S. Hungerford Museum Fund, 1999.70.0

Plate 2
John Trumbull, American, 1756–1843
Self-Portrait, 1777
Oil on canvas, 30¼ x 24⅛ in. (76.8 x 61.3 cm)
Museum of Fine Arts, Boston, bequest of George Nixon Black, 29.791. Photograph © 2024 Museum of Fine Arts, Boston

Plate 3
John Trumbull
The Death of General Warren at the Battle of Bunker's Hill, June 17, 1775, 1786
Oil on canvas, 25⅝ x 37⅝ in. (65.1 x 95.6 cm)
Yale University Art Gallery, Trumbull Collection

Plate 4
John Trumbull
The Death of General Montgomery in the Attack on Quebec, December 31, 1775, 1786
Oil on canvas, 24⅝ x 37 in. (62.5 x 94 cm)
Yale University Art Gallery, Trumbull Collection

Plate 5
John Trumbull
The Declaration of Independence, July 4, 1776, 1787–1820

Oil on canvas, 20⅞ x 31 in. (53 x 78.7 cm)
Yale University Art Gallery, Trumbull Collection

Plate 6
John Trumbull
The Capture of the Hessians at Trenton, December 26, 1776, 1786–1828
Oil on canvas, 20⅛ x 30 in. (51.1 x 76.2 cm)
Yale University Art Gallery, Trumbull Collection

Plate 7
John Trumbull
The Death of General Mercer at the Battle of Princeton, January 3, 1777, c. 1789–c. 1831
Oil on canvas, 21 x 30¾ in. (53.3 x 78.1 cm)
Yale University Art Gallery, Trumbull Collection

Plate 8
John Trumbull
The Surrender of General Burgoyne at Saratoga, October 16, 1777, c. 1822–32
Oil on canvas, 21⅛ x 30⅝ in. (53.7 x 77.8 cm)
Yale University Art Gallery, Trumbull Collection

Plate 9
John Trumbull
The Surrender of Lord Cornwallis at Yorktown, October 19, 1781, 1787–c. 1828
Oil on canvas, 21 x 30⅝ in. (53.3 x 77.8 cm)
Yale University Art Gallery, Trumbull Collection

Plate 10
John Trumbull
The Resignation of General Washington, December 23, 1783, 1824–28
Oil on canvas, 20 x 30 in. (50.8 x 76.2 cm)
Yale University Art Gallery, Trumbull Collection

Plate 11
John Trumbull
General George Washington at Trenton, 1792
Oil on canvas, 92½ x 63 in. (235 x 160 cm)
Yale University Art Gallery, gift of the Society of the Cincinnati in Connecticut

Plate 12
John Trumbull
Hopothle-Mico, or *The Talasee King of the Creeks*, 1790
Pencil, 5 x 3⅞ in. (12.7 x 9.8 cm)
This drawing is owned by the Fordham University Library as an item in the Charles Allen Munn Collection

Plate 13
John Trumbull
Reclining Nude, late 18th–early 19th century
Black and white chalk on blue paper, 14 x 22⁷⁄₁₆ in. (35.6 x 57 cm)
Yale University Art Gallery, gift of the Associates in Fine Arts

Plate 14
John Trumbull
Self-Portrait, c. 1802
Oil on canvas, 29¾ x 24⁹⁄₁₆ in. (75.5 x 62.4 cm)
Yale University Art Gallery, gift of Marshall H. Clyde, Jr.

Plate 15
John Trumbull
Sarah Trumbull with a Spaniel, c. 1802
Oil on canvas, 30³⁄₁₆ x 25³⁄₁₆ in. (76.7 x 64 cm)
Yale University Art Gallery, gift of Marshall H. Clyde, Jr.

Plate 16
Andrew Robertson, *Lieutenant John Trumbull Ray,* 1814
Watercolor on ivory, 3³⁄₁₆ x 2½ in. (8.1 x 6.4 cm)
Yale University Art Gallery, gift of Maria Trumbull Dana

Figures

Figure 1. The house of Governor Jonathan Trumbull, Sr. © William Frucht.

Figure 2. John Singleton Copley, American, 1739–1815. *A Boy with a Flying Squirrel (Henry Pelham),* 1765. Oil on canvas, 30⅜ x 25⅛ in. (77.15 x 63.82 cm). Museum of Fine Arts, Boston, gift of the artist's great-granddaughter, 1978.297. Photograph © 2024 Museum of Fine Arts, Boston.

Figure 3. Benjamin West, *The Death of General Wolfe,* 1770. Oil on canvas, 60¹⁄₁₆ x 84⁷⁄₁₆ in. (152.6 x 214.5 cm). National Gallery of Canada, Ottawa, gift of the 2nd Duke of Westminster to the Canadian War Memorials, 1918; Transfer from the Canadian War Memorials, 1921.

Figure 4. John Singleton Copley, *The Death of Major Peirson, 6 January 1781,* 1783. Oil on canvas, 99 x 144 in. (251.5 x 365.8 cm). Tate, London. Photo: Tate.

Figure 5. Jacques-Louis David, *Oath of the Horatii,* 1784. Oil on canvas, 129¹³⁄₁₆ × 167³⁄₁₆ in. (329.8 cm × 424.8 cm). Musée du Louvre. Scala / Art Resource, NY.

Figure 6. The First Congregational Church, in Lebanon, Connecticut. © William Frucht.

Figure 7. John Trumbull, *Maternal Affection, Tenderness, or Love,* 1809–after 1815. Oil on canvas, 24⅜ x 20³⁄₁₆ in. (61.9 x 51.3 cm). Yale University Art Gallery, Trumbull Collection.

Figure 8. John Trumbull, *Benjamin Silliman,* 1825. Oil on wood, 19¼ x 15¾ in. (48.9 x 40 cm). National Portrait Gallery, Smithsonian Institution; gift of Alice Silliman Hawkes.

Figure 9. A trespasser totes the Speaker of the House's lectern through the Capitol Rotunda. Photo: Win McNamee via Getty Images.

Figure 10. National Guard members stand in the Rotunda with the U.S. Capitol tour. Photo: Rod Lamkey / CNP / MediaPunch; MediaPunch Inc /Alamy Stock Photo.

Index

Page numbers in italics refer to figures.